Invested Indifference

Kara Granzow

Invested Indifference

How Violence Persists in Settler Colonial Society

UBCPress · Vancouver · Toronto

29 28 27 26 25 24 23 22 21 20 5 4 3 2 1

Printed in Canada on FSC-certified ancient-forest-free paper (100% post-consumer recycled) that is processed chlorine- and acid-free.

Library and Archives Canada Cataloguing in Publication

Title: Invested indifference : how violence persists in settler colonial society / Kara Granzow.
Names: Granzow, Kara, author.
Description: Includes bibliographical references and index.
Identifiers: Canadiana (print) 20200198440 | Canadiana (ebook) 20200198521 | ISBN 9780774837439 (hardcover) | ISBN 9780774837446 (softcover) | ISBN 9780774837453 (PDF) | ISBN 9780774837460 (EPUB) | ISBN 9780774837477 (Kindle)
Subjects: LCSH: Indigenous women—Violence against—Alberta—Edmonton. | LCSH: Indigenous women—Alberta—Edmonton—Social conditions. | LCSH: Violence—Alberta—Edmonton.
Classification: LCC E98.W8 G73 2021 | DDC 305.48/8970712334—dc23

Canada

UBC Press gratefully acknowledges the financial support for our publishing program of the Government of Canada (through the Canada Book Fund), the Canada Council for the Arts, and the British Columbia Arts Council.

Printed and bound in Canada by Friesens
Set in Garamond and Meta by Sharlene Eugenio
Copy editor: Robert Lewis
Proofreader: Helen Godolphin
Indexer: Judy Dunlop
Cover designer: Alexa Love

UBC Press
The University of British Columbia
2029 West Mall
Vancouver, BC V6T 1Z2
www.ubcpress.ca

How does one encounter the past as an anteriority that continually introduces an otherness or alterity within the present? How does one then narrate the present as a form of contemporaneity that is always belated? In what historical time do such configurations of cultural difference assume forms of cultural and political authority?

– HOMI BHABHA

Contents

Preface

I HAVE HEARD IT IS often the case that, by the time a book like this is published, it is out of date and so fails to fully deliver on what it set out to do. In this case, the majority of the research for this book was conducted between 2005 and 2008, so in some ways it arrives too late, although in other ways it arrives too soon.

What I describe as the production of an affect of societal indifference in this book does not look the same now as it did prior to the eventual onset of a national inquiry into the cases of missing and murdered Indigenous women and girls in Canada in 2016. Although I do not argue that the initiation of this inquiry marked the beginning of an era of deep and generalized concern over the issue of violence toward Indigenous women and girls – since it is true that such a concern both preceded this introduction and has never really materialized as a kind of national sentiment as a result – it is still the case that, with the introduction of this official inquiry, a kind of line was drawn that is relevant to the ideas addressed in this book. Rather than resolving the problem of what I pose as a deep national investment in ongoing colonial violence, the inquiry has been effective in transforming and reconfiguring affect even though it is not likely to prove to be very effective at moving the nation toward producing decolonial and material conditions of greater safety for those rendered materially vulnerable as a basic operation of settler colonialism. Although it is in many ways too soon to assess the impact of the inquiry, which released its final report and recommendations in April 2019, while this book was still in production, criticisms of the inquiry's shortcomings were already being expressed by advocates, Indigenous leaders, Indigenous organizations, and family members (see Canadian Press 2017a, 2017b; Galloway 2017; and Palmater 2016).

Over the past decade, excellent work has been produced that aims to address and intervene in ongoing settler colonial violence in Canada – much of it by Indigenous scholars, writers, and activists. Staying abreast of such a burgeoning field has been among the challenges of working within teaching, research, and service contexts where one is stretched always thinner. The pressures I describe are all too familiar to academics today and have resulted in movements toward a slower, more thoughtful form of scholarship. At the same time, and given the specific issues that concern me, perhaps more time is not necessarily what is needed.

The concerns expressed in these pages took root for me in 2004 through news stories that would occasionally interrupt my quiet life. As I struggled to find my footing as a doctoral student and to establish this work as a proper "study," these concerns functioned for me as an intervention into what I saw as the Eurocolonial trend in the social sciences of finding *the object* of and for analysis *elsewhere*. This elsewhere found different forms, sometimes in the past and sometimes in the "less civilized" and the less sophisticated, always being presumed inferior in relation to the place from which the social scientific gaze emanated. I sought to escape that tendency and wanted to address an issue of local concern: the occurrence of violence in the city where I lived. For this reason, prior iterations of this book began with the following quotations as epigraphs:

> This is a socially authorized death, mundane and unaccounted for, and we partook of it in our foreign and native gazing, in our blend of learned indifference, sense of intolerability, and failed witnessing. (Biehl 2001, 134)

> Of course that's elsewhere, always elsewhere, you'll want to say, not the rule but the exception, existing in An-Other Place like Northern Ireland, Beirut, Ethiopia, Kingston, Port au Prince,

> Peru, Mozambique, Afghanistan, Santiago, the Bronx, the West Bank, South Africa, San Salvador, Colombia, to name but some of the more publicized from the staggering number of spots troubling the course of the world's order. But perhaps such an elsewhere should make us suspicious about the deeply rooted sense of order here, as if their dark wildness exists so as to silhouette our light, the bottom line being, of course, the tight and necessary fit between order, law, justice, sense, economy, and history – all of which them elsewhere manifestly ain't got much of. (Taussig 1989, 3)

These anthropologists' words spoke volumes to me when I began this work, and they are still important reminders to critically examine who and what we think we are here. They directed me to look around the city where I lived in order to recognize how I had learned *not* to see the "dark wildness" that "silhouettes our light" here so that I too might maintain the story of my field of study (sociology), a story that is often about desperation and cruelties elsewhere. This book thus became about the elsewhere *here* through which the mirage of a benevolent Canada gets produced again and again.

But even as I turned my gaze to what was occurring where I lived, I had no guarantee of the effects of my work. We know good intentions are as suspect as the rest. This book is a result of my experience in the neoliberal institution that is the modern university in Canada. It is shaped by over a decade of training in sociology as a student in three postsecondary institutions in Canada. Although this training was often exciting and exhilarating, it was also narrow. With some important exceptions, it was primarily a training in learning to read, interpret, and respond to texts written by the fathers and forefathers of the discipline, all of whom themselves cite a remarkably uniform history within the discipline. To some extent, with this work, I have been successful in fulfilling the imperative of my disciplinary heritage. I have learned to read, interpret, and write through institutions, and in turn, I have fortified these institutions. I build upon the lineage of the same writers whom I have been taught to read, understand, and cite. In its earlier stages, this book was full of settler scholars. It still carries the heritage of their work onward. But now, more than a decade after I began this project, it begins to draw on scholarship produced by Indigenous, feminist, anti-colonial, and queer writers, too, whose work also sometimes uses, radically challenges, and undermines the authority of those enduring figures. So, although I had originally hoped to investigate the tenacity and seemingly infinite flexibility of settler colonial practices, this work is itself also an expression of that tenacity and flexibility. That I write, with security, as a socially recognized and affirmed subject, and that I write with citizen rights, in a national language that is also my first language, English, are circumstances ensured by settler colonial conditions. These conditions are inescapably woven into this text.

When beginning this book, I took anthropologist Michael Taussig's (1989) words literally and decided that I needed to build a bridge to the elsewhere here that denied me my usual sense of safety and protection. So I started to volunteer at a drop-in centre for women, transgender, and two-spirit people involved in street-level sex work in Edmonton. I was interested in proximity, specifically in whether physical distance had anything to do with my sense of having some safety from danger and in whether it perhaps explained the larger trend that was being called "societal indifference" to violence. If I was indifferent to violence happening in the city where I lived, was this affect due to a lack of awareness and/or the distance between me and the elsewhere here? Was this distance provided by the river valley between Mill Creek (where I lived) and Jasper Avenue in Edmonton? Was the affect of indifference due to the distance between my basement apartment and the spaces of danger I had imagined to be somewhere else in Edmonton, like along 107th Avenue? To begin to consider these questions, I started volunteering one day a week at the drop-in centre. Women who sold sex on the street already had a place in my imagination – a place in part informed by materials like those I examine in the upcoming chapters. Each day when I arrived to volunteer, I hoped there would be no violence. And each day when I left, I had learned again and again that such unsubstantiated fears were what hid the ongoing social abandonments that produced the real dangers for the women with whom I had spent my day. The violence was not already present there, but actually emanated from the much greater certainty of safety elsewhere.

My time at the drop-in centre was immensely important to me, although this is the first time I have written about it, and it does not find its way in explicit form into this book beyond this preface. I know now that the director allowed me to be there not because I was needed but because she is a profoundly compassionate and generous person who knew I had a lot to learn. I was remarkably unnecessary. I was nonetheless tolerated – another middle-class white woman with "a research interest." I wasn't the first and wouldn't be the last. While I was there, I swept the kitchen, did the dishes, cooked, or watched episodes of *Ellen* in the common room. In general, the place was characterized by a sense of immediacy. It was a place where needs were met, whether the need for sleep, warmth, and food or the need for a reprieve, laughter, comfort, and friendship; and it was a place where people shared their lives, sometimes for days, weeks, or months and sometimes for years.

I do not address these experiences except here in the preface because I do not want such experiences to be read as though they somehow absolve me of accountability as a producer of texts and knowledge. My time there was not research, but it shaped my thinking and kept me feeling. What I offer here are pieces; to be certain, they are partial and flawed and will have effects that I have not predicted and that may work precisely against the very politics I hope to advocate. Having paused for a moment prior to the publication of this work, I think now that there is no way to do this work without also doing damage. As I am a person whose life and career are literally made to matter in part through the attention I give this issue, my attempt to address how settler colonial violence routinely positions people as living lives that matter more or less than the lives of others feels impossibly paradoxical and highly unethical. But not attempting to draw further attention to how settler colonial violence operates as a flexible, tenacious, and ongoing series of everyday forces also presents a problem. At best, I see what I am doing in this book as working always from within a problematic position, one that I cannot sidestep but must attempt to face in order to try to understand the history and thus the contemporality of this position. In the work of social critics

Fred Moten and Stefano Harney (2004, 101), I find words to guide my practices:

> It cannot be denied that the university is a place of refuge, and it cannot be accepted that the university is a place of enlightenment. In the face of these conditions one can only sneak into the university and steal what one can. To abuse its hospitality, to spite its mission, to join its refugee colony, its gypsy encampment, *to be in but not of* – this is the path of the subversive intellectual in the modern university. (Emphasis added)

Before turning to the book itself, I reiterate that it fails on many fronts. Its intervention into "contact zones" is best characterized as an accumulation of pieces that do not convey a coherent story. Perhaps it is something of a plaiting of strands. I hope, however, that together these pieces or strands tell us something of the flexibility and tenaciousness of investments in settler colonialism – of the facade of order and justice *here* – so that we might begin to produce something that interrupts the relationship between everyday acts of settler colonial violence and what is too easily dismissed as a widespread indifference to it.

Acknowledgments

FINANCIAL SUPPORT FOR THIS WORK came from a number of provincial and federal grants and fellowships. I am grateful for support from a doctoral scholarship awarded by the Social Sciences and Humanities Research Council of Canada. My training in qualitative methodology was supported by a fellowship from the Canadian Institute for Health Research. Financial support also came from the Province of Alberta, the Department of Sociology at the University of Alberta, and the International Institute for Qualitative Research. I am also grateful for the institutional and financial support provided by the Faculty of Arts and Science at the University of Lethbridge. The Provincial Archives of Alberta and the City of Edmonton Archives provided vital assistance in locating, accessing, and interpreting archival materials. In particular, I thank Michael Gourlie at the Provincial Archives of Alberta who has been an enormous help to me in the last moments of pulling this book together. In addition, I am grateful for the last eight years of support provided by the University of Lethbridge, which is located on the lands of the Siksikaitsitapii people.

I want to thank Darcy Cullen, my editor; Ann Macklem; copy editor Robert Lewis; cover designer Alexa Love; indexer Judy Dunlop; and the staff at UBC Press for their support and publication of this work. I am also enormously grateful for the thorough work done by two anonymous reviewers. This book would not have been published if not for folks willing to work the way you have to contribute to a community of scholarship. Thank you. I also want to acknowledge that parts of Chapter 1, co-authored with Amber Dean, have been previously published as "Revanchism in the Canadian West: Gentrification and Resettlement in a Prairie City," *TOPIA: Canadian Journal of Cultural Studies* 18 (2007): 89–106. These are reprinted here with permission from University of Toronto Press © 2007.

I have had several amazing mentors over the years. Bill Ramp and Pat Chuchryk ignited my interest in sociology and continue to guide my work as a teacher. Nancy Theberge played a pivotal role in my training as a sociologist, teaching me essential skills and giving me valuable opportunities to explore them. Nancy's confidence in me came at a crucial moment, and I am grateful for her support. I will always be grateful to Jim Curtis (1942–2005), who was a generous, light-hearted, and much beloved teacher and mentor. I am so lucky to have known him during my time at the University of Waterloo.

I thank Drs. Susanna Luhmann, Daphne Reed, Jan Newberry, and Karen Hughes, whose contributions to improving this project are deeply appreciated. I am deeply grateful to Dr. Amy Kaler, who supported me in this work from the beginning. Amy is a strong advocate for students and an excellent mentor whose thoughtful and brilliant questions were enormously helpful as I worked on this project.

This book owes its existence to Dr. Sharon Rosenberg (1964–2010), who was a dedicated and inspiring teacher and had a radical impact on the direction and content of my work. Sharon gave me the opportunity and courage to do difficult research. She lives in my heart and in my work, as well as in the work of so many who were lucky enough to know her.

While in Edmonton, I met amazing people and learned so much. I am grateful for my time with Bavie Sara, Amorette Chase, and Rebecca Lock. I am deeply indebted to Shawna Hohendorf for welcoming me and offering friendship, encouragement, and strength. I am enormously grateful to have known Veronica Desabrais (1970–2007), a woman whose generosity and warmth deeply impacted my life and my work on this project.

During the early writing of this book, and since then, I have been surrounded by friends and colleagues who have taken an interest in my work and have helped to guide me through it. I want to thank Carly Adams, Michelle Helstein, Catherine Kingfisher, and Carol Williams for their encouragement and advice. I am so grateful to Jason Laurendeau for reading a prior draft of this manuscript, for providing invaluable feedback, and for urging me to keep working at its publication. I am lucky to have worked with many outstanding students at the University of Lethbridge and these students have enriched my thinking and scholarship. In particular, I thank Rachel Shields, Tessa Penich, and Emily Kirbyson.

I would have given up on this work long ago without the love, support, and friendship of some truly incredible people. I am grateful to Julie and Henry Klok for happy hours, pie crusts, fairy letters, and friendship. I feel so fortunate that Vanessa Maxwell arrived at an important time in my life, reminding me to breathe and to bend when I can. I am deeply grateful to my dear friend, Suzanne Lenon, for her thoughtfulness and care. Anne Winkler delights and surprises me with her humour, dedication, and love. I could not have continued this work without my brilliant collaborator and cherished friend, Amber Dean. Amber has been an unwavering companion, supporting me through some of the hardest moments I have faced. I am so thankful also to Kim Mair, who has been with me for even longer than this project, who encouraged me from the start, and whose brilliance has influenced my thinking and writing profoundly.

I owe everything to my parents, Friederike and Carl Granzow (1943–2009), an amazing team who gave their children an incredible family. My dad had every confidence in each of us; he urged us to seek freedom and to pursue our interests, always. He was full of passion and had a robust and enthusiastic spirit. My mother, like her mother before, is the heart of our family. I am deeply thankful for her amazing strength and for her ongoing attention and care. With my siblings, I am lucky to share so much. My sister, Andrea, is my hero, a load that she has endured with grace and love. John has shared his unique humour, encouragement, and affection, which has meant so much to me. Michael gives with such ease and open friendship, and I cherish that deeply; a conversation with Michael never fails to delight me. Mark, Madeleine, Erica, and Lesley, you have each made our lives so much more abundant than they were before. I am especially grateful to Tom and Linda Perks – your love and support has meant so much to our family.

I am deeply thankful to my partner, Tom, whose love has held strong. Thank you for the life we share. Words cannot express my gratitude for and to my children. Thank you for teaching me so much. You give me so much joy and so many reasons to play.

I am so fortunate to share in all of your lives. Thank you.

Introduction

IN 2004 THE NATIVE WOMEN'S Association of Canada (NWAC) reported that more than 500 Indigenous women had gone missing or been murdered in Canada since the mid-1980s (cited in Amnesty International 2004, 4). That year, Amnesty International reported that in the city of Edmonton, Alberta, alone, there were eighteen ongoing investigations of "unsolved murders of women in the last two decades" and that these murders were disproportionately of Indigenous women (Amnesty International 2004, 4). In 2009 NWAC (2009, 88) stated that the number of Indigenous women missing or murdered in Canada was 520. The organization's 2010 report states that 582 Aboriginal girls and women were missing or had been murdered (NWAC 2010, 18). And by 2013 it had "documented over 600 cases where aboriginal women have been murdered or gone missing between 2005 and 2010" (cited in CBC 2013). The numbers are imprecise but growing. In 2014, after decades of social activism to draw attention to the issue and numerous calls for such an accounting, Canada's national police force, the Royal Canadian Mounted Police (RCMP), reported 1,181 Indigenous women and girls as either missing or murdered in this country since the 1980s (RCMP 2014, 7). In 2016 Canada's federal minister of Indigenous affairs characterized the actual number of missing or murdered women as significantly larger than reported by the RCMP (cited in Kirkup 2016). Still considered an underestimation, these numbers, and the degree to which their accuracy has been obscured, are provoking increasing alarm in Canada (see NWAC 2015, 2019).[1]

In 2016 the newly appointed Liberal government of Canada, under Justin Trudeau, launched a national inquiry to investigate the "unacceptable overrepresentation of Indigenous women and girls as victims of violence" in Canada (Government of Canada 2016, 135). In its 2016 budget, the government proposed to invest $40 million over two years in this inquiry. This federal recognition of the problem and the dedication of significant funds to its redress marked a radical departure from the approach of the outgoing Conservative government, under Stephen Harper, which for years had refused numerous pleas for such a national inquiry and had in fact cut funding to the Native Women's Association of Canada approved by the prior government (Chase 2014).[2] This prior funding, first provided in 2005, had been directed toward several NWAC initiatives to address the problem of disappeared Indigenous women. The report *Voices of Our Sisters in Spirit* (NWAC 2009), for example, was the outcome of $5 million allotted for a five-year research project. The NWAC's broader Sisters in Spirit initiative was established to work with the Canadian government and with Aboriginal women's organizations in order to improve the provision of human rights, and it included working to protect Indigenous women from disproportionately high rates of murder and abduction.[3] Part of the initiative was also directed at ascertaining a more accurate tally to determine the extent of this emergency in Canada. Such a comprehensive assessment, however, was not possible given the limited political support for this project.

The NWAC's website explained that the objectives of the Sisters in Spirit initiative were "to address violence against Aboriginal (First Nations, Inuit and Métis) women, particularly racialized and/or sexualized violence, that is, violence perpetrated against Aboriginal women because of their gender and Aboriginal identity." The NWAC noted that "this type of violence typically occurs in the public sphere, where societal indifference often leaves Aboriginal women at greater risk."[4] "Societal indifference" is the phrase used to characterize a notion of the public sphere in Canada and to explain the disproportionate danger faced by Indigenous women. With this idea of societal indifference, the Native Women's Association of Canada referred to a kind of violence that is targeted at Indigenous women, and it articulated a perceived lack of public concern or apathy as instrumental to the perpetuation of this violence.

This claim of Canadian societal indifference was not made exclusively by the NWAC. The same year that it reported its estimate of 500 missing or murdered Indigenous women and a full decade prior to the RCMP's report and the announcement of a national inquiry, the international human rights organization Amnesty International (2004) published a thirty-seven-page report entitled *Stolen Sisters: A Human Rights Response to Discrimination and Violence against Indigenous Women in Canada*. Describing nine incidents of racialized and gendered violence, all of which occurred in the country's western-most provinces, this report suggested that Canadian authorities were failing to provide the protections that would keep Indigenous women safe (Amnesty International 2004, 2). The report went on to outline four factors that have long played into the "heightened – and unacceptable – risk of violence against Indigenous women in Canadian cities":

> [1] The social and economic marginalisation of Indigenous women, along with a history of government policies that have torn apart Indigenous families and communities, have pushed a disproportionate number of Indigenous women into dangerous situations that include extreme poverty, homelessness and prostitution. [2] Despite assurances to the contrary, police in Canada have often failed to provide Indigenous women with an adequate standard of protection. [3] The resulting vulnerability of Indigenous women has been exploited by Indigenous and non-Indigenous men to carry out acts of extreme brutality against them. [4] These acts of violence may be motivated by racism, or may be carried out in the expectation that *societal indifference* to the welfare and safety of Indigenous women will allow the perpetrators to escape justice. (Amnesty International 2004, 2; emphasis added)

With these factors, Amnesty International set up a broad and historically situated consideration of how and why, and apparently with little social concern, some people are disproportionately subject to discrimination and violence in contemporary Canada. Yet, despite all the issues (e.g., social, economic, and historical) that these factors seem to address, they also obscure. Words always operate to both express and conceal, and I propose that in this context what is hidden is highly relevant to the idea that a nation, or city, or citizen might have the capacity to care for or to fulfill an obligation to protect those already rendered "Other" from within.

So the question is what (almost) disappears with the outlining of these four factors? Not Indigenous women. They are there, as they are in this introduction – written in as the missing and murdered, as "at risk," and as potential victims. Some police are there too; they have *neglected* those potential victims. Some Indigenous and non-Indigenous men are there too; they have *exploited the vulnerabilities of women* – known again as victims. And then there are the social, economic, and historical factors that have *pushed* Indigenous women (again, victims) into marginal, dangerous situations. But as might already be apparent, I wonder whether there is much more here. Is there something more to the clearly complicated contemporary emergency than some categorical distinction between the victims, the perpetrators, the indifferent, and a backdrop of "social and economic marginalisation" and problematic "government policies"? Such a scenario rings very familiar but leaves us with little ability to see or intervene in this violence as anything beyond the tragedy of individual cases, individual victims, and individual perpetrators. The account presents us with one-dimensional assessments of responsibility and with contextual factors construed as abstractions, namely social, economic, and historical maginalizations, but in conceptualizing them as such, it distances readers from realizing their salience as material realities and thwarts forms of action that might be taken against these realities.

The fourth factor identified by Amnesty International perhaps takes us furthest in our understanding of racialized gendered violence in Canada by pushing us to revise the oversimplifications implicit in the prior three factors. With this fourth point, we are drawn to consider the expectation or likelihood that violence against racialized women in a racist society might be met with indifference. Societal indifference, here, relates to and might be conflated with racist violence. But these are not the same things.

To repeat, Amnesty International (2004, 2) identifies the following as a final instrumental factor in the ongoing racialized and gendered violence in Canada: "racism" or "the *expectation* that societal indifference to the welfare and safety of Indigenous women *will allow the perpetrators to escape justice*" (emphasis added). Amnesty International's fourth point is extremely productive for thinking about racialized and gendered violence in Canada, not only for its attention to an expectation of indifference but also for the way that it moves thinking from expectation to considering the social contours of this phenomenon that Amnesty International names as *both* an expectation and an indifference. Something operating at or beyond the level of "the social" is obscured by such naming. But what is operational is not an absence or a lack. However imperceptible it may be, I suspect that it is something active, something at once beyond and inside of individual expectations, something too often referred to in sociological terms that also obscure its operations, terms like "power" and "structure," and something that demands a more thorough, local, and practice-based form of theorizing. If there is a learned expectation and indifference *here* in Canada, as there is in anthropologist João Guilherme Biehl's (2001) ethnographic account of social abandonment in Brazil, then perhaps we must consider how such an expectation and indifference materialize, how they are learned, who is implicated, and with what effects such affective realities are made.

It seems important to ask early on what it means to suggest that indifference might be considered *the* reaction to news of a person gone missing or found murdered. It also seems important to ask what it means to suggest that this indifference might even be *the message* in the news media about this missing woman's fate? Some academic work and media examples support Amnesty International's claim that, indeed, there might be some generalized indifference to the welfare of some Indigenous women and girls, particularly to violent acts against them (Ferris 2015; Jacobs and Williams 2008; Jiwani and Young 2006). Media headlines are especially known for their callous and alarming descriptions; one that ran in the *Edmonton Journal* (2009) read, "Murdered Aboriginal Women 'Not Garbage.'" This headline not only states the obvious but also requires us to imagine that it actually has an addressee who might already see murdered Aboriginal women as just that. The statement requires at least a prior knowledge of some association between the two, or else it is unintelligible. If no such association yet exists, such headlines might function to instruct readers on this association. In her work, cultural theorist Amber Dean (2015) argues that the use of mug-shot-like images of women missing from Vancouver signals that these women are already criminal – "inherently bad or deviant persons" (Ferris 2015, 48) – and hence not worthy of care. There is something at work here beyond an *absence* of affect. There is a logic. Biehl (2001, 134) suggests that in Brazil some deaths are "socially authorized," and Michael Taussig (1989) describes the "terror as usual" of something that is happening in the *here,* and although neither is writing of Canada, both strike me as approaching what is disavowed in Canada and perhaps also in the NWAC's and Amnesty International's designation of a society-wide form of indifference. In this book, I argue that this logic is rooted in contemporary settler colonialisms at work both in the violence of disappearance and in the affective possibilities for responses to that violence in Canada. I suggest that this logic has been difficult to address outright but that it nonetheless can be made apparent through a consideration of what indifference means and how it might work to repeatedly secure a national (and nation-based) complicity in the ongoing disappearance of Indigenous peoples, lands, and nations. I think that the claim of societal indifference has worked to hide what is there instead of indifference and an absence of care. What if instead of such a lack, disappearance has been managed in particular ways, including on some occasions through (what have been defined as) protective or benevolent practices? This book takes up the concept of societal indifference as a question and probes the possible meaning and utility of the notion of indifference in relation to the actual disappearance of Indigenous peoples, specifically women and girls, and in relation to the contemporary and long-term project now called Canada. In the pages that follow, I cautiously critique the postulate of an absence of care at the level of the societal, questioning both the conditions for and the performative effects of Amnesty International's (2004) declaration of the possibility of a national sentiment – or, more accurately, the precursors and effects of the declaration of the *absence* of a national sentiment. I claim that there is some kind of national sentiment here. In fact, it might be this feeling that undergirds projects undertaken to address disappearance more generally. In this way, I bring Amnesty International's four factors together, demanding that *specific* historical, economic, legal, social, and individual aspects of Indigenous and settler colonial relations be thought of in practical terms and brought to bear on the claim that there is *anyone* here who is indifferent to this particular kind of violence.[5]

It is important for me to state that I engage in this research and this writing summoned as I am by the very discourses I critique. Like all forms of discourse, the one that mobilizes societal indifference affords me particular positions as a subject of this discourse, just as it affords positions to those rendered victims through this discourse (Hall 1992). In part, what I have struggled to investigate in this work are the contours of my being situated both amid and at a distance from the forms of violence I examine.

Amiskwaciwâskahikan/Edmonton

I have tied my writing to places within the bounds of what has been officially designated Treaty 6 territory since 1877. My writing refers to places in the area asserted as the city of Edmonton by settlers in 1904. But these are places where people have lived and gathered for much longer; there have been people in or moving through these places for at least 10,000 years. Among the Indigenous nations that have gathered and lived in the surrounding areas are the Cree (Nehiyawak), Saulteaux, Niitsitapi (Blackfoot), Métis, Tsuu T'ina, and Nakota Sioux.[6] Edmonton is still contested terrain; the Cree word for the city is Amiskwaciwâskahikan, which means "beaver mountain house" (*Online Cree Dictionary* 2019). In its most recent history, the city has been called the provincial capital of Alberta, which is part of the country officially designated by settler colonial subjects as Canada, and it is home to nearly 1 million people (City of Edmonton 2019). It is a place thought of as economically rich as a consequence of a boom directly tied to the extraction of oil from the Athabasca oil sands, one of the largest reserves in the world, which is located just 500 kilometres north of the city and in Treaty 8 territory. Many people know Edmonton today for its festivals, its extensive green spaces, and its world-renowned recycling program. In 2007 Canadian Heritage named Edmonton the Culture Capital of Canada (City of Edmonton 2007). But the economic boom has also been tied to a marked increase in things less celebrated, like an increase in the involvement of Albertans in sex work, including in Edmonton (Mahaffy 2007). More alarmingly, five years after Edmonton was crowned the Culture Capital of Canada, the *Edmonton Sun* named it the country's "murder capital" (Roth 2012). And indeed, in preceding years, the media had reported that the city was facing something of a killing spree. Describing a location where several women had been found dead, a front-page headline in the *Edmonton Journal* on June 13, 2004, reported the presence of a "Grisly 'Dumping Ground' Discovery" (Kleiss and Farrell 2004). This news story chronicled the fate of nine women whose "bodies [had been] found in rural areas around Edmonton" since 1988. Then, in 2005, the Canadian national newspaper the *Globe and Mail* ran the headline "The 'Killing Fields' of Edmonton" (Harding 2005a). Subsequent reports were more specific, identifying ten of Edmonton's unsolved murder victims as "women who had been found dead in fields near Edmonton in the preceding 16 years" (Pruden 2011). Indigenous women were considered to be at particular risk of violence in Edmonton, which had reportedly joined Regina, Saskatoon, Winnipeg, and Vancouver as cities in Canada where there is a heightened danger of violence against Indigenous women (Ferris 2015; Jacobs and Williams 2008).[7]

I learned about these distressing aspects of Edmonton only after I turned my research to the topic of disappearance and indifference in the city. Initially, I focused on Edmonton because it was where I lived from 2002 to 2008 while engaged in doctoral studies at the University of Alberta in the Department of Sociology. During those years, I spent a lot of time alone. I walked or I rode my bike to school and back most weekdays. In those days, I was lucky enough to be inspired by wonderful friends and by thoughtful and generous scholars and mentors, like Drs. Sharon Rosenberg and Amy Kaler. At Sharon's urging, I fumbled through and eventually read feminist poststructural and anti-colonial theories for the first time. I had a strong interest in qualitative research, so I accepted a fellowship at an international institute for qualitative research and tried to work through the ethics of research with human subjects and the politics of representation. These issues, in fact, became something of a fixation for me; and I continue to be caught up in the knots of how to come to know ethically, regarding it as a problem that should not be resolved but maintained. During a precious time that bridged my twenties and thirties, I was safe, doing what I liked, and looking for purpose in my work.

In those days, in my little basement suite just off 99th Street and 83rd Avenue, CBC Radio One was almost always on. Radio One was my primary source for news, so I did not see newspaper headlines, but I did occasionally hear of women found murdered or reported missing, and what I occasionally heard started to feel like a pattern. It was on my radio that I also heard of Amnesty International's (2004) account of societal indifference to violence against Indigenous women, and seeking an answer to the questions of how and why such apparently patterned forms of violence could persist, I read Amnesty International's online report *Stolen Sisters.* Then, one particular morning, awoken as usual by my clock radio tuned to CBC, I heard a report about a woman's body found just a few blocks away from where I lived.[8] Because I was in Edmonton and studying sociology when I heard this terrible news and heard about this apparently *social* phenomenon – an expectation of indifference – Edmonton became the site of my research activity. From then on, this place became the context for my scrounging around in search of what I now propose is something not at all like indifference but something that mattered enormously – historically, politically, socially, intimately, and affectively. This was something so deeply invested in the present that disappearance occurred *as usual,* so that some people seemed authorized to die in Edmonton, and the language of societal indifference was the best that Amnesty International could do to draw attention to a collective implication of the ongoing pain and murder of many.

As I worked, I came to theorize that if societal indifference was indeed actually a form of investment, it had to have features. Or, if not features, perhaps more accurately, it had to occur through practices. One might not *actually feel* indifferent; rather, one might feel momentary despair, outrage, or fear, or one might even feel the kind of contentment I allude to as I describe the purpose that I sought in my work. But if indifference was in operation as a settler colonial investment or as a logic of complicity, it had to be enacted and re-enacted for patterns of violence to continue. And all the while, the features of its enactment may have had to apparently disappear so that all that seemed to be left (depending on where one was situated) was the notion of not caring much or for long or on any significant scale, while those in the *elsewhere of here* were apparently being abandoned, disappeared, or murdered. And so I began this work.

In the following chapters, I specifically address aspects of Edmonton's local context while both considering the claim of societal indifference and examining how social and historical practices operate with meaningful effects in relation to the issue of violence against Indigenous women and girls in the present. Debunking the individualistic factors often used to explain and address this violence (e.g., so-called high-risk lifestyles or the likelihood of a serial killer) as distractions productive to maintaining the violent status quo, I demonstrate how they effectively function as social and political strategies that very often disavow what I argue is an underlying and enduring social and colonial commitment to racialized and gendered violence in Canada, even as these commitments are expressed in different times and places and in different practices within the contexts of settlement, treatment or care, and violence or police control. In this book, I use research conducted at three moments in time to provide support for the controversial claim that, when examined at the socio-historical level, the perpetuation of violence against Indigenous peoples in Canada is not due to indifference at all, as Amnesty International (2004) suggests, but to precisely the inverse. Violence against Indigenous women and girls is state violence, and it is an effect of contemporary, entrenched, and enduring *commitments* to the perpetuation of racialized and gendered oppressions as part of attempts to maintain a settler colonial social order. Political anthropologist Audra Simpson (2016, 1) states it plainly, "Canada requires the death and so called 'disappearance' of Indigenous women in order to secure its sovereignty." The problem is not that individual people happen not to care or that they feel indifferent to this violence but that this violence occurs in myriad forms and is actually congruent with the much larger and much-celebrated project of making and remaking the nation-state as a legitimate and sovereign entity (Simpson, 1). And in this book, I suggest that this project might *feel* for those who are bolstered by it – who are legitimized by it – very much like *comfort from the inside*. Part of home, after all, is its familiarity, repetition, reinstatement, celebration, and assurance.

Theorizing Societal Indifference

The *Oxford English Dictionary* defines the word "indifferent" as Latin in origin and as meaning either "having no particular interest or sympathy; unconcerned" or "not particularly good; mediocre." It notes that the word originally meant "making no difference." The *Oxford American Dictionary* adds that in its origins the word communicated an element of "being neither good nor bad." The word's definition thus presupposes an a priori subject who *has* no particular interest, sympathy, or concern and from whom indifference emanates. Based on this definition, a basic reading of Amnesty International's (2004) claim suggests that Canadians are people who might be expected to have no particular interest, sympathy, or concern when it comes to the occurrence of violence against Indigenous women and girls. Such events make no difference, are neither good nor bad, and provoke no particular concern among those living in Canadian society. There is an absence here – a lack. Read with this definition in mind, Amnesty International's claim of an expectation of societal indifference has particular effects. The discourse positions those who face racialized and gendered violence as on the *outside* of a society expected to be indifferent to this violence. Such an expectation of indifference is possible only if the indifferent subject sees the victim of violence as already *not* a member of this society. The claim thus signals the prior social exclusion of women and girls who were disappeared or who experienced harm. Moreover, it signals that those who know and love the kidnapped or murdered are also *not* contained within the idea of "Canadian society." That is, the utterance of "societal indifference" expels from a generalized notion of "the social" specifically those people who are not indifferent at all. In this case, as a national problem, those excluded by such an utterance are excluded too from a Canadian public whose members, by Amnesty International's assessment, are expected to be impervious to these particular acts of violence.

Assuming that a person would not be expected to be impervious to violence that they themselves are subject to, this discourse points to a very clear conceptual divide regarding who is a citizen of Canada and thus worthy of protection and who is left out. This interpretation positions those disappeared as already excluded from "society" even prior to their disappearance. With this fairly basic reading, Amnesty International's fourth factor can be understood both as a condemnation of Canadians for violence and harm against Aboriginal women and as key to the construction of those subject to violence and harm and their social networks as existing outside of the context of "Canadians" and thus outside of a right to or requirement for protection and concern from the Canadian state. This construction in fact explains and justifies Amnesty International's (2004, 2) second factor: "police in Canada have often failed to provide Indigenous women with an adequate standard of protection." Those people not imagined as indifferent are also not imagined as members of the Canadian society, so in practice, they are perhaps the ones deemed not to warrant the protections otherwise apparently on offer by the state.

There is also the question of what a postulate of societal indifference does to those situated as of *the social*? What of those who (intermittently) hear reports of women or girls disappearing from Edmonton? What of those who also read Amnesty International's (2004) account of an expectation of general indifference? In this case, to be indifferent is perhaps also an indication of safety or protection from violence considered by Amnesty International to be "racist violence" (Amnesty International 2004, 2). Thus, in summoning an indifferent society, does Amnesty International speak specifically of and to a society that is *not* subject to racist violence, a society that has benefited from historical practices and politics that privilege its members' typically nonracialized status? How is it possible, then, for such a proclamation to provoke widespread concern?

None of the interpretations I put forth are in keeping with the mandate of Amnesty International. And my readings of this report are not those expected or intended. However, I suggest that the use of "societal indifference" to address a perceived lack of political or social mobilization in the face of racist and gendered violence has implications that exceed, and perhaps even work counter to, Amnesty International's more explicit call to attention. I worry that these consequences might function to contain or limit the possibilities for how we think about and address racialized and gendered violence in the Canadian present. Perhaps more urgently, I worry that in its worst manifestation, the account works to name but also to maintain systems of structural state violence.

However, there is also a second interpretation, one that relates to "societal" as a modifier of "indifference."[9] With "societal" characterizing this type of indifference, and thereby distinguishing it from other types of indifference, there are more possibilities for theorizing what is happening. Distinct from, for example, a natural, learned, or individual indifference, "societal indifference" is specific only to the societal context. It is not what one feels or does not feel in relation to a report of violence. The individual is not its locus. Such an understanding cannot work in keeping with a definition that assumes the individual as the source and indifference as only a feeling. With this elaborated interpretation, Amnesty International (2004) might be attempting to discern an indifference that is contingent on the existence of a societal unit or level, an indifference that is unique from whatever apathy or sorrow is felt or not felt by single people, an indifference that has the social as its source. Indifference here is exclusively social. It cannot be otherwise. The claim of societal indifference, then, is not a chastisement but a claim through which to articulate a more elaborate understanding of how a particular affect (or lack thereof) can be social, tied to matters of life and death, and learned even though it remains unconscious or only part of the background to some experiences of daily life. But again, the "societal" relied upon here is an abstraction. And within a mainstream modernist discourse, such a "social" is hard to think with. Questions remain regarding what "the social" is and how we can intervene in social affect. Is the social that is made through this discourse realized only in and by virtue of such proclamations? Is this same social particularly attuned to its historical makings – in this case, to histories of violent settler colonization?

Additional questions abound regarding the capacity in which the social can exist at all and toward what ends. Is calling upon the societal in effect like calling upon no one? Is doing so an escape from responsibility or a failure to assign blame to anyone in particular? Is an affective expectation of indifference (i.e., a moment of shared affect) one of the ways that a society might actually be said to cohere in discursive practice? With these questions in mind, and returning to Biehl's (2001, 134) description of a woman left to die of poverty and disease in Vita, Brazil, I wonder what the distinction is between language and practice – that is, between an apparent indifference to death and its social authorization? Is societal indifference a depoliticized version of, a prerequisite for, or perhaps the consequence of the social authorization of death? What does public belief in the postulate of indifference do? Are Canadian cities such as Edmonton, Regina, and Winnipeg, which have been noted for "clusters of activities" where Indigenous women and girls face heightened risks of violence (Jacobs and Williams 2008, 134), similarly depoliticized, their strangely neutral naming obscuring pasts that still presently inflict violence as something historically and socially usual?

There are so many of these questions. And so, in this book, I attempt to work against allegations of societal indifference that rely on a modernist distinction between the social and the individual, and I wonder what happens when the question of who is left to die is asked in alternative terms. What happens when an attempt is made to name societal indifference to violence outside of the language of modernity? What happens when violence is framed as a historical and colonial investment in particular practices that have predictable ends? Is this the historical authorization of present-day violence? Along the same lines, how does societal indifference work not as a response but as an idea with no real referent that can nonetheless actually neutralize what might otherwise arouse a reaction to violence? How does the circulation of the concept allow for certain deaths? And how does it work to potentially erase processes of violent colonization, past and present? Does the claim of societal indifference work to keep some Indigenous women and girls in vulnerable and past positions in relation to an unuttered *rest of the nation* by positing them as supposedly unloved and forgotten and perhaps, as this book warily considers, as either not fully living or already on the cusp of death?

If so, how might the claim of an expectation of societal indifference be thought to work the same as or differently from nationalist colonialist strategies of the past? Might it work differently from or in coherence with, for example, the passing of legislation like the Indian Act, which, for more than a century and until Indigenous women successfully fought its overt discrimination, functioned to systematically dissolve Indigenous women's status and rights in Canada (Lawrence 2003)? Is that how the past works – "as an anteriority that continually introduces an otherness or alterity within the present" (Bhabha 1990, 308)?

Another question that incessantly nags is one that considers the relationship between the expression of a societal affect of nonresponse and the occurrence of actual incidents of violence. Although it would be overly simplistic to think that certain kinds of disappearances and deaths are entirely separable from various reports on reactions to these deaths, it is also problematic to assert a straightforward causal relationship between the two. Discourse and practice are inseparable. I attempt to decipher the contents and effects of this discourse in a Canadian contemporary context, questioning what societal indifference means in practice, how it appears or fails to appear, how it might authorize the deaths of some, and how it might function as an iteration not only of who is allowed to die but also of who is made to belong in Canada's present and who is made to belong only partially or only to the past.

Ultimately, I theorize that if we are interested in protecting women and girls of Indigenous heritage, then an uncritical acceptance of Canadian societal indifference is a constraining place to begin. A postulate of societal indifference would be appropriate only if it were intended to simplify and depoliticize what are otherwise complicated and time-honoured, yet ostensibly reprehensible, parts of the Canadian national story. Despite how the discourse is used by Amnesty International and the Native Women's Association of Canada, I argue that we must be very careful with the term "societal indifference." As an expression of regulatory powers, the idea of societal indifference might actually neutralize contemporary violence toward Indigenous women and girls and erase or ease the Canadian state's and its citizens' historical and contemporary roles in this violence. Amnesty International nonetheless provides a place to begin, and throughout the analysis that it conducts, its four factors prove highly relevant to pursing an understanding of the present as standing *in* the past since these four factors prove relevant to the structured vulnerability that some women and girls might face in a contemporary colonial Canada due to indifference and otherwise.

My thinking about how some lives are made to matter more or less than others is deeply informed by the work of poststructural social theorist Judith Butler. In the context of wars instigated by the United States since September 11, 2001, Butler's (2009, 50) work has been concerned with examining what she describes as a "differential at the level of affective and moral responsiveness" to violence. All lives are not valued equally, and this differential valuing is not explained only by individual relationships to the dead – these relationships are not the only thing that makes lives matter – but also by an affect that is communicated and shared. As Butler writes, "Affect is never merely our own: affect is, from the start, communicated from elsewhere. It disposes us to perceive the world in a certain way, to let certain dimensions of the world in and to resist others" (Butler 2009, 50). Butler describes affect as regulated and as dependent "on social supports for feeling" that are embedded in particular practices (Butler 2009, 50), such as the claim itself. That is, the claim of an expectation of indifference not only names but also prepares and instructs. However, beyond this observation, I have begun to theorize that the notion of societal indifference actually contains its inverse, which suggests that it contains a primary and basic interest in the production of particular subjects for subjugation. In Butler's (2004, 148) terms, I am suggesting that the claim of societal indifference might function as a basic support for the production of particular subjects for "dehumanization." This support, I suggest, actually necessitates what I identify as racialized state violence.[10] Societal indifference, in this case, becomes a practice and outcome for the achievement of dehumanization and is perhaps itself the evidence of successful racialization.[11] As such, societal indifference to an act of violence may be akin to what Butler describes as "the derealization of loss – the insensitivity to human suffering and death [as] the mechanism through which dehumanization is accomplished" (Butler

2004, 148). But if insensitivity to human suffering is a mechanism through which dehumanization is accomplished, I wonder how we might examine it. How do we examine affect as more than our own? How do we find the social supports that Butler (2009) identifies?

In this book, I analyze a variety of texts toward understanding what I have come to see as the historical logics of recent violence in Edmonton. I postulate that practices of dehumanization occur through claims of societal indifference and that these practices seem to share a number of consistencies. I propose further that these consistencies are in fact supported, maintained, and reproduced by the metaphysics of a settler colonial logic and context. The world defined by this ontology has specific components, including that it is singular, that it is Euclidean and inert, that it has a linear and progressive model of history, and that it has a "natural" and hierarchical organization, such as in terms of the Great Chain of Being, gender and "race," or biology (Law 2004; L. Tuhiwai Smith 1999). Theorized as a social support for feeling (indifferent), dehumanization might therefore occur with an implicit acceptance of actual violence when specifically tied to socially constructed categories of biological distinction and hierarchy; that is, by virtue of these distinctions, some people are positioned as a priori dehumanized victim subjects. A temporally singular rather than historically embedded or entrenched theory of time also supports this idea since what bears upon us in the present is considered to be dislocated from an equally singular and prior time. A Euclidean and naturalized conception of space as empty and inert – which determines that, in realist terms, there *is* actual proximity to violent events that occur in certain spaces – means that we do not need to examine the meanings made in and attached to human places and that we do not need to see these places as themselves active as social supports. Accordingly, distance is purely geographical. And finally, a progressive social teleology means the endurance of a narrative of history in which the nation is articulated as morally good or, perhaps more accurately, as having once made mistakes but as now redeemed – often by apology or just by the passage of time.

If dehumanization is a predecessor or companion to enactments of societal indifference, and if it occurs, in part, through these four mechanisms, each a feature of our contemporary and recent historical episteme (Foucault 1970; Law 2004) – that is, through the consistent invention and naturalization of biologized categories *for* the relative valuing of life, through a historical forgetting en masse, through the invention and binding of spaces of safety and danger, and through a national storyline that functions to create the present as an always improved upon version of the past – then I expect that there are historical materials as well as symbolic indicators of such coalescences. That is, these features are latent in material conditions and indeed haunt practices of dehumanization as they occur in the contemporary context. I expect that these social mechanisms produce certain absences and presences that are indicative of such hauntings (Gordon 1997). If an apparent societal indifference to the disappearance of Indigenous women in Edmonton is haunted by (or occurs via) the features outlined above, then I suppose not only that these features of the colonial present can be assessed empirically but also that these features have made some prior appearances as more or less tried and true repetitions. Although I suspect that these characteristics are often not explicit in our practices – neither in official memory nor in official historical productions of the past such as history texts and museum exhibits – they are nonetheless there. They are discernible in careful analyses of cultural productions of and from the past. Therefore, to examine these four as they haunt contemporary moments and the disappearances now occurring, I isolate and take up several moments in the making of violences in particular places in the city known as Edmonton.

There are many ways to conceptualize violence, but it is perhaps most common to think about violence while assuming a basic victim-perpetrator dyad. Such conceptions permeate everyday understandings of violence and function as justifications for various forms of policing and police institutions. But understandings of violence are asociological when limited to assessments of individual motives or events and when conceptualized as existing in a vacuum of social meaning. Violence, like affect, is never merely individual. Rather, when examined sociologically, violence is always found to have certain social, historical, and relational precedents.[12] In the context of this book, I examine violence beyond the limitations of a dichotomous and individualized definition and in much more expansive terms, addressing both targeted and specific aggressions against particular bodies in particular places as well as the sometimes impalpable, and nearly impossible to study, damages of historical objectification and erasure. Although typically conceptualized as physical harm committed by one person against another, violence here is instead understood as existing in individual experience but also as exceeding individual experience since it exists in and surpasses the moment of its most apparent manifestations, with always a much more complicated story to tell.

Sociological conceptions of violence have addressed how violence operates in ways that transcend the individual, often framing violence as a structural feature of a social and historical context (Farmer 2004; Galtung 1969). Violence, too, has social supports. Anthropologist Paul Farmer (2004, 307) describes violence as an outcome of multiple axes of oppression, with combined effects that cannot thoroughly be discerned using a linear, modernist, and individualist approach. Attempts to understand violence only in the present historical moment and only in terms of individual experience and positions will always fail to capture what is operating as a social force: "Structural violence is exerted systematically – that is, indirectly – *by everyone who belongs* to a certain social order" (Farmer 2004, 307, emphasis added). As structural, not individual, the concept offers no relief from implication in violence. There is no retreat to some false distinction between a victim and perpetrator. Instead, the concept of structural violence defies "moral econom[ies] still geared to pinning praise or blame on individual actors" (Farmer 2004, 307). Structural violence thus describes a kind of general or collective implication in the particular violent practices occurring in a certain social order, partly through *belonging*. Within that order, there is no position of freedom from responsibility for violence.

Yet this is an extremely challenging way to think about violence. In part, that is because achieving belonging has included collective practices of forgetting or denying all but an individualized implication in violence (Farmer 2004). Farmer's work addresses "the erasure of historical memory and other forms of desocialization as enabling conditions of structures that are both 'sinful' and ostensibly 'nobody's fault'" (Farmer 2004, 307). Making a specific tie to the founding of settler colonial societies like Canada, historian Lorenzo Veracini (2010, 80) writes that "only a sustained disavowal of *any* founding violence allows a seamless process of settler territorialisation" (emphasis in original). The arrival of settlers and their attempts at the permanent takeover of land have required an ongoing denial of the violence in these processes. Thus, for an analysis of patterned forms of racial and gender violence and of what appears as "societal indifference" to such violence in Canada, structural violence offers the beginning of a way to think through how harm occurs without overt recognition and historical memory – and hence without reproof. How violence may occur in everyday contexts without being recognized as violence, how it might even be socially condoned and supported in some contexts, how it eludes redress or how it changes, and how it escapes anything more than the individual assignment of responsibility can be elucidated only with a concept of violence that operates at a distance from, yet remains directly tied to, people's experiences.

Neither structural violence nor the notion of a societal indifference can be considered without addressing settler colonialism in Canada as a form of colonialism characterized by the intention of settlers to stay and make "a new home on the land, a homemaking that insists on settler sovereignty over all things in their new domain" (Tuck and Yang 2012, 5; Vowel 2016).[13] This assertion of sovereignty is most centrally an assertion of control and ownership of land, and it is a control that radically disrupts vital relationships between Indigenous peoples and the land (Tuck and Yang 2012, 5; Watts 2013). For this reason, scholars of settler colonialism have identified violence as inherent to the structure of settler colonialism and to its daily iterations (Veracini 2010; Wolfe 2006). This violence not only exists at the level of incongruent worldviews and relations with land but is also fundamentally about the elimination of the Indigenous subject, *constructed* as "Other," through whom colonial sovereignty is achieved and maintained (Mbembe 2001; A. Smith 2005; Tuck and Yang 2012; Veracini 2010; Vowel 2016; Wolfe 2006). Philosopher, political scientist, and public intellectual Achille Mbembe (2001, 25) enumerates three forms of violence embedded in the kind of claims to sovereignty made through settler colonialism: "the founding violence of conquest; the legitimating violence of transforming conquest into moral authority; and the ordinary and banal violence necessary for the maintenance of colonial sovereignty." Although the last of these forms appears most obviously aligned with the questions of concern in this book – such as how violence against Indigenous women is constructed as though it were original and banal, provoking no response – I suggest that, even though disavowed, the founding and the legitimating of violence, here postulated as historical forms of state violence, remain in operation in ways that eventuate the perception of some violence as ordinary and banal. Settler colonial sovereignty is deeply invested in making some forms of violence ordinary for the maintenance of sovereignty, and among these types of violence, gendered and sexualized violence are key mechanisms through which settler colonial power and entitlements are visualized and re-enacted (Deer 2015; Hunt 2017; Razack 2000, 2016; A. Simpson 2016; L.B. Simpson 2014; A. Smith 2005; Watts 2013).

In this book I address settler colonial violence as manifest in the disappearances of people, specifically of women and girls, and in the emergence of a notion of indifference to these occurrences. But among the major limitations of this work is my failure to elaborate on the full complexity of the power relations in operation in relation to these specific events. Societal indifference and racist and state violence against Indigenous women and girls are not predetermined occurrences. The perpetuation of, or continual return to, violence in Canada is not inevitable, and the events that I theorize as part of a structural state violence are not without multiple, active, and effective modes of Indigenous defiance, resistance, strength, and transformation. These stories, however, are not the stories that many Canadians hear (see A. Simpson 2014; L.B. Simpson 2016, 2017; L.B. Simpson, Nanibush, and Williams 2012; Tuck 2009). Kwakwaka'wakw scholar Sarah Hunt (2017) critiques the too common representations of Indigenous peoples as "at risk" rather than as strong, resilient, and powerful. This book does not describe the multiple, active, and effective modes of defiance, resistance, strength, and transformation within Indigenous communities. Here, I concern myself with the question of *how* it is communicated that some lives are not considered full and legitimate within a Canadian nation and hence are subject to disregard and violence. This is a question of how. It is not a question of which specific lives and their particular matterings. The practices that I examine in the book do produce a uniformity of *type,* but they do so precisely, I argue, so that those lives made "typical" can also be rendered less than fully human. The phrase "societal indifference," however, only falsely asserts that the disappeared were not loved or cared for and that their disappearances are not deeply mourned. Yet with this phrase, a Canadian constituent is being produced and told of "disposable" lives or of lives that matter less than others; the practices that support this instruction are what I am most interested in discerning. It is these practices that I hope to unsettle. I do not take up this research in relation to particular accounts of lived human experiences, and I neither interview or talk to people as though they were subject to racial and gendered oppressions nor speak with them as active agents of resistance, subversion, or modification of such forces. Instead, my focus is on discourses, those discernible in mostly public texts. I examine how such texts position us and how we might position ourselves, how we are made through discourses in relation to one another, and how these processes occur in ways that subsume some realities and produce others, largely in keeping with implicit settler colonial understandings and with narratives of progress, individualism, and history. Nonetheless, I will continue to argue that disappearances and the supposed "societal indifference" to such profound losses in Canada are not the inevitable present but are made possible only by ongoing practices that are part of the project of making a supposedly modern benevolent version of this nation in what we consider *the present* time and place.

Names and Places

In this book, I overgeneralize and distort. One of the ways that I do this is when I refer to diverse peoples in very homogeneous terms. This is a practice I both critique and perpetuate in this book. This homogenization occurs most problematically in relation to how I refer to different nations of peoples whose kinship networks and stories extend for millennia in parts of what is now commonly called North America. However, as legal scholar and member of the Muscogee (Creek) Nation Sarah Deer (2018) describes in her work on the relationship between violence and settler colonialism, there is no consensus on one set of appropriate terms to refer to the great diversity among Indigenous populations. In the book *Peace, Power, Righteousness: An Indigenous Manifesto,* Mohawk activist, scholar, and writer Taiaiake Alfred (1999, xxv) situates the problem of naming as a contemporary one, stating that "as Native people relearn the languages stripped from us in the past, we are coming to realize the gross insult of most common 'Indian' names." Many of these are names that early settler colonizers used to refer to First Nations, Métis, and Inuit peoples, and their contemporary repetition can re-enact a kind of colonial entitlement to name, to appropriate, and to know, and it can continue the legacy of colonization. Alfred outlines the use of these various terminologies:

> "Indian" (it should be noted that the area now known as "India" was still called "Hindustan" in the fifteenth century; the term "Indian" as applied to indigenous Americans is derived from Columbus's original name for the Taino people he first encountered, "una gente in Dios," or "Indios," meaning "a people in God"; "Indian" is also a legal term, and in common use among indigenous people in North America), "Native" (in references to the racial and cultural distinctiveness of individuals, and to distinguish our communities from those of the mainstream society), "American Indians" (in common use and a legal-political category in the United States), "Aboriginal" (a legal category in Canada; also to emphasize the primacy of the people who first occupied the land), and "indigenous" (in global contexts, and to emphasize natural, tribal, and traditional characteristics of various people). All are quite appropriate in context and are used extensively by Native people themselves. (Alfred 1999, xxvi)

There is no route to purity here. There is no possible assurance of correct or ethical use of language here. We cannot step outside of the language histories through which we communicate and act today. In this work, in attempting to adopt a context-specific approach, I primarily use "Indigenous peoples." The plural here is important, as it indicates that there are many different nations of Indigenous people and that similarities between diverse groups should not be assumed (Vowel 2016). My frequent use of "Indigenous peoples" emphasizes the primacy of the land's First Peoples and of their relations, and reflects a common usage in a variety of Canadian texts, including those generated by Indigenous communities as well as by scholars, governments, and activists. In some parts of the book, I also use the terms "Aboriginal," "First Nations," "Métis," and "Inuit." "Aboriginal" was used as a legal designation in Canada in the Constitution Act, 1982 (Vowel 2016), is a very general term, and does not indicate legal Indian status (27). The terms "First Nations," "Inuit," and "Métis" are also commonly used in government publications and are the three Aboriginal groups recognized in Canada's Constitution. I occasionally use these terms when referring to a group that has historically been demarcated as such. I use the term "Native peoples" to refer to a multitude of different communities whose members identify them as distinct from what are now commonly considered mainstream Canadian communities. I also use the term "Indian" when such usage reflects the language used in historical texts.

When I have been able to access the traditional or chosen names of important territories or figures, I have used them in this book. When I have been unable to do that, I have attempted to make reference to the territories and figures in ways that nonetheless undermine Eurocentric naming practices and assumptions and foreground the diversity and complexity of humans and groupings. However, it is the case that language changes, names are contested, and the boundaries that seem to be demarcated by particular namings are always blurred. The language I use in this book does reflect my own social positions and ignorance; I do not always know – nor perhaps, importantly, *should* I always know – the traditional, contemporary, or chosen names of the places and peoples that feature as significant in this work. I recognize that I cannot know all of the implications of my writing. Such a knowing seems anyway to be too much aligned with the certainties that a Eurocentric ontology might guarantee. I take some reassurance in the idea that this particular politically oriented historiography of violence in a settler colonial contemporary context could not be written without some collapsing of diverse peoples into more homogeneous groupings. This simplification also applies to those people I broadly characterize as settler colonial subjects, as white settler subjects, or as colonizers. This work suffers from a lack of specificity there, too, although in this case it works quite differently. I know few details of the early settlers. I argue, however, that the construction of the Native-settler dyad has been a crucial and ongoing component of the making of a Canadian national history and that these two categories have been instrumental to the (provisionally) successful making of a particular Canadian nation (Mackey 1999; Veracini 2010). A most essential exclusive dichotomy produced through settler colonialism is "the one separating the coloniser and the colonised" (Veracini 2010, 16). Thus part of the work includes at once a use of and an interrogation of those terms. But the uses of these two overly general categorizations are not equivalent in their effects since all of the terms I use to describe those who arrived in this place and established Canada from French and British colonies are terms used by Euro-Canadians to write and speak of themselves, they are not historically derogatory, and although certainly overly general (as with the term "Euro"), they serve to locate the movement and spread of a certain form of Western power and knowledge that accompanied the footsteps of (various) settler colonial subjects. Among settler colonizers, I name fur traders, explorers, settlers, and immigrants. Notice that the array of terms used to describe those who colonized the country function to distinguish between people based on their activities, not on their *being* or their bodies, and thus function differently from terms that suggest or emerge from a notion of ethnic or racial difference. I use the term "white" when speaking specifically of a racial politics that has effectively naturalized the privilege of one group by situating its members as in opposition to or as inherently different from an "Other."

Throughout this book, the language used in reference to the missing and murdered women and girls of Edmonton and elsewhere in Canada is deliberate and requires particular attention. As has been done thus far, I often refer to these cases as instances in which people have been "disappeared." This is a dangerous reference and an allusion to those more commonly known as the *desaparecidos,* those who were disappeared from a number of Latin American countries from about the mid-1960s to the early 1980s (Gordon 1997). The disappearance of people in countries like Guatemala, Chile, and Argentina was an exercise of state power to deter public resistance. Sociologist Avery Gordon (1997, 72) describes these processes as consisting of "illegal abduction by the police, military and paramilitary squads, detention in secret centres, torture, usually death and improper burial and denial by the authorities ... These were the horrifying characteristics of the organized system of repression known as disappearance." In Argentina 30,000 people were disappeared between 1976 and 1983, but disappearance has also occurred as an exercise of state power in other places, such as Nazi Germany, where 7,000 people were disappeared under the Night and Fog Decree of 1941 (Gordon 1997, 72).

Using disappearance to frame what is happening in Edmonton risks suggesting that the type of state repression and violence exercised in Latin America or Nazi Germany is comparable to what is happening in Canada. This is neither the point nor the case. Rather, Gordon (1997, 72) is clear that disappearance is a "worldwide phenomenon." I follow anthropologist Dara Culhane's (2003) use of the term in her account of how Vancouver activists adopted a strategy famously implemented by the movement Las Madres de Plaza de Mayo in Argentina to draw attention to the disappearances of loved ones. In 2001, during an annual procession held on February 14 to draw attention to Vancouver's missing and murdered women, participants carried pictures of the missing, just as was done by members of Las Madres de Plaza de Mayo (Culhane 2003). The terms "disappearance" and "the disappeared" are used in this book for several reasons. First, they circumvent what has in recent years become the arguably too easy iteration of the phrase "missing and murdered Indigenous women," which is found specifically in Canadian media and social media – a repetition that I argue has something important to do with what has been identified as the "societal indifference" to violence against those identified as Indigenous women. Second, they radically redefine the cases of missing and murdered women as public and political rather than private occurrences and thus implicate the nation-state in these violences. Third, they lack the abstract meaning of the word "missing" and instead point to real actions taken by real people to effect another's disappearance (Gordon 1997, 75). Fourth, their use as a theoretical tool in one of the historical moments I analyze in this book seems only to illuminate their applicability to the other two, thereby contributing to how we might understand the possibilities that temporally drawn-out, highly obscured, but nonetheless systematic forms of disappearance were occurring across colonial time in Canada. Finally, this use of "disappearance" and "the disappeared" operates to refuse death for those whose lives have been taken away, whether through kidnapping or murder. "Death exists in the past tense, disappearance in the present" (Gordon 1997, 113). Whereas death in the modern moment marks a life as though it were past, disappearance does not (Gordon 1997, 113). "Disappearance" can in fact ward off death, and in so doing, the term also keeps at bay a tendency or desire or imperative to mourn, to forget, or to get over the violence of a life taken.

So, although the disappearances occurring in Canada are not at all equivalent to those that occurred in Latin America, at least in the most immediate present, and although the state roles in these violences may not appear to be direct, immediate, or obvious, I argue that the use of disappearance as a framework reveals some startling and important parallels (Culhane 2003; Dean 2015). Since I argue that the implication of the state in Edmonton's disappearances is particularly nuanced, hidden, or – as will be discussed – recognized as existing only in the past, the analysis here does much to further our understandings of disappearances and how they might work to produce a settler colonial nation of the present.

1

A History of the Present: Methodology

> *Imagine how you as writers from the dominant society might turn over some of the rocks in your own garden for examination. Imagine in your literature courageously questioning and examining the values that allow the dehumanizing of peoples through domination and the dispassionate nature of the racism inherent in perpetuating such practices. Imagine writing in honesty, free of the romantic bias about the courageous "pioneering spirit" of colonialist practice and imperialist process. Imagine interpreting for us your own people's thinking toward us, instead of interpreting for us, our thinking, our lives, our stories.*
>
> – JEANETTE ARMSTRONG, "THE DISEMPOWERMENT OF FIRST NORTH AMERICAN NATIVE PEOPLES AND EMPOWERMENT THROUGH THEIR WRITING"

IN THIS BOOK, I ATTEMPT to disrupt a specifically western and Euro-American temporal ontology and epistemology. I seek to loosen conventional, individual, and ingrained attachments to structures of knowing that automatically situate a past-present-future progression, to instead provide what French philosopher Michel Foucault (1977, 3) deems a "history of the present," and to then pursue another story as a consequence (Law 2004; Thrift 1999). As much as this is a scholarly endeavour for the purpose of pursuing an alternative politics, it is also an exercise in the abandonment of my (individually learned and socially produced) form of knowing, which situates the past as prior, the present as current, and the future as anticipated, encroaching, and lucky for us, always an improvement. The approach I employ here is taken precisely against a mainstream, Western, Euro-American politics of clear and progressive temporal distinctions (Brown 2001; Law 2004; Thrift 1999) but without a set alternative. It attempts to grapple with colonial legacies in Canada in the present while refusing the limitations inherent in offering either an analysis of seemingly isolated events or an analysis isolated in time. This work includes pulling together mostly public texts and images that are likely more commonly considered separately and regarded as unrelated. In no modern archive would they be shelved in proximity. This work offers a synthesis across time to refute the notion that a progressive lineage is the natural and only human conceptualization of order – because, of course, there are others (see Gell 1992). Although a synthesis in this sense, this work also aims for fragmentation or incoherence throughout, as I attempt to be sensitive to the problems of creating an integrative (and integrating) account. In this effort, I repeatedly attempt to defamiliarize (myself with) conventional Western constructs of time, and because a linear temporal organization is frequently made into or conflated with causation, I attempt to defamiliarize (myself with) that too.[1]

In this book, I do not attempt to produce an overarching theory or explanation of settler colonial violence. Rather, my analysis is specific and local; I offer up fractured *descriptions* of what practices might be embedded in the cultural productions I examine (Thrift 1999). I momentarily grasp at a series of what critical theorist and filmmaker Elizabeth Povinelli (2011, 144) calls "quasi-events" and attempt to juxtapose or plait what I characterize as three spatial and temporal episodes: (1) European settlement in the area of Edmonton circa 1870; (2) the treatment of First Nations, Métis, and Inuit peoples in the Charles Camsell Indian Hospital in Edmonton beginning in 1946; and (3) the contemporary disappearance and murder of numerous Indigenous women and girls, some reportedly involved in survival or street-level sex work in downtown Edmonton. I frame these spatial and temporal episodes as "contact zones" to signal that each one offers "the space of colonial encounters, the space in which peoples geographically and historically separated come into contact with each other and establish ongoing relations, usually involving conditions of coercion, radical inequality, and intractable conflict" (M.L. Pratt 1992, 6). I add that none of these episodes functions as an initial or original point of contact but that each one occurs within a network of relations and includes returns to or continuations of these relations. I work with the notion that the separating-out and the coming together of people are not limited to one point in time and do not occur as singular events but as series of practices that constitute a (dialectical) process. Consequently, they must be considered at various moments that are not exclusive to the slow arrival of "the Europeans" as though such arrivals were singular (Veracini 2010). Contact zones exhibit the interactivity characteristic of a coming into relation with and they reject a reliance on pervasive "conquest and domination" accounts. Contact zones postulate the effects of contact as established, struggled over, and practised in different ways and always in relation (M.L. Pratt 1992, 6). Contact zones are times, places, and relations of interactivity and struggle and thus of mutual transformation, and I propose that as such, these three contact zones haunt one another.[2] In conventional delineations of events as differently situated in empty time and in empty space, the specific practices undergirding such framings are nearly impossible to discern. Using haunting as a methodology, however, we can attempt to grasp both the practices and the ontology upon which they rely (Gordon 1997).

The notion of the contact zone is useful not only for the challenges it poses to a Eurocentric colonial narrative of time as linear and progressive but also for how it works to expand understandings of the scope and range of the relationships, exchanges, objects, bodies, and subjects of colonization. Although the conceptual tool of the contact zone is used here first and most broadly as a mechanism to pull together rather large and amorphous chunks of a conventionally linear narrative of history for their juxtaposition, it is also used to demonstrate that relationships of facilitation, struggle, and exchange in settler colonization occurred and occur materially on and through bodies, particularly on and through women's bodies. "Women occupied the spaces of colonial encounter between Aboriginals and newcomers as both colonizers and the colonized, transgressing restrictive boundaries and making history ... Colonial relationships of power were expressed locally and in different times and places that were grounded in the materiality of women's day-to-day lives" (Pickles and Rutherford 2006, 1). This insight is important, but it is perhaps as important to see the emergence of some taken-for-granted notion of "women" as an *outcome* of that colonial encounter rather than as a pre-existing reality. This is the case both for those attempting to settle the new nation and, perhaps more obviously, for members of Indigenous communities, whose gender became a prime concern for the emerging nation-state, as is clear in the regulation of gender and marriage through legislation such as the Indian Act (Vowel 2016). Thus the use of contact zones works as a way to specifically tap into this coming together as something that is not only deeply intimate and embodied but also occasioned by a more macro-level movement of peoples across and within the ongoing making of a Canadian nation. Although I am ultimately concerned with settler colonial violence against Indigenous women and girls, this issue can be addressed only if we look at the ways that colonization and nation building across time in Canada are realized spatially and on bodies specified as such. I propose, then, a sketch of the structural and colonial violence within each contact zone through a consideration of dislodged, everyday, and present sites of struggle and exchange.

I take these contact zones out of what might be imagined as their prior configuration in a colonial order. I dislodge them and hence interrupt what might otherwise be their arrangement as discrete and coherent. I presuppose that the moments I take up haunt each other. The selection of each one was due less to a specific knowledge of *how* they might haunt each other and more to a certain confidence in the idea *that* they might haunt each other (Gordon 1997; Thrift 1999). I presuppose that a "modern" era produces hauntings as ubiquitous, and those projects that forge temporal orders as though they were natural and discrete cannot but betray (Foucault 1977). Because the rigid imposition of temporal distinctions between the past, present, and future is so fundamental and foundational to the idea of modernity, I suspect that such divisions are profoundly functional in the bolstering of contingent projects like individualism and nationalism and that they are fundamental to ensuring exploitative (i.e., capital-oriented) relations among societies and between people and nations (Benjamin 2002; Brown 2001; Gregory 2004; Moses 2005; Stoler 1995). If, then, temporal distinctions are recognized as an ideological apparatus, there might be something to learn from their attempted suspension – or at least from their recognition as such an apparatus. What might happen due to a refusal of such colonial temporality in exchange for the assumption of its opposite? That is very hard to imagine. But I think that this is the task, as described by anthropologist Ann Laura Stoler (1995, 5): "Post-colonial scholarship has been precisely [intended] to disassemble the neat divisions that could imagine a European history and its unified collectivities apart from the externalized Others on whom it was founded and which it produced." Thus, within a period of just over one hundred years and in a broadly circumscribed place, I have wagered on the notion that, whatever moments are selected, they will, with concentrated research and an attention to present absences (Gordon 1997; Van Wagenen 2004), speak to each other, refer to one another, and perhaps even anticipate and expose each other's arrival or presence (Thrift 1999). It is important to state clearly that my selection of contact zones did not follow methodological rules for systematic or representative sampling in any way, as I was not preoccupied with the guarantees that such practices are said to deliver. These guarantees would have been suspect. Instead, I chose to look at the disappearance of women and girls from Edmonton because this was the news that kept interrupting my thinking during my doctoral coursework. It was what was going on in the city where I lived. Yet, partly through the discourse of social indifference, a discourse deployed ostensibly to activate outrage and response, such disappearances seemed not to matter or, perhaps more accurately, not to have occurred at all. These disappearances seemed to lack the weight of historically meaningful events, and this very observation seemed to further stymie any response or reaction that would deem them to be meaningful.

It is important that I be clear that my observations reflected my social position at the time. I was a young settler scholar actively taking up all of the advantages that such a positioning afforded me, and so if I thought that such disappearances did not seem to matter, this perception had everything to do with the fact that they did not seem to matter to *me*. Each disappearance and each murder mattered to those who loved and lived with the people who had been disappeared or harmed. Their pain was not in question. But to stop at proximity seemed unsatisfactory. We do collectively and publicly mourn the deaths of some people that we have never met. I did not think Amnesty International was just describing a *lack of relationship* between those subject to harm and those indifferent to it. I proposed that there was a relationship there. And to understand the relationship between these positions, I felt compelled to "turn over some of the rocks in [my] own garden for examination" (Armstrong 1998, 240) in order to see myself as a socially inscribed subject through whom indifference is made to operate as though it came *from me* rather than operating as a discourse, as what Povinelli (2011, 8) describes as affective and "cosubstantiating practices." The question to ask, then, was how this process occurs.

I chose to examine cultural documents produced in 1870 during an early era of settler colonialism in Edmonton because the relationship between Indigenous disappearance and settler colonial arrival seemed a necessary one to elaborate; I had already learned of early legislative efforts that worked and still work to disappear Indigenous peoples generally. Moreover, my training in sociology demanded that a historical account be provided, so some examination of what remains of "early contact" seemed to matter. I investigated the Charles Camsell Indian Hospital because one of my supervisors knew of my interests in medicine and in haunting, and she thought of this place and urged me to visit it. When I finally saw it, the hospital occupied the landscape like a demand. The hollowed-out place seemed to still be standing only as a kind of appeal or a claim. The Charles Camsell Indian Hospital was a specific site where relationships between settlers and Indigenous peoples were of prime importance and where these relationships were managed as such through the celebration of colonial notions of medical treatment, technology, and care. This investigation into an institution that was commonly considered one of benevolence offered opportunities to consider how settler colonialism might operate within logics of apparent care as well as of containment. The Charles Camsell Indian Hospital, then, was to offer something of a counter-site for analysis. It was a place that could not be characterized as indifferent, given the specific attention, treatment, and care offered there.

In my analysis of settler colonial violence in Edmonton and of the unique and apparent social contours of indifference to this violence, I take up these times and spaces as practices rather than containers, as productive rather than idle, and as entrenched in prior practices there rather than as neutral or empty (Thrift 1999). I take from geographer Nigel Thrift, who describes places as "'passings' that 'haunt' us" (Thrift 1999, 310). Key to his understanding of places is that they are dynamic and disclosive. Places take "shape only in their passing," they "can never be pre-ordained," and "whilst places may be designed to elicit particular practices ... all kinds of other practices may in fact be going on within them which they were never designed to admit (but which may become a vital part of those places' intelligibility)" (Thrift 1999, 310–11).

Places are also "disclosive" (Thrift 1999, 310–11), taking form through the intelligible practices enacted there. Thrift draws on another geographer, Theodore R. Schatzki (1996, 115), for the following example: "When a tree is understood as something to climb ... it becomes a place at which climbing is intelligible." Thus I consider the contours of these three times and places through the practices rendered intelligible there. I admit into my investigation multiple aspects of each contact zone that might otherwise appear singular or isolated to offer something of a description of colonial and racialized gendered violence and of their constitutive invisibilities.

In taking these contact zones out of their assumed configuration in a colonial spatial and temporal order, I forge links between them according to a strategy of "blasting" (Gordon 1997, 66). I break with the linearity of Western ontology and overlay historically specified vaguenesses into events to see what their coalition produces. The effect that I hope for is inspired by cultural theorist Walter Benjamin's (1968, 263) concern with "the oppressed past" and with drawing the past out of the present, where it seems to be hidden or is apparently dead but where its resonances still echo and move (Gordon 1997; Harootunian 1996). Elaborating on this component of Benjamin's methodology, Gordon (1997, 66) describes "blasting" as

> a method of dialectics that reconstructs a lifework by following the scrambled trails the ghost leaves, picking up its pieces, setting them down elsewhere. Blasting might be conceived as entering through a different door, the door of the uncanny, the door of the fragment, the door of the shocking parallel. Entering one place, another often emerges in juxtaposition, along the lines of a defamiliarization coalescing into a moment of connection, a configuration. Through this door a certain kind of search is established, one that often leads along an associative path of correspondences ... This path of correspondences is not like the causality associated with social science or related modes that share its basic epistemology: it blasts through the rational, linearly temporal, and discrete spatiality of our conventional notions of cause and effect, past and present, conscious and unconscious.

This project, then, is something of a montage. It dislodges linear temporality. It is "dedicated to 'blast(ing) from the continuum of history'" and conceives of "the task of 'construction' as a performance that must seek to produce a certain concrete effect, the coming together of the 'Then *(das Gewesene)* and the Now *(das Jetzt)* ... into a constellation like a flash of lightening'" (Harootunian 1996, 77, quoting Benjamin). I enter and re-enter contact zones from a number of times and places to defamiliarize through a kind of juxtaposition but without the kind of separation that juxtaposition would perpetuate. I do so in part because I also take seriously Lorenzo Veracini's (2010, 14) contentions that there are features specific to settler colonial projects and that a mimetic character is among their traits. There must be repetitions in settler colonial projects, and with repetition comes a recurrent need for their disavowal so that settler societies are rendered legitimate and benevolent over and over again. In its details and in its design, this book is a blasting aimed at tapping the uncanny, the parallel, and the fragment while dismantling a linear temporality that commonly structures formally learned and reproduced understandings that distinguish present struggles from the past and thus, I postulate, ensure the endurance of settler colonial violence in the contemporary context.

In this book, I seek to set down the elements of blasting elsewhere and to bring together that which has not been made into history both for what it might offer in terms of an alternative understanding of the past, present, and future and for how such understandings might challenge the fortitude of oppression. I consider how such an effort might provoke potential anti-colonial interventions into these sites such that we can no longer talk about racialized and gendered violence as though such violence were independent of authorization by, disconnected from, and unrelated to the settler colonial present and to each of our situations here. In practical terms, the focus is one that sketches out social and historical factors operational in the contemporary emergency of violence against Indigenous peoples generally and against women and girls specifically. As I write toward describing the hold of a Eurocentric metaphysics that imposes spatial and temporal orders as neutral and passive and that frames bodies as though they naturally and individually harboured their own inherent worth or worthlessness, I focus on how such systems of thought are materialized in violence against people in everyday social practices and locales. To do so, I focus on three contact zones in a city where this violence has been realized for well over a century.

I have noted that my study of these contact zones also represents my individual attempts to render strange a previously taken-for-granted reality. And this concern returns me to an earlier point: all and any form of research occurs as already interested and already particularly situated (Haraway 1991; Law 2004; L. Tuhiwai Smith 1999). Human knowledges are limited "because of the way human subjects are embodied as beings in time-space, because of their interconnected position in multiple social relations, and because there are numerous perspectives on, and metaphors of, what counts as knowledge, or, more precisely, knowledges" (Thrift 1999, 303).

But I have not yet thoroughly addressed my own situated and interested positions in the present work. I know it may read as though I address my own historical and relational positioning as a mode of confession or to resolve the complicated nature of my ongoing and everyday embodiments, relationships, and practices (Pillow 2003; A. Smith 2014), but such confessional modes, I think, tend to mask what are still complicated and complicit forms of settler colonial relations (A. Smith 2014). Instead, this brief sketch offers insight only into how this text came to be made, how it might be taken up, the presences that continue to haunt it, and the conditions of its production.

The work I do now and here is a matter of history and relations. We are here because my parents came here, because their parents came here, because members of their extended family came here. My mom arrived on the Canadian prairies when she was eight, only eighty-five years after the nation of Canada itself was apparently founded. It was this new nation that granted my mother and her family a home. They had fled their farm near what is now the city of Gdańsk during the Second World War, and after living as refugees for seven years near Hamburg, my grandparents, my mother, and her two brothers took a ship to Canada to join my grandfather's brothers, already settled on the western prairies. There are few details offered up to describe the difficulties of these times, but I have always understood the story of my mother's family's arrival here to be one of great fortune and their prosperity here to be the result of luck as well as incredible hard work and perseverance. I know less about my father's family. The Granzows came to the United States of America from Europe several generations before my dad was born in Chicago, Illinois, in 1944. My grandmother used to say that they came from France, and although we know much less about our relations on that side, there is apparently also a German and British connection there. My parents met in British Columbia, where my mom worked as a teacher and my dad was visiting his brother, who had fled the US draft and become a teacher in Canada. My parents married in 1972 and lived for several years in Phoenix, Arizona, where my sister and I were born. In 1975, when my dad was hired by the University of Lethbridge, my mom returned to the Canadian prairies and to her extended family, now with her own young family. Here, my father worked for thirty-four years at the same postsecondary institute that now supports me and my partner in our work. The work I do now and here is a matter of history and relations.

Lethbridge is where I spent my childhood. I have lived in Alberta for much of my life, but I did not officially become a Canadian until 2005 while living in Edmonton, the province's capital. Despite my American citizenship, I had always felt like I belonged in Canada. Although the rights and responsibilities of Canadian citizenship were not legally mine, it seemed to me that even without this legal status, I was recognized as though I belonged in my everyday life and received the benefits of such status. I was never asked where I came from. I learned that the belonging I experienced in everyday contexts was contingent on something other than where I actually came from. My writing of this book has been about how I am situated both as belonging as an immigrant to this country and in relation to the events and materials I take up. On a daily basis, I realized – as I still do – various advantages afforded to me in part because they had been afforded to people deemed to be "just like me" in the past. These advantages are easy to access. They seem always, in fact, to be on offer. When I began writing this book, I had no children and was living in Edmonton, enrolled as a graduate student in the social sciences and living on funds from scholarships, including one provided by the Government of Canada. For all of these reasons, I was able to research and write extensively about these particular matters of other peoples' lives and deaths with so much support, from afar, and under conditions of security. More precisely, I was able to read and write about matters that I thought were necessarily vitally relevant *not* to my own life but to the lives and deaths of the women I had heard about on the radio. At the same time, I felt pursued by the notion that my life and my security were actually intimately implicated in the lives and deaths of those I had heard about. I felt like I was both at a distance and implicated. I felt like I was part of some silent public contract, perhaps Michael Taussig's (1999, 2) "public secret," a collective commitment to carry on as though there were no stories of women found dead. And I felt like I had long ago developed the resources for such indifferent comportments in my daily practices, such as by leaving my little apartment and going into the world – by carrying on. The conditions that make possible my life here and my research and writing are not external to the project; they are part of the apparatuses undergirding both my writing and my position in relation to the subject matter. That I might take up the subject matter as research in this way is an indication of my own removal and of my own indifference. How could it be otherwise?

I am attempting to write against my own orientations both as an intervention into the preconditions, practices, or structures that support an apparent indifference and as a recognition and interrogation of my own material and psychic attachments to this topic. What we might frame as a "public secret" goes beyond a kind of collective knowing to practices that effect a mutual making. I have used the notion of attachment in the past but am now thinking of the ways that we are actually co-made or co-substantiated (Povinelli 2011, 8) through such practices. This type of deep implication is highly charged by the fact that I lived for much of my life in a small city in southern Alberta. In this city, it seems racism was and is not an anomaly but a central mechanism for ordering daily life and for establishing the righteousness of certain already established communities of belonging.[3] I argue that, while always resisted, this dynamic and the practices that support it are central to the production of a broader, perhaps even national, politics of indifference that is realized in everyday practices and through which we might all be collectively made.

In closing this chapter, I want to reassert that instead of offering an authoritative or single "truth" in this work, I offer a particular production – an assemblage of "data" and ideas – for what its components might inspire. I take up conventional objects of sociological analysis as "haunted" objects of inquiry (Gordon 1997). I take up "history" as a story that is situated and interested, and I dispute its modern characterization as inherently progressive and constant (Brown 2001; L. Tuhiwai Smith 1999). And I investigate "space" as alive, as productive, as invested with meaning and power, and as operational as social matter (Lefebvre 1991). For an escape from the demands to produce more authoritative and conventional sociological "truths," I am inspired by Foucault's (1980) offering-up of a particular type of "fiction." About his own work, Foucault writes,

> [It] does not have the function of a proof. It exists as a sort of prelude, to explore the keyboard, sketch out the themes and see how people react, what will be criticised, what will be

> misunderstood, and what will cause resentment ... As to the problem of fiction, it seems to me to be a very important one; I am well aware that I have never written anything but fictions. I do not mean to say, however, that truth is therefore absent. It seems to me that the possibility exists for fiction to function in truth, for a fictional discourse to induce effects of truth, and for bringing it about that a true discourse engenders or "manufactures" something that does not as yet exist, that is, "fictions" it. One "fictions" history on the basis of a political reality that makes it true, one "fictions" a politics not yet in existence on the basis of a historical truth. (Foucault 1980, 193)

I engage in this project of producing fictions in the context of already established truths and of their politics and am highly interested in the effects of such productions, particularly in the political possibilities they inspire. As will be seen, criticisms, misunderstandings, and resentments may be among the effects that this work inspires precisely because of the truths that this work rejects, like the constructs of "race" as biological, science as "truth," and the nation as "good." Thus, in these pages, I examine just how histories have already been fictioned by their political foundations. Taking up the present temporal moment as an expression of these fictions, this assemblage might provoke (or itself fiction) a kind of political response that, as one of its multiple effects, eventually gestures toward the deconstruction of "societal indifference" and toward more just human socialities.

2

"It in no way makes you safer" Contemporary Policing and Remaking the City

IN 2002 AND 2003 the *Edmonton Journal* ran these headlines: "Every 'Date' Can Be Her Last: Death Stalks Women Who Stroll City's Underworld" (Sinnema 2002) and "Murder Puts Prostitutes on Edge: Dead Woman Could Have Been Any One of Them, They Fear" (Sinnema and Purdy 2003). The *Globe and Mail* ran the headline "Edmontonians Fear Serial Killer Preying on Sex-Trade Workers" (Fowlie 2003). In fact, an analysis of sixty-one relevant articles published in 2005 in the *Edmonton Journal* and the *Globe and Mail* reveals an underlying trend in the mainstream media during that year: women who had gone missing or been found murdered in Edmonton were frequently identified in these texts as involved in prostitution. This association resembles the dominant representation of Vancouver's missing women in print media coverage, which women's and gender studies scholar Shawna Ferris (2015, 7) argues consistently "constructs the victims as criminals who are classed, racialized, *and* of poor moral character" (emphasis in original). Moreover, media accounts of the cases of abduction or murder in Edmonton reported that such kinds of violence occurred with some regularity to women involved in street-level sex work more generally. Examples from that year are "Dead Woman Was Prostitute: Eleventh Death in City Sex Trade" (Cormier and Farrell 2005), "Latest Body in Farm Field Another Prostitute" (Loyie and Cormier 2005), and "Another Sex Trade Worker

Declared Missing" (Audette 2005). "*Eleventh* death," "*latest* body," and "*another* sex trade worker" – each of these phrases points to a link between ongoing violence and street-level sex work. Although I do not conduct a detailed analysis of news media here, Ferris's (2015, 51) study suggests that media representations of the murdered in Edmonton "cultivated interest not in the suffering and deaths of multiple women, but in the tracking of a serial killer or group of killers who had ... eluded Edmonton Police for more than twenty years."

In 2012, even as the *Edmonton Sun* reported that police could see "no discernible pattern whatsoever" in the killings in the country's "murder capital," it paradoxically noted that in 2011, "even as the death toll rose, police maintained *Edmonton was safe* since most of the killings involved those who lead a high-risk lifestyle" and that ten of the forty-seven people murdered that year were Aboriginal (Roth 2012, emphasis added). The callousness of this claim is not unique or isolated to the media. Nor is it uncommon for the press to conflate multiple and complex factors for the purposes of putting forth an impactful headline. In this case, police reportedly asserted that "Edmonton was safe." But clearly, it was not safe for those who fell into some variation of leading "a high-risk lifestyle" and being "Aboriginal." Being at high risk and being Aboriginal are decidedly and categorically excluded from the assertion of a safe city. Yet the danger faced by those excluded from such safety was extremely high. Aboriginal people, at the time, made up less than 6 percent of the city's population, but more than 20 percent of the murdered that year were Aboriginal. Thus, for the claim that Edmonton was safe to be meaningful, it had to be understood that Edmonton was a city that did not include either those leading "a high-risk lifestyle" or "Aboriginal" people. This strategy of pairing "high-risk" with some reference to Indigeneity also worked to offer particular readers a kind of story with which they might already have been familiar – one that is found throughout the other texts considered in connection with the other historical moments examined in this book – but what it did not do was accurately describe some truth about the correspondence between the two.

In this chapter, I examine some seemingly disparate practices through which the ground is prepared for ongoing indifference to the deaths of some people in Edmonton; I suggest that this foundation is laid, in part, through various makings of the city of Edmonton. Among these practices are representational strategies used by major newspapers, as briefly touched on above, but in this chapter, I specifically examine discourses circulating through online materials that outline the practices and mandates of both the federal and the municipal police and discourses occasioned by the City of Edmonton's project to gentrify a downtown neighbourhood. I refer to these practices with spatial metaphors, like setting the foundation, and do so intentionally; this chapter addresses how affective indifference is prepared in and through social conceptions and productions of place, such that the relationship between a lack of concern and an association with particular places in the city appears natural. I argue that through such practices a temporary coherence is apparently forged between place and population with regard to degeneracy. In later chapters, I move on to consider how such associations have been made in two other contact zones, demonstrating that although unique in their specific manifestations, the colonial violences of settlement and legitimation have long undergirded and naturalized contemporary assertions of indifference to the well-being and to the disappearance of high-risk peoples, including some Indigenous women and girls.

The Paradox of Kare

In October 2003 the Edmonton Police Service and Alberta divisions of Canada's national police force, the Royal Canadian Mounted Police (RCMP), established Project Kare, a special unit to investigate the eighty-two cases of "unsolved homicides/high risk missing persons" in the Edmonton and Calgary areas.[1] The project initially focused on cases from the 1990s and 2000s but went as far back as the 1970s (Pruden 2011). By 2011 the Kare team was made up of twenty-eight officers, was involved in numerous other investigations, and had been instrumental in charging three men with murder (Pruden 2011). Project Kare has also resolved missing-persons cases and worked "proactively" to develop "databases of personal information about people in high-risk lifestyles in Alberta" (Pruden 2011). In 2011 the head of the task force stated, "I think that we've made a big impact" (Sgt. John Respet, quoted in Pruden 2011).

But the question of what kinds of impacts are even possible might be considered through an analysis of the project's basic operating framework, some of which it made available to the public through online formats. In this section, I examine some of Project Kare's online material related to the investigations of high-risk missing persons and unsolved homicides from 2006 to 2010. Although since then it seems that the project has changed and "expanded considerably" and now includes a proactive component (RCMP 2015), the consideration here is limited to an analysis only of material online during that time. To be clear, I conducted this analysis from a distance, and I offer only an interpretation of some of the project's online materials as well as of secondary sources reporting on the project. I do not report on direct or firsthand research conducted with members of the project. Rather, I take up these texts as public documents given that they were produced for the public and were intended to be read without consultation with those who produced them. I had no consultation with any representative of the police.

On its website, Project Kare explicitly stated that its goals were to

> identify, collect, collate, evaluate, and analyze all high-risk missing person and unsolved homicide cases in Alberta, Saskatchewan, Manitoba and the Northwest Territories, to determine if any cases were potentially linked and if possible, identify offenders. The case criteria for inclusion in the project was: A missing person or homicide victim whose lifestyle, behaviour, profession, or circumstances placed them at high or extreme risk to be a victim of violent crime.[2]

The project's range was huge, and so were its tasks, namely investigating all cases of high-risk missing persons and unsolved murders, making connections between cases where they existed, and identifying offenders – all undertaken across an enormous geographical expanse. To be included under Project Kare's purview, missing persons and unsolved homicides had to be considered high-risk cases, which according to this excerpt, was a matter of lifestyle, behaviour, profession, or circumstances.

In 2005, two years after Project Kare was established, the RCMP and Project Kare announced that they suspected a serial offender was responsible for the murders of women involved in the sex trade in Edmonton, and they offered a $100,000 reward for information that would lead to an arrest and conviction.[3] They also issued a "profile" of the offender:

> The RCMP's behavioural science department in Ottawa believes the person who is behind the gruesome crimes probably likes to fish and hunt, enjoys the outdoors, drives either a truck, van or sport utility vehicle and may clean the vehicle at odd times. He may also live or work, or have friends or family, in places south of Edmonton such as Leduc and Camrose. (Harding 2005b)

In both the project's goals and its profile of the killer, we see violent disappearances and murders framed as individually committed and ahistorical events. The victims were described as individuals at high risk, and the killer was described as a person with particular interests, hobbies, and habits. This framing of the killer paralleled the framing offered in the media at the time. Media headlines reflected a concern that a "serial killer" might be responsible for these crimes.[4] Among sixty-one articles in 2005 relevant to Edmonton's violence, sixteen carried headlines indicating the presence of a serial perpetrator.[5] Only three of these headlines did *not* refer to the perpetrator in the singular as the "killer," "serial killer," "predator," or "multiple murderer," and only one headline made reference to "predators" in the plural. So, although the media seemed to indicate that *women* – in the plural – involved in sex work were at high risk of violence (e.g., "*another* sex trade worker"), the perpetrator of such violence seems to have been most commonly cast as a lone and potentially familiar man.

Rendering the killer a singular man precludes a consideration of this violence as a structural or social phenomenon. A focus on the individual – on the psychological monstrosity of a serial killer – maintains a historical consistency in regard to the murder of those involved in sex work in the city and in regard to a refusal to recognize killings as actually an "outgrowth of a misogynist, classist, and deeply racist culture operating within (and effectively exploiting) a marginalized, neglected population who inhabit a disastrously inadequate urban infrastructure" (Ferris 2015, 36). If Project Kare really were designed to *prevent* the murders of those it deems at "high risk," it would be necessary to reconceptualize such violence in the way that Ferris suggests – as social in origin – despite the fact that it may be committed against and by individuals. And although the project's individualizing approach may be considered necessary for everyday policing and for the punishment of individual criminal behaviour, this approach has other, more insidious, effects. For example, rendering violence purely individual further fosters an already established social amnesia regarding the various systemic and social antecedents of such violence. The structural nature of such violence is ignored. If such crimes were reconceptualized as containing strong and sustained social elements, perhaps prevention and prosecution at the level of the individual might also be reconsidered as insufficient and as arriving always too late. They do not prevent the reoccurrence of such violence. Moreover, they do not actually tackle what I postulate are social investments in the disappearance of women and girls, many Indigenous, from cities now governed as "Canadian."

Project Kare's website materials did not identify missing or murdered women in Alberta as disproportionately of Indigenous heritage. The Amnesty International report from 2004, however, did. And, in 2014 an RCMP report followed the lead of numerous Indigenous organizations, loved ones, and scholars in documenting that, at the national level, having Indigenous heritage was indeed a salient factor and that the rates of violence against Indigenous women were extremely high. That report estimated that 1,181 Indigenous women had gone missing or had been murdered in Canada since 1980 and stated that Aboriginal girls and women faced a disproportionate risk of violence compared to non-Aboriginal girls and women (RCMP 2014, 7). This point is most significant. The disappearance of Indigenous women from Canadian cities is critically tied to the politics of the nation-state and to a particular iteration of a nation that at once apologizes for and denies the violence and trauma of colonialism here.[6] My analysis of Project Kare's 2006 online materials suggests that rather than an atrocity that the nation-state attempts to prevent, the disproportionate disappearance of Indigenous women and girls is a form of state-sanctioned violence that augments the legitimacy and authority of the Canadian nation (Dean 2015; A. Simpson 2016). Why else were the demands made by Canadian citizens that the government attend to this urgent crisis of missing or murdered women and girls met with such sustained refusal on the part of Prime Minister Stephen Harper and the Conservative government of Canada? There is something considerable at stake here.

Writing about the exercise of power within totalitarian states, Italian philosopher Giorgio Agamben (2005, 2) argues that implementation of a "state of exception" "allows for the physical elimination not only of political adversaries but of entire categories of citizens who for some reason cannot be integrated into the political system."[7] Perhaps this is a useful consideration in relation to the disappearance of Indigenous peoples in Canada. Audra Simpson (2014) identifies Indigenous peoples in Canada as long refusing assimilation and catalogues such refusals as occurring since before their national sovereignties were ostensibly enshrined in nation-to-nation treaties and later refuted in practices of aggressive colonization and assimilation on the part of the Canadian government (Palmater 2011, 119). Indigenous peoples refuse to disappear and instead continue to "insist on being and acting as peoples who belong to a nation other than the United States or Canada" (A. Simpson 2014, 2). These refusals pose a fundamental and ongoing problem to the claim of Canadian nationhood and hence might be the impetus toward state-sanctioned eliminations of Indigenous peoples.

The elimination of those who refuse to integrate does not necessarily take direct or obvious forms (Agamben 1995). Rather, withholding legal protections from those unable or unwilling to integrate effects another form of disappearance. Agamben writes that such withholdings constitute certain positions as comprising "bare life": "Bare life remains included in politics in the form of the exception, that is, as something that is included solely through an exclusion" (Agamben 1995, 11). This kind of theorizing a position of and for allowable yet illegal violence has already been extended to understanding the violence faced by women involved in street-level sex work (Hubbard, Matthews, and Scoular 2008). In their article on the regulation of sex work in the European Union, researchers

Phil Hubbard, Roger Matthews, and Jane Scoular claim that the law exercises this kind of inclusion through exclusion specifically with regard to women selling sex on the street, stating that "the female sex worker stands on the threshold between the human subject and the inadmissible 'animal,' and ... this is reflected in legal geographies of exception that render them visible to the state and law, yet stripped of rights as worker-citizens" (Hubbard, Matthews, and Scoular 2008, 138). Separately, women engaged in street-level sex work and Indigenous women each seem to signify a refusal to integrate into a patriarchal, colonial economy of capitalism, in which resources and women are subject to exploitation in systemic ways. When the two categories of women are conflated, as they have been in the media, some readers may assume that women involved in street-level sex work are also likely Indigenous. Positioned as involved in informal economies of sex, Indigenous women are seen to subvert the economic, national, and indeed supposedly moral order in multiple ways. Hence their actual protection is framed as being at odds with ongoing projects of nation building in Canada. And it is indeed at odds "with a coercive land grab that has been 500 years in the making" in Canada (Wyatt 2013). What is *not* at odds with the ongoing project of nation building in Canada, however, is the symbolic work that Project Kare does via its own online materials.

Are Project Kare's strategies implicated in the execution of the "state of exception" and thus limited in their capacity to actually prevent the murder of high-risk missing persons? If the state of exception works in practice such that some people are omitted from public protections (and public political life), then can it be said that these strategies maintain the hoax of democratic equality in Canada? In theorizing strategies used by law enforcement agencies as effective in the production of the state of exception, I reconsider these strategies because I think that, as a guiding framework, they are failing to protect the lives of some people with alarming endurance and consistency, even though they are commonly thought to be key and effective instruments for protection. Moreover, I suggest that appeals made to the state by Indigenous peoples for protection are, in a context of ongoing settler colonialism, at best circumscribed by sets of contrary interests and assumptions. At worst, such appeals result in a renewed exposure to violence, this time directly at the hands of the state. In an attempt to examine whose lives get made to matter, Judith Butler (2009, 26) writes about this paradox: "They [precarious populations] appeal to the state for protection, but the state is precisely that from which they require protection. To be protected from violence by the nation-state is to be exposed to the violence wielded by the nation-state, so to rely on the nation-state for protection *from* violence is to precisely exchange one potential violence for another." This paradox exists despite and even in keeping with individual state actors' (e.g., judges, social workers, officers) intentions and actions toward offering individual protections. And so Butler takes us beyond states of exception to the paradox embedded in the provision of such protections. For this reason, it is crucially important to analyze how violence is wielded by the nation-state precisely *through* its provision of protections.[8]

There is little information available on the naming of Project Kare. Official RCMP webpages state only that the name refers to the RCMP's Division "K," which has 107 detachments and is responsible for the province of Alberta. In 2005, however, Alberta's solicitor general, Minister of Public Safety Harvey Cenaiko, reported that the name "reflect[s] the philosophy of care and concern and compassion that goes on in the investigations of missing and murdered women. The 'K' in Kare is the initial for the lead agency, the RCMP in Alberta, which is K Division" (Legislative Assembly of Alberta 2005, 1523). Other than Cenaiko's statement, no such claim to "care" is made. Nonetheless, the name of the special task force suggests a foregrounding of concern and compassion. The claim that Project Kare cares, however, is specifically missing from the project's official mandate, which focuses on minimizing the risk of murder to and investigating the murders of "high risk missing persons." If Project Kare is assumed to *care,* then the initiative might better be aimed at ensuring safety in order to protect and secure lives.

Situated in the historical context, however, the protection of Indigenous peoples has not been an obligation of Canada's national police forces. The North West Mounted Police are the forefathers of today's Royal Canadian Mounted Police and first arrived on the western prairies to found Canadian rule here (S. Carter 1993). Historically, the police presence in the West made it possible to open up the area for settlement and to establish and control that "new world" as part of the sovereign nation of Canada (S. Carter 1993). A police force with the goal of establishing the authority of a new nation here has always been incompatible with the goal of fostering and protecting the lives of the peoples and nations that predated the arrival of British and French settlers (Veracini 2010). But it was not only a matter of incompatibility. As a poem published in the *Saskatchewan Herald* in 1878 stated, the North West Mounted Police were there to "protect the pioneer" and to "restrain the lawless savages" (quoted in Graybill 2007, 5), which they ostensibly did in many ways, including through their roles in relation to the policing of borders, the operation of Indian residential schools, the administration of treaty obligations, and the institutionalization of numerous Indigenous peoples (S. Carter 1993; Razack 2002; Regan 2010).

Government policies reflected the now infamous words uttered by the deputy superintendent of Indian affairs, Duncan Campbell Scott, in the early twentieth century: "I want to get rid of the Indian problem ... Our objective is to continue until there is not a single Indian in Canada that has not been absorbed into the body politic and there is no Indian question, and no Indian Department" (quoted in Palmater 2011, 119). Mi'kmaw citizen, lawyer, activist, and scholar Pamela Palmater describes this motive as an enduring "cornerstone of Indian policy" and argues that "despite apologies to the contrary, various provisions in the *Indian Act,* originally intended to speed up assimilation, are still in effect and in fact, vigorously defended by Canada" (Palmater 2011, 119). The Canadian nation has long attempted to eliminate the "Indian" problem by eliminating "Indians" (Palmater 2011, 119). And the RCMP's nefarious role in relation to the policing of Indigenous peoples is not only in the past; although Project Kare may be applauded in Alberta, a recent inquiry into RCMP responsibility for the freezing deaths of several Aboriginal men in Saskatchewan reveals that "Aboriginal death in [police] custody is banal" (Razack 2014, 80). In a report by Human Rights Watch (2013) titled *Those Who Take Us Away: Abusive Policing and Failures in Protection of Indigenous Women and Girls in Northern British Columbia, Canada,* the officers of the RCMP are described as abusive and violent in their treatment of Indigenous women, as they have not only failed to protect but have also been actively involved in direct violence against Indigenous women and girls. The RCMP, conceived of both as an organization and as many individual officers, needs further investigation to examine its implication in genocidal policies and practices of the past and present.

Even without a comprehensive consideration of the specific and ongoing practices through which the RCMP has worked to attempt to deliver Canadian national sovereignty over Indigenous sovereignty and nationhood, a careful analysis of Project Kare's publicly available online materials hints at an insidiousness within a name that proclaims care. The project's mandate is neither to protect particular "high-risk" people nor to minimize those "high-risk" persons' vulnerability to abduction. It certainly does not aim to reduce risk status given that these risks are largely understood as arising from individual choices or circumstances. Rather, the project's explicitly stated primary task is to reduce the *risk that those already missing will be murdered.* Given this discrepancy, it seems that Project Kare's name works as a first-level signifier for precisely that which it specifically omits: care.

In 2006 each of the project's linked webpages stated the following official mandate: "The 'Project KARE' Task Force will pursue strategies to minimize the risk of having additional HIGH RISK MISSING PERSONS (HRMP) murdered within the Provincial Capital Region. Furthermore, investigational strategies have been developed to investigate all leads, [and to] capture and prosecute the offender(s) responsible for these murders."[9] This mandate proclaims that the project's objective is "to minimize the risk" of the murder of people who are both at "high risk" and already missing. This mandate structures the project in the most futile of terms given that, once a person is missing, it is very hard to protect them from murder. This framing limits the population for whom the project takes responsibility to those considered not only to be at "high risk" but also to have already (been) disappeared. Such a framing reveals that Project Kare is not concerned that those deemed to be at "high risk" are missing; their status as missing may in fact already be implied as inevitable through the deployment of the concept of "high risk." The determinants of high risk, after all, seem to be mostly matters of individual choice, like lifestyle, behaviour, or occupation, with circumstances coming to bear only as an imprecisely sociological fourth factor. In this account, "high risk" seems to signal its presence as an individual attribute, one that, for the way it signifies outside of what it means to be a rational and autonomous human subject, already foreshadows an unreliability or a propensity on the part of the problematic subject to be missing. Perhaps the coupling of "high risk" with "missing persons" in "high risk missing persons" effects a kind of normalizing of "missing persons." The two together – "high risk" and "missing" – explain and absolve social responsibility for the individual's arrival at this precarious state. "High risk" circulates as part of a larger discourse deployed with regularity in contemporary neoliberal contexts to flag difference and to position one outside the realm of the rational citizen subject. "High risk," then, names the subject's failure at responsible and disciplined conformity to bourgeois, Christian values as the justification for her own and embodied vulnerability.

I argue that, although not explicitly addressed as such by Project Kare, this failing subject, the subject whose status as "missing" is not a public concern, is also already racialized. Consider that in the context of colonizing the North American continent, a major project and assumption has been that "the Indian" is on the brink of death. The notion "that Aboriginal people are a dying race" has been the colonial state's "most enduring fiction" (Razack 2014, 52). Academic and activist Andrea Smith (2003, 72) refers to Indigenous education professor Kate Shanley's observation that "Native peoples are a permanent 'present absence' in the ... colonial imagination, an 'absence' that reinforces at every turn the conviction that Native peoples are indeed vanishing and that the conquest of Native lands is justified." In terms of the arrival of Europeans and Americans in this area, the context is one in which the eradication of Aboriginal peoples has long been a priority and historically an overt objective (Razack 2014; Regan 2011; A. Simpson 2014; Veracini 2010). With regard to the Mohawks of Kahnawá:ke, who refuse Canadian nationalism and instead assert their "precontact Indigenous polity," Audra Simpson (2014, 3) writes, "As with all Indigenous people, they were supposed to have stepped off the beam that they walked on and plummeted to the ground several times through the course of their historical lives." That Aboriginal peoples should go missing is exactly what settler colonial projects have aimed for.

The Canadian state can no longer hide its organized attempts of the past and present to exterminate "the Indian," whether through genocide, institutionalization, assimilation, or policy (Razack 2002, 2014; Regan 2011; A. Simpson 2014) – a contemporary example being the deaths of Aboriginal men at the hands of RCMP officers during "starlight tours," a term that refers to the practice of dumping Aboriginal men outside of the city in subzero temperatures (Razack 2014, 62). Of the effects of such practices, Canadian postcolonial scholar Sherene Razack writes, "Through the surveillance, arrest, detention, and brutalizing of Aboriginal peoples, to say nothing of outright murder, colonial power is made tangible" (Razack 2014, 60). Historically, through disappearance, colonial power is realized in material terms. In this context, the status of the Indian as missing becomes all the more irrefutable and all the more natural – predating the missing of people in particular. Examined against a background of state efforts toward the vanishing of Indigenous peoples, racialized women constituted as missing might be *thought of* by those who do not know them as already long gone – as absent even prior to their disappearance.

The moment at which Project Kare is mandated to intervene, then, is a moment at which the effective prevention of murder is already at its most improbable point. Those comprising the population that is the official concern of the project and that it was established to help keep alive – "high risk missing persons" – are pushed close to the brink of death prior to the project's mandated intervention. Those for whom the project is mandated to minimize the risk of murder are first marginalized through notions of "high risk" and are also identified as already no longer belonging to the social world – as never really being here or as having severed their connections to the state, family, and friends – given that they are lost, or "missing." The project's directive situates those whom it is to protect as already in the final stages of life. These strategies hence deliver the facade of a state interest in preserving life generally, but they also secure a more deeply held state imperative in legitimizing the differential valuing of life and death in Canada.

I suggest, then, that the wording of the project's mandate is significant to the construction of a readership that might recognize itself as indifferent to structural settler colonial violence and begin to practice that indifference, the effect being that when committed against those already easily constituted as lost, violence itself loses its moral burden. When a population is already firmly established in the public imaginary as missing, or as comprising "bare life" (Agamben 1995), or life that is not really life, no atonement is necessary. If there is a form of "care" embedded in the project, perhaps the work of anthropologist Lisa Stevenson (2014) offers a suitably revised and specific definition. Stevenson asserts that settler colonial interventions, medical and otherwise, into Inuit lives did not represent a specific form of caring for specific people but tended actually to manifest a kind of "anonymous care ... a regime of care that requires life to become an *indifferent value*" (Stevenson 2014, 7, emphasis added). In this regime, "it doesn't matter *who* you are, just that you stay alive" (Stevenson 2014, 7, emphasis in original). Such a conceptualization works too for the kind of care embedded in this project.

Before closing this section, it is necessary to add that I am not advocating for more police intervention in the lives of people prior to their disappearance. Increased intervention offers no easy alternative to that critiqued here. There are numerous mechanisms through which life might be rendered bare, including through strategies of care, and this analysis illustrates only a few. The matter most importantly at hand is not *when* the state seems to intervene in its supposed attempts to prevent murder but how, for whom, and with what effects? How are categories of peoples repeatedly subject to ineffectual, even dangerous, simulations of state protection?

Project Kare collects information on, or "registers," people considered to have a "high-risk" lifestyle (Dransfeld 2012; Pruden 2011). In its online video *Ride Along with Project Kare,*[10] members of the special force describe the information collected from women considered to be at high risk as including their "name, address, phone numbers, tattoos, where they work, how they dress, [and] ... a DNA sample." In 2008 the *Toronto Star* newspaper reported, "In Edmonton, where another serial killer is preying on women, sex trade workers are voluntarily giving police samples of their DNA so their bodies can be more quickly identified if they're killed" (Fong 2008). Pointing out that we should be struck by the odd priority expressed in these practices, Ferris (2007, 105) addresses these tactics as actually a technology of death: "Project Kare gives lip service to the prevention of violence against these vulnerable populations, but the task force ultimately serves the interests of murder victims' families after the fact: they offer to pursue kidnappers and murderers when registered women go missing, and to provide closure by identifying victims' remains." If the information collected is useful, it sounds like this usefulness emerges only after the fact of disappearance and murder. This situation provokes questions regarding how the project works to define the protection of some people in terms of a conglomerate of facts – the production of a catalogue of as many high-risk persons as possible (Ferris 2007).

Project Kare's website gave no indication that women were protected through strategies that would reduce exposure to desperation and danger, nor does the National Film Board of Canada's documentary *Who Cares,* in which filmmaker Rosie Dransfeld (2012) rides with project officers who are attempting to gather personal information and several strands of hair from women on the street, while also providing them with food and water. Speaking with one woman after collecting her information and DNA, one corporal states,

> All it takes is one bad date. A lot of the girls we had registered ended up being our victims, and a number of our girls, their bodies are so decomposed you can't identify them through fingerprints or by looking at their face 'cause some were bones. Some were decomposed. It helps give your family some closure. You know, knowing that you have been found ... It in no way makes you safer. The only way that I can help protect you is to help to get you off the street. (Dransfeld 2012, 0:28:00)

But getting women off the street was not at the time apparently in Project Kare's mandate. The extent to which the project actually helps women to get off the street is not identified either in the film or in online materials. Rather, Project Kare's registration of women seems relevant only posthumously. In the film, one corporal involved in the project states, "Another thing we do at Kare is we register people that live high-risk lifestyles. Until we can identify a body dumped in a field, we can't even start a file. Where do we start? Who do we talk to?" (Dransfeld 2012, 1:52:00). Through the collection of biomatter, living people are catalogued as bodies that are sufficiently near death to already be recognized as future corpses, that are useful for their DNA, and that will eventually be "dumped in a field," the recognition of which will supposedly give loved ones closure.

This amassing of data on who might die, Ferris (2007, 109) identifies as specific and anticipatory:

> Certainly the "accounting" systems developed by ... Project Kare to monitor street sex work and to identify the bodies of murdered women mimic to a certain extent the recordkeeping of an efficient prison system ... An imprisoning nation-state reserves the right to control the fates of its imprisoned, and to restrict access, violent or otherwise, to prisoners' bodies to a select few state representatives.

The system of accounting for bodies enacts a form of biopower (Foucault 2003). In this case, power is deployed to delineate proximity to death, rationalizing both the fact that some murders are already anticipated due to the victims' prior characterization as at "high risk" and the callous assertion that no file can be started until the body is "dumped" and "identif[ied]." Rather than making women safe, the creation of a DNA database both effectively legitimizes a police presence on the street – "A lot of the girls we had registered ended up being our victims" – and rationalizes these murders before they occur, while also absolving the project of responsibility prior to the actual murder. Far from being a neutral archive of information, Project Kare's database is an example of what Michel Foucault calls "power's hold on life" and, more specifically, it exemplifies a modern "'biopolitics' of the human race" (Foucault 2003, 242–43).

Biopolitical practices often appear to be oriented toward protecting a population from a form of death that, in modernity, has become all-pervasive. In the case of disappeared women, I suggest that within a biopolitical field, strategies like collecting DNA or taking photographs of tattoos come to replace or symbolically affect a sense of secured or protected life, while remaining highly isolated from and in essence disavowing the intimate or warm features of the living women from whom such information is gathered. The product is not a secured life; maybe it is a life enacted as though it were of "*indifferent value*" (Stevenson 2014, 7, emphasis added), or maybe it is only a database – useful only after the women who provided the data are dead. Although heralded as protective, this database does little to guard the lives of the living. Its value is in fact proven only when those women whose DNA has been collected actually turn up dead. In this way, the database's (and Project Kare's) success is premised on the assumption that more women involved in street prostitution will both give up their DNA and die. Evidence of the project's accomplishment or utility is realized only when the DNA of another body matches a profile in the database.

It is curious that racialized women who have on occasion sold sex on the street might appear in this particular database after having escaped some of the more conventional systems of accounting, such as through completing annual income tax forms.[11] For those who live and work on the street, the information that is so imperative to engaging in normative practices of consumption and that is indeed required to access various systems of social support is less likely to be held in concrete forms like a driver's licence, social insurance card, healthcare card, bank debit card, birth certificate, or list of employment and landlord references. Life on the street is materially light; it can be insecure, and often identity cards and other cards are lost or stolen. Without these cards and without permanent addresses, activities like opening a bank account, renting a suite, or accessing social services are often made impossible. Indeed, accessing most forms of social assistance in Canada without such evidence of identity is exceedingly difficult. So in the absence of the usual paper trail – produced via *compliance* within a formal economy of production and consumption– the information collected from women on the street takes account of their physical bodies, a feature itself of their exclusion both from the society in which they live and from its protections.[12] Such a tallying of information regarding names, dates, hair, and flesh may also work pedagogically, then, to communicate that exclusion through death is ultimately what awaits you here. Or in the case of those watching the videos, this form of exclusion is what awaits *them* (people who live high-risk lifestyles) *there* (on the street). And what becomes clear is that what awaits people who live high-risk lifestyles on the street is not a random act of individual and anomalous violence; if that were the case, we could *not* anticipate it. Rather, it is an expected violence, one already symbolically tied to specific people, specific bodies. It is difficult to interpret this violence as not socially sanctioned. Indeed, the corporal's comment that "all it takes is one bad date" is likely read as a statement of fact, a warning. But it also disavows the reality that if this were not already a socially sanctioned murder, we could not know of the need to add that name to a database, the effectiveness of which will be confirmed only when the individual is eventually found in a field. The corporal is clear that the collection of one's DNA "in no way makes you safer."

Agamben (1995, 3) writes, "For the first time in history, the possibilities of the social sciences are made known, and at once it becomes possible both to protect life and to authorize a holocaust." For Agamben, building on the work of Foucault, the dual effect that he describes is neither exclusively the protection of bodies nor the sanctioning of death but the way that our formulations of knowledge, of biopower, work concurrently to do either or both given that they can sometimes protect life and sometimes enact murder not randomly but at the will of the state. I argue that it is precisely because these effects seem so contrary that the name of Project Kare, when combined with some attention to vulnerable populations, is sufficient to brand it publicly as protective and thus as primarily oriented toward lifesaving. That is what is most obviously signified. The point is that although these practices might protect someone, the very same techniques concurrently anticipate or sanction the murder of another. And the effects of such framings are not limited to those on the street – they work also in relation to those women not out at night, who such strategies effectively situate as among those who are "safe." To be clear, I understand these as among the varied and concurrent effects of the particular practices considered.

The (at minimum) twofold mechanism at work in the project's practices illustrates what Butler (2009, 26) has identified as a paradox. Summarizing Ann Laura Stoler's (1995, 84) description of this as the paradox that Foucault sees in the modern state more generally, geographer Geraldine Pratt (2005, 1053) writes, "The paradox is that there is a positive relation between the state's assurances of life (eg, protecting the rights and freedoms of citizens, as well as the health of the nation), and the state's right to kill." Stoler (1995, 84) quotes Foucault directly: "The more you kill [and] ... let die, the more you will live."[13] The safety of those who are not racialized as "high risk missing persons" is augmented by the practices that Project Kare engages in for the ostensible protection of those racialized as high risk and missing. And I argue that the project works not primarily to minimize the risk of violent death for those most vulnerably positioned, but to keep an account of them, to identify them as bodies, and to maintain the project of death that at once secures life. On its own, the collection of information stands in for real, material, protective interventions from the state and nonetheless works as evidence of the very care that the state seems to promise. The collection of information from women in life gets posited as evidence of the attempt to protect "high risk missing persons" from murder. Worse, the information collected is symbolically substituted for a woman, such that the human subject is now a composite of anatomical details regarding such things as hair colour and height and is even further reduced to her particular genetic material. She is a body (to be) accounted for. She is specific and anonymous – that is, specifically identifiable as an individual and as a member of a family and history via her DNA, but anonymous in terms of who she was, beyond her vulnerability. Even more unsettling is that this collection of information about and for the identification of bodies works to symbolically anticipate or map the violent death of certain bodies. These are the particular women defined as at high risk, the ones who will become missing, and this fate is known in part according to their positioning within geographies deemed degenerate. The database, then, is an official assessment that identifies and keeps for the purpose of future identification bits of the bodies of those women whom the state recognizes/positions as already close to dead.

But more than the future here, there is also the past. I want to suggest that we read DNA as historical text. In the cases where DNA was collected from those racialized as Indigenous, one can understand how the past might bear on the present in vital ways. As this book develops I will suggest that the DNA stored by Project Kare might find family in the bones desecrated and dug up from a sacred burial site near the old Fort Edmonton and stored in a university archaeology department for more than forty years. It might seem uncanny that kinship relations that can be evinced in DNA might also be read through the imaging of bones via mobile X-ray units that led to the forced institutionalization of many people indigenous to this land at the Charles Camsell Indian Hospital. That is to say, the analysis of these three contact zones suggests that bodies figure as central in enduring attempts to settle the West and the Edmonton area and in ways that identify specific populations whose disappearance might deliver settler colonial security.[14]

Project Kare's website again demonstrates its contradictory orientation toward life in the video *Ride Along with Project Kare.*[15] This video is filmed from the perspective of someone riding in the passenger seat of the project van, so the viewer is positioned as within, not outside, the van and therefore as safe and not at high risk. As well as being positioned as a member of Project Kare, the viewer is positioned in the same way as a potential client inside a car and therefore as someone interested in purchasing sexual services. As a potential client, this person is also, according to both the RCMP profile and an analysis of several newspaper headlines in 2005 in Edmonton, always potentially the serial killer among us. "The killer" is represented as any man "lurking out there ... watching" and, as the headline for one two-page spread asserts, is likely "somebody's neighbour" (Withey 2005). As a representative of Project Kare states in the same article, "He may be somebody's brother. But he likely will not look like the monster we see in the movies. He is likely going to blend in with the rest of society, possibly never having had any interaction with the police" (Withey 2005). In the context of such statements made by the RCMP, *Ride Along with Project Kare* is filmed from the point of view of a potential killer *and/or* a perceived protector. The two are not mutually exclusive here, and for a few seconds, the technology reveals the project as one for establishing both life and its unprotected outside, or bare life. In the same way that the Canadian nation-state has historically positioned itself in relation to Indigenous peoples as both their protector and annihilator, these two are not incompatible. There is no avoiding the titillation that the video offers viewers, enabling the moralizing and the menacing to cruise the stroll virtually and anonymously and as if they were a member of the good working folks at Project Kare. With the national police force at the fore, the work of colonialism continues, and all the while those whose safety is ensured by such practices congratulate themselves for the state's protective work as they "ride along with Project Kare."

As a further assertion of the distance between vulnerability and safety, a member of the project's team drives the van while explaining the project in terms that almost repeat verbatim the first two of the four investigational objectives listed on the website.[16] She goes on to state that in an unmarked van, members of the "insurgence team" "dress down, and so we can come down to their level." The constable continues, "One of the strategies that we have is we register the girls by getting tombstone information from them, such as name, address, phone numbers, tattoos, where they work, how they dress. We also ask them for a DNA sample, which is nonintrusive by asking them for some hair, and we also take their pictures." Repeating prior points here cannot overemphasize the significance of the strategies at work on this website and specifically contained in the video. Most alarming is that members of the team "come down to their level," then "register" and gather "tombstone information" from "the girls" whom they encounter on the streets. The language overtly invokes a hierarchy, symbolically identifying women and girls who provide information as beneath, as already dead, even as they stand alive and offer details and parts of their bodies – *information* that is gathered ostensibly to protect lives but functions primarily to ease the state's postmortem identification of bodies (Ferris 2007; 2015). If some people are more or less proximate to death, then indeed these women, through their treatment in this case by a state agency of protection, inhabit a location that we might recognize in this way. They appear to be seen by the state as at risk of murder and yet unprotected from that murder –

abandoned and socially authorized for death. The gathering of information thus becomes a survey of those identified as dying; it becomes a catalogue of their DNA, family history and information, tattoos, height, weight, and so on.

The constable's use of the term "tombstone information" offers a particularly startling exposure, something psychoanalysts might see as a form of public parapraxis, given that it communicates multiple intentions at the same time and potentially reveals a truth otherwise unknown or disavowed (Freud 1914). There is little information on the history, meaning, and use of the term "tombstone information," but it seems to occupy a place in police work and among federal agencies to refer to basic information about a person, like name, address, and phone number.[17] The term might be commonplace in bureaucratic settings, but its use in this way in this video – meant as public relations material for Project Kare – is eerie, unsettling, and revealing. Moreover, when address and phone number are replaced with DNA, the term intimately invokes the body and its identified precarity here. An email submitted to Library and Archives Canada inquiring about the term elicited this response: "Obviously, the term is in common use at both federal and provincial levels as well as elsewhere but so accepted is it that a definition is not always provided" (Healy 2008). Yet, used in this context, it signifies excessively. Although the use of a term that seems to reveal so much may be considered coincidental, I urge its consideration as the "open door [that] stops us in our tracks" (Gordon 1997, 67) and calls for recognition. How close to death must the living be in order for us – Project Kare as well as those "riding along" – to collect their tombstone information? Is it sufficient to be a woman walking down the street at 11:00 p.m.? Does this use of language reflect something about those protecting lives as well as about those we might begin to see as dead on the street, already missing, even before they are gone?

Although the video gives viewers some access to Project Kare's procedures, it does not depoliticize or defuse the term "tombstone information" in this context. The term in this video seems to reference an anticipated violence, something that viewers might hear for its literal meaning and whose shocking effect might seem to divulge a "public secret" (Taussig 1999, 2) among Edmontonians and Canadians in general. The secret is that Indigenous women and girls have long been positioned by the colonial state as at risk of violence and that the risk of death faced by Indigenous people through sexual colonization is contemporary and commonplace despite a lengthy history of resistance (A. Smith 2003; 2005). This type of colonization does not occur in the span of a lifetime but extends its reach through generations; this transtemporal aspect of colonization might be the most secret part of our knowledge of the Canadian present.

Project Kare's philosophy also works to guarantee settler colonial legitimacy. The project's philosophy appears on all of its webpages.

> No greater honor will ever be bestowed on an officer or a more profound duty imposed on him than when he is entrusted with the investigation of the death of a human being. It is his duty to find the facts regardless of color, lifestyle or creed without prejudice and to let no power on earth deter him from presenting the facts to the court without regard to personality.[18]

This philosophy reveals the primary concern as resting with the officer, not with the already dead human being. The officer here is specific: *he* is honourable, entrusted, and objective. In this philosophy, the living officer and the dead human being work as a crucial dyad for what I argue is ultimately the elevation or expression of the officer's honour or humanity. The dead human being is significantly the officer's "Other," although *her* death is critical to the project of realizing the officer's honour. Because "no greater honor will ever be bestowed on an officer" than through his "investigation of [a] death," it becomes apparent that it is actually the officer who requires the dead for the achievement of honour. His honour requires her death, just as the law requires the "state of exception" (Agamben 2005). And whereas the dead human being is specifically not identified as anything other than dead, the officer is not only specifically gendered, with a gendered pronoun being repeated four times in this short excerpt, but also specifically white. The last few sentences of the project's philosophy insist, however, that the dead will not be subject to prejudiced assessments regarding "color, lifestyle or creed." Although this philosophy is perhaps most superficially read as an assertion of fairness, it also already cordons off those dead as potentially suspect, or "Other," in colour, lifestyle, or creed and silently normalizes those whom we tend to think of as unmarked by colour, lifestyle, or creed. The claim that officers are impartial is made with the suggestion that there might indeed otherwise be something suspect about being marked by colour, lifestyle, or creed, and thus it repeats the same racializing, marginalizing, and individualizing assignment of blame found in the assessment of those missing as high-risk women and of the killer as a single and seemingly ordinary man.

Each of Project Kare's materials analyzed here can be read in a number of ways. Most commonly, each is taken up separately and understood as benevolent in its assumed orientation toward protecting a national citizenry. But then again, the nation and the citizenry have always been contested. Further, there is very little evidence that such protection has ever occurred for Indigenous peoples in Canada or that it is occurring now. In fact, the establishment of settler colonial nations requires precisely the opposite (A. Smith 2005; Veracini 2010; Vowel 2016; Wolfe 2006). An analysis of Project Kare's own documents, mandate, philosophy, and select practices reveals deep investments at hand and suggests that the project inadvertently or otherwise sanctions or anticipates certain disappearances. The human beings whose murders the project is mandated to investigate – "high risk missing persons" – are not actually only missing persons. As *Ride Along with Project Kare* demonstrates, these missing women and girls are already constructed as absent from a national citizenry, whether as missing, as sources of DNA, or as sources of "tombstone information." An analysis of this selection of Project Kare's materials exposes Canada's public secret – that disappearing "the Indian" is an ongoing, although failing, colonial project – and situates this particular type of missing person as inherently so and as missing primarily due to factors that are the responsibility of the missing and dead human being herself. As noted in the Introduction, this is a form of violence at work in settler colonialism that includes "the erasure of historical memory and other forms of desocialization as enabling conditions of structures that are both 'sinful' and ostensibly 'nobody's fault'" (Farmer 2004, 307). Thus, for an analysis of patterned forms of racial and gendered violence and of what appears to be societal indifference to this violence in Canada, structural state violence offers a means to think through how harm occurs within a context of social amnesia and hence without reproof. How might violence occur in everyday experience? How might it even be socially condoned in the very practices that are said to prevent it? How does it elude redress? And how does it escape the assignment of responsibility? A notion of settler colonialism that acknowledges the central role of state violence turns these questions on their heads, exposing that it is the ongoing repetition of violence and the facade of its contemporary redress that deliver the "Canadian" nation again and again to the future.

Frontiers for Gentrification

"Revitalization" is a euphemistic term used to refer to gentrification projects like the one that began in 2006 in downtown Edmonton.[19] Revitalization promises new life: a rejuvenation or renewal. And in practice, it usually signals a radical change to a neighbourhood. Such rhetoric is directed at a location, a place, as the site of revitalization (e.g., the downtown), and physical modifications are among the various changes that proceed with gentrification efforts in urban neighbourhoods. But there is often much more going on: "The gentrified term (revitalization) is perfect for Canadian politesse, stating one thing officially, yet suggesting exactly its opposite beneath the surface" (Blackwell 2005, 30). Just as the name Project Kare covers over more complex and varied practices, so too does the term "revitalization." In practice, revitalization often includes changes to who occupies these places. These changes mean that it often includes the introduction of a new kind of precariousness to those who had lived their lives where such a revival is occurring. Often, the people who live where such urban renewals are planned are marginalized and eventually ejected from their homes, being subject to powers "expressed in the monopolization of space and the relegation of weaker groups in society to less desirable environments" (Sibley 1995, xi). The vulnerability of people who, through gentrification, are relegated to less desirable places is made invisible by the use of terms like "revitalization," whose opposite is actually what is signified;

a city's renewal and a space's revival are celebrated while particular people grow increasingly vulnerable through gentrification and then are disappeared from the neighbourhoods that were their homes.

In early 2006 the City of Edmonton began a round of public consultations called "a community visioning process" in order to "kick-start the revitalization" of a neighbourhood that had been newly dubbed "the Downtown East." By September of that year, City Council had approved "The Vision" for the area (City of Edmonton 2014, 2). The Downtown East Project targeted 97th to 92nd Streets, from the bank of the North Saskatchewan River to 103a Avenue. Pamphlet advertisements for "public" involvement in the process carried the following slogan: "What would it take for YOU to live in the Downtown East area?" This particular downtown area is one where the unjust and uneven effects of urban poverty and neglect are deeply felt, where at least 2,425 people live, and where some of Edmonton's most critical social services are housed. In public consultations on the gentrification plan on February 2, 2006, the public was asked this question again, and with this question the city articulated *who* was specifically invited to contribute to plans to revitalize the neighbourhood. Those invited – the "YOU" in the address – were specifically those who currently *did not* live in the area and thus *not* those who already called the area home. Stretching over eighteen city blocks just east of the downtown core, the area referred to as the Downtown East is home to many of Edmonton's most impoverished and/or homeless citizens. A disproportionate number of the most impoverished in Edmonton are Indigenous, a trend consistent in other Canadian cities (Culhane 2003).[20] At least three homeless shelters operate in the area, including the only residence offering emergency shelter to single women. A resource centre specifically for women involved in street-level sex work operates in the neighborhood. Some of the women who must on occasion use these services might also on occasion work selling sexual services within a few blocks of the shelters and the resource centre. Although this downtown area also encompasses some single-family dwellings and a portion of Edmonton's Chinatown, much of the neighbourhood consists of rooming houses, small businesses, and parking lots geared toward cheaply accommodating those who commute to downtown.

A feature of this city-sponsored revitalization project was the exclusion of many local residents from the redevelopment of their neighbourhood. Not only were those who lived in the Downtown East absent from the advisory committee, which included only politicians, city bureaucrats, a real estate agent, and a developer, all from outside of the area (Phillips 2006), but they were also not asked to contribute to "The Vision" for changes to the place they called home.[21] Instead, they were *imagined away* in an effort to gentrify part of what had for many years been known as the Boyle Street community. This virtual erasure both legitimized the decades of neglect to which the area had already been subject and portended actual dispossession.[22]

This was not the first time that the land in and around Edmonton had been (re)constituted for the purposes of appropriation. Although nineteenth-century Europeans initially deemed the Canadian West unfit for civilized settlement due to its long winters and extreme geography, the expansionist movement revisioned the West as a land of agricultural opportunity and thus as a site of vast potential both for European settlement and for the appropriation of natural resources (Dickason 1984; Owram 1980). Whereas the first European settlers were utterly dependent on Indigenous people for survival (S. Carter 1999; Mackey 1999), the new arrivals and trading companies eventually assumed ownership of lands despite the presence of Indigenous peoples, and ultimately the vast western territory was sold to the Canadian government. In the late 1800s, the federal government offered incentive programs for settling the West, and more and more people, mostly Europeans, arrived to colonize Canada's frontier in the image of their homelands. Since then, the Canadian government's colonial policies and practices have endeavoured to assimilate or eliminate Native peoples and their claim to the lands. Treaty agreements and scrip certificates were used to usurp land from First Nations bands and Métis families; by 1877 what is today considered the city of Edmonton was bound by Treaty 6. Significantly, despite these practices and policies, activists and advocates continue to dispute national claims to entitlements to the land and its resources across the country.

The white settlement of western North America has been characterized by historian Sheila McManus (2005, xx) as "the dominance of 'whiteness'

... reinforced by its association with masculine nationhood and the rightful possession of femininized land." Accordingly, the mapping and usurping of lands symbolically brought under European control a terrain deemed not only uncharted but also empty or "fallow" and, by extension, feminine. Via the imposition of borders, a nation was bound, and the violence of this binding was an exercise analogous to the enforcement of a European gendered and sexual normativity in the West (McManus 2005, xx). McManus writes of the early settlers' "colonial journey and text – the anticipation; the long distance between 'here' and 'there'; the assistance of technology; some 'never before seen' scenery at the end; the blend of beauty and utility; and a landscape conveniently empty of other people to allow the gaze of the white, male writer to enjoy unimpeded vistas of his desired object" (McManus 2005, 1). This description of the pioneer's appropriating gaze is evocative of that employed by city planners and contractors in the re-visioning of Edmonton's downtown given that in both situations the landscape was cleared and the current residents were imagined away. McManus characterizes such imagery as one of the "regulatory tools" used by Canadian policy makers to conquer western North America (McManus 2005, xvi–xvii), and the value of this tool seems timeless, employable again today by city planners, contractors, and those deemed legitimate "stakeholders" in gentrification as they seek to conquer what are now urban spaces. McManus's insight predicted the appraisal of the land east of Edmonton's downtown as "fallow" by those pushing for gentrification. Indeed, the Boyle Street neighbourhood was deemed "fallow," and with this assessment, thoroughly ingrained imperatives of conventional colonialist, patriarchal heteronormativity were mobilized; the *land* was deemed to be unseeded, infertile, unproductive, and ready for its cultivation, its production, its insemination. With this metaphor, the appropriation of a particular space is sedimented in the violence of patriarchal (and capitalist) terms: the land is feminized and its theft imbued with the same sense of naturalness and inevitability characteristic of established orders. Just as early government-sponsored and corporate representations of these inhabited lands portrayed them as spaces open and empty for settlement, Edmonton's Downtown East project regarded the residents of the Boyle Street area as absent and the space itself as uncharted terrain, "fallow" ground open for the taking.[23] Those spearheading the city's revitalization used other metaphors, all of which can be understood as further contributing to the cohesiveness of the western Canadian scene: for example, a consultant on the project suggested that private developers did not want to invest in the area as "pioneers" but would rather be part of the "wagon train." The violent appropriation of land through treaty arrangements, subsequently misinterpreted and dishonoured, is echoed in the contemporary reappropriation of this land in the interest of increasing corporate investment and instilling commodity culture.

Although the formal imperatives behind efforts to re-vision the downtown were not, on the surface, even similar to those that affected the nineteenth-century theft of Indigenous lands in the West (i.e., the downtown initiative was not a federal government agenda, whereas colonial expansion was), McManus (2005, xvi–xvii) could well be writing about the gentrification of Edmonton's eastern downtown area when she describes early settlement practices and policies in southern Alberta:

> First, federal authorities used the processes of surveying and mapmaking to "reimagine" the West in terms of European agricultural production; second, they attempted the spatial, social, and sexual regulation of western aboriginal peoples like the Blackfeet; and third, they geared their immigration policies toward the need to "settle" the West with newcomers dedicated to Euro–North American agricultural, spatial, and gender norms.

Replace the references to "agriculture" with "urbanization," and what we are left with is an apt description of contemporary efforts to resettle inner-city urban neighbourhoods. At the second and third public meetings for Edmonton's downtown revitalization, attendees were informed that zoning issues would not impede the kind of consumer/consumption of culture that a dramatic increase in neighbourhood-wide reinvestment would generate; in other words, the city's policy would be modified to encourage the resettlement of the neighbourhood by those dedicated to the sorts of Euro–North American norms that McManus describes.

Although staggering in its constancy and consistency, the use of frontier mythology to justify the reappropriation of urban land is characteristic of innumerable efforts to displace people and appropriate land in large North American cities and, more recently, internationally (N. Smith 1996). "It is a highly resonant imagery bound up with economic progress and historical destiny, rugged individualism and the romance of danger, national optimism, race and class superiority" (N. Smith 1996, 189). Not only did this imagery work to reference a particular historical conquest, of which those constituted as "Albertans" appear particularly proud (Rosenberg, Dean, and Granzow 2010), but it also supported the contemporary consensus that Alberta was indeed in the middle of an economic boom. In the context of the oil boom, the commitment to this ideology both worked as evidence of the boom itself and confirmed that the prosperity that the boom brought to some (at the expense of others) was deserved.

At the same time that the neighbourhood was repeatedly constituted as fallow and empty ground, gentrification efforts also rendered the area east of downtown a degenerate space. Those in attendance at the "public" meetings on February 2 and March 8, 2006, both uttered and heard veiled assaults from the audience calling for the "regulation" of current residents of the area, frequently referred to as "those people," because of the purported "problems" they posed to "revitalization." As well, the city's decision to refer to a portion of the Boyle Street community as the "Downtown East" area at the same time that it began planning this revitalization seems hardly accidental; indeed, it was a renaming that the local mainstream press followed, calling the neighbourhood "Edmonton's seedy downtown eastside" (Mah 2006). Each of these references performed a rhetorical trick that conjured images of the illicit drug use, widespread HIV infection, and missing and murdered women associated with Vancouver's now notorious Downtown Eastside neighbourhood. The seemingly contradictory practices of articulating the space as both empty *and* degenerate worked together to further legitimate the practices of gentrification and resettlement. Moreover, such a framing disallowed affective opposition to the practices. Once such images were conjured, the city needed to do nothing more to make its case for the necessity of cleaning up and improving the neighbourhood. This work was done through the act of naming. So in some Edmontonians' imaginations, the neighbourhood began to occupy the space of a new frontier, one that demanded the taming and settlement necessary to replace degeneracy with civility and modernity – in short, with progress. The city planners involved in this process of gentrification provided further evidence of this claim: once the case for "cleaning up" the area had been made and the process was begun, the city renamed the area yet again, this time calling it "The Quarters" – a dignified name with inescapably bourgeois undertones, one that would presumably help to "sell" the neighbourhood to the middle and upper classes once the cleanup was completed (City of Edmonton 2008).

The characterization of a space in a certain way has effects that exceed the obvious, and the pervasiveness of frontier mythology and degeneracy in descriptions of the Downtown East area is intimately tied to the violence that has occurred there in recent years. Razack (2000) shows the ongoing significance of a dominant white, colonial, masculine presence in western Canadian cities through her analysis of the trial and eventual conviction of two men who brutally murdered a Saulteaux woman named Pamela George. The trial transcripts used in Razack's analysis demonstrate that contemporary violence against Aboriginal women is a significant and still-sanctioned colonial act. Razack explains such murders as colonial accomplishments that effect the arrival of perpetrators' manly identities through their voyage into, and safe return from, terrain conceptualized as foreign and degenerate. Two young men, both white university students and athletes, enacted a contemporary symbolic travel into and return from spaces considered at once "Native lands" and lands to which Aboriginal people no longer have a right, and this travel fostered in the men colonial, masculine identities that have been written into the authorized history of the West (Razack 2000). In Steven Kummerfield's and Alex Ternowestsky's pursuit of "the stroll" and in their eventual murder of George, they enacted a kind of spatial story that conferred on them a highly revered colonial masculinity (Razack 2000). The imagined colonial and masculine frontier remains a psychic (pre)occupation among those living in the West. This focus is illustrated not only in the discourses relied upon to generate support for gentrification, but also, as Razack describes, in particular forms of violence faced by Indigenous women. It is in and through such frontier spaces that incidents of gendered and racialized violence function as contemporary repetitions of colonial appropriations (Razack 2000). "The city belongs to the settlers ... and the sullying of civilized society through the presence of the racial Other in white space gives rise to a careful management of boundaries within urban space" (Razack 2000, 97).

Removed from the particular murder of George and from what eventually must be recognized as a national trend in violence against Indigenous women and girls, we are confronted with the frightening scenario, as Razack's (2000) analysis suggests, that this violence is the inevitable and predictable outcome of a particular past. Although such brutal violence may be a particular outcome, it is not the only outcome. Yet when city planners and developers propagate a discourse that frames an urban area as fallow, as requiring cultivation, or as a new frontier awaiting insemination or conquest and when a city addresses its residents as absent, degenerate, removable, and apparently expendable, perhaps we should not be surprised by such parallels.

The murder and violent removal of people who occupy the spaces slated for redevelopment should give us pause about any actions that might further perpetuate or exacerbate such violent displacements. Yet efforts to raise concerns about how changes to traffic flow stemming from the revitalization would affect the safety of women doing sex work in the area were met at each of Edmonton's public-consultation meetings with stony silence, dismissal, or outright scorn and derision. This was one way that the women who lived and worked in this neighbourhood were cast as less than human, their displacement being deemed inevitable and thus an irrelevant concern in the drive to generate "culture" and to "create a vision" for a future wiped clean of its past. Displacing these members of the community to new and unfamiliar areas likely heightened their vulnerability. Thus the casting of Indigenous women in this neighbourhood as subhuman was a specific refusal to allocate value to human life, and this refusal effected a real corporeal threat. To be constituted as less than human is to face treatment in those terms, and thus the City of Edmonton is implicated not only in past deaths but also in the future deaths that this gentrification process itself advanced. In this case, it appears that gentrification has created spatial boundaries, delineating those within the downtown eastside as nonhuman since it is those outside – the "YOU" in "What would it take for YOU to live in the Downtown East area?" – who are constituted as relevant human subjects for address here.[24]

If the city's gentrification process made bare a landscape and made absent or degenerate a whole constituent in the city, then the Edmonton Police Service's webpage "Anatomy of a Stroll" may have worked to further elaborate a presumed natural spatial relationship between "race," degeneracy, and proximity to murder. Just as the gentrification process asserted the empty degeneracy of peopled and built spaces, the police website asserted the particular character of a second place in Edmonton referred to as "the stroll" and demonstrated how that place was markedly identifiable as different from other social spaces in the city. Like Edmonton's Downtown East, the stroll also emerged as both the outcome of and the perpetuation of what postcolonial theorist Edward Said (1979, 49) calls a particular "imaginative geography"; it emerged as a construct "that fold[ed] distance into difference through a series of spatializations" (Gregory 2004, 17). Although the Downtown East and the stroll did not overlap exactly in geographical terms, they worked together to produce coherence about the normative conduct and character of the city.

Anatomy of a Stroll

In 2005, the Edmonton Police Service's webpages "Anatomy of a Stroll" and "The Prostitution in Edmonton Resource Centre" offered "a discussion of the social and environmental characteristics that define an Edmonton stroll" and provided maps of "the stroll" and of where so-called "johns" and "prostitutes" lived in Edmonton.[25] These webpages identified prostitution as involving these two parties – prostitutes and johns – and asserted that the two were spatially locatable in or near the area geographically surveyed and mapped as "the stroll." The notion of "the prostitute" was deployed as though *to be* a prostitute was to be naturally criminal, despite the fact that the law exercises no formal regulatory power over prostitution as an occupation or an identity; it is no longer the case that being declared a prostitute is sufficient for legal prosecution (Backhouse 1985).[26] Indeed, in 2016 the Edmonton Police Service's webpage "Legalities of Prostitution"[27] explicitly stated that *being* a sex trade worker is not illegal for those over the age of eighteen. Canadian law regulates most of the behaviours or practices associated with sex work but *being* a prostitute (whatever that means) is not an offence. The language on the webpage "The Prostitution in Edmonton Resource Centre" was, however, reminiscent of an era in Canadian history when "it was the 'status' of being a prostitute that was unlawful" (Backhouse 1985, 389). From the first sex work legislation in 1839 – which authorized the arrest of "all common prostitutes or night walkers wandering in the fields, public streets or highways, not giving a satisfactory account of themselves" (quoted in Backhouse 1985, 389) – until the 1970s, prostitution was a status offence under Canadian law. With the introduction of the soliciting law in 1972 and the communicating law in 1985, the legal focus, however, shifted from the identity or occupation of the prostitute to the criminalizing of particular behaviours associated with sex work.

With its attention to prostitution as something one *is* rather than something one does, the Edmonton Police Service's website diverted attention from what is illegal about sex work in Canada and instead postulated a category of people to whom the law is oriented. The language construed the offence as though the person who engaged in sex, rather than the behaviour, were in violation of the law and thus the proper object of legal attention. This postulate of categories of citizens is common in the modern biopolitical order, according to Agamben (2005), and it functions as a basis through which the *suspension* of law can occur (G. Pratt 2005). Indeed, categories are required in this context. As noted by ethnic studies scholar Lisa E. Sanchez (1997, 549–50), who shows how such categories work precisely to enable the suspension of legal protections specifically in relation to sex workers in the northwestern United States, "Modern law categorizes women in prostitution – 'prostitutes' – by their sexual conduct and makes their involvement in prostitution *the* central component of their identity. [Consequently,] 'prostitutes' stand outside the law" (emphasis in original). Such categorization foregrounds a notion of a stable identity and backgrounds or erases action, so in a very dangerous way, what seems to become illegal in practice is "being *identified as* a 'prostitute'" (Sanchez 1997, 550, emphasis in original). Despite the fact that such identification is not written into the law itself, with this language the Edmonton Police Service suggests such a categorical definition of prostitutes and, by plotting their location on a map, also showed the viewer where to find them.

It is important to note that the effects of categorization were not necessarily the same when the Edmonton Police Service identified sex workers' clients, or as its website described them, "johns." To understand why this is the case, it is necessary to consider the particularities of the assumed, universal, and lawful subject embedded in the emergence of modern law; only particular identities have been sanctioned for inclusion within the modern moral order (Mitchell 2006). More explicitly, the rights and freedoms of the assumed humanist subject embodied as a white man with property are not trumped or challenged by his consumption of sex; they may even be buoyed by it (Razack 1998b, 2000). Moreover, the relationship between place and exception from law becomes apparent in a closer examination of where we might find those rendered "prostitutes" and those called "johns."

Some attempts seem to have been made on the Edmonton Police Service's website to obscure the location of the neighbourhood (e.g., street signs were blurred out or indiscernible in some images). Other features seemed to pinpoint the exact location of the Edmonton stroll. The webpage "Anatomy of a Stroll" included photographs and maps showing city streets, parks, and businesses. With such photographic specificity, the site did not actually offer the anatomy of *a* stroll but the anatomy of *the* Edmonton stroll. Thus an effect of this representation is that real and locatable places were spatialized as degenerate – as places where immoral or illegal subjects existed. Through the contents of "Anatomy of a Stroll," social realities were inscribed onto physical places (Bourdieu 1999, 124) but not permanently or without contest. In (always temporary and contested) attempts to bind space by drawing boundaries, the more defined these boundaries, the clearer are the inscribed distinctions between the degenerate place and its moral opposite. And the more legitimate is the exercise of law in those places and with respect to those people defined as outside the moral order (Lowman 2000; Sanchez 1997). I suggest that once places and people *seem* to have been so defined, these definitions demarcate places for police activity in the control of what consequently seems to be always already occurring: immoral practices such as those considered to be simply described rather than actually inscribed by "Anatomy of a Stroll."

Social and cultural geographers argue that space is unfixed, being remade over and over again through various practices (Blomley 2004; de Certeau 1984; Thrift 1999). Maps are not neutral or ample reproductions of space but can be read as "strategies" (de Certeau 1984) for actively forging the distinctions they seem only to report and for reifying the categorical organization of people and places in terms of the normal and the deviant. And although the title of Edmonton Police Service's website – "The Prostitution in Edmonton Resource Centre" – seems to have indicated a concern with prostitution generally, another look suggests a concentration on identifying, mapping, and hence effectively claiming and criminalizing the places and people actively positioned as involved in street prostitution. The website framed prostitution in terms of its most criminalized and often most desperate forms – survival and street-level sex work – which are forms of sex work thought to constitute about 20 percent of the sex trade (Ferris 2015, xix).[28] It did not address escort services or online commercial sexual transactions. It did not address forms of sex work associated with the middle or upper classes. In this case, the important social symbolic power of "the prostitute" was more accurately the important symbolic power of "the street prostitute," or as Ferris describes, the "trope" of the "Lone Streetwalker" (Ferris 2015, 43). The Edmonton Police Service's lack of attention to off-street sex work in the city prompts the question of whether, rather than preventing various forms of prostitution in Canada, its website actually functioned to forge, reinforce, and naturalize associations between certain kinds of sex work and particular kinds of people and places, and the occurrence of violence. This analysis of the website's contents suggests it realized this outcome, first, by demarcating a particular landscape, one that, by virtue of its deviance and immorality, functioned to effectively define the remainder of the city as normative and moral (Hubbard and Sanders 2003, 75); second, by producing women as though they were, by virtue of where they resided, deviant, immoral, degenerate, and perhaps even less than fully human; and, third, in the worst interpretation of the website's strategies, by situating women there to be legitimately policed, removed, apprehended, hurt, or killed.

One can read the Edmonton Police Service's account of prostitution on its website, then, as tautological given that it posed a scenario from which the immoral "Other" could not emerge except to affirm the morality of the self (or the reader). As speech, this account effectively said, *the prostitutes are here, and here are the prostitutes.* Such representations demonstrate Razack's (1998, 356) point that bodies and spaces are put into "a dialectical relationship" when it comes to street-level prostitution, each posited to define the other although not in a predetermined or inevitable way. In other words, enacted places – in this case, the place of street-level sex work – cultivate or discipline consonant subjectivities, although not stably or uniformly (Blomley 2003; Razack 1998b, 2000).

"Anatomy of a Stroll" can thus be read as an instance in which the stroll and particular people were established there *as though* it and they existed as such *prior* to their representation. This webpage mapped the stroll as a feature of the landscape prior to whatever interpersonal interactions or transactions may momentarily have occurred there. With streets, parks, and parking lots defined as the stroll, the effects bled into the possible realizations of people and places there. The mapping of prostitutes as residents naturalized both residents' status as (always potentially) sex workers and the geographical location as (always potentially) the stroll. Moreover, with the identification of this place as the stroll, other places became *not* the stroll. Since this place was immoral, elsewhere became moral. Such mapping practices operate as a means of geographic confinement, being efforts to establish these precise boundaries (Hubbard and Sanders 2003, 75).

However, enactments of place are momentary, subject to change, and in flux (Blomley 2004). Hence the contents of the Edmonton Police

Service's website could not settle the question of the moral order, nor could they cement the boundaries of degeneracy. Nonetheless, they precluded certain important questions about the role of policing and sex work, namely what is the relationship between the surveying and mapping of a place and the people we imagine to be there, how are those people gendered and racialized, and to what ends do we designate that a stroll and prostitutes exist in the absence of enacted sex work?

The Edmonton Police Service's website seemed to proclaim that *a* prostitute was always already standing in the space of the stroll, always already signalling her degeneracy and immorality, and always already defining the stroll. The prostitute, however, as I have addressed, was not the only characterization to emerge from "Anatomy of a Stroll." There were those identified as degenerate by virtue of where they were, and there were those identified as vulnerable to the threat of the stroll by virtue of having come from elsewhere. This webpage can thus be read as having had the further effect of ensuring that those who were constituted as being from elsewhere were not deemed responsible for the buying of sex and hence for its causes and outcomes. The webpage stated that both prostitutes and johns lived "all over the city," but then for johns, it specified that they are "concentrated in areas where prostitution is a problem." Prostitutes also apparently live all over the city; they are, however, "concentrated around the strolls." Although subtle, such an account might be read as spelling out that the john's arrival was subsequent to the prostitute's arrival and that the prostitute's presence constituted the stroll; the stroll was framed as the prostitute's natural environment and as securing *her* social definition as degenerate. There was an implicit, asymmetrical, and relative social valuing in this idea. Mobility here was the privilege of those not defined by their environments.

This asymmetry was evident on the Edmonton Police Service's website in a second way. Despite the fact that the text identified where prostitutes and johns lived in Edmonton as being nearly identical, the two accompanying maps were different: whereas the area of the prostitutes' residences was demarcated with an icon of a house, the area of the johns' residences was signified both by the same icon and by large black arrows pointing from outer neighbourhoods in toward the stroll areas.

I suggest that the map of the johns' residences animated their arrival on the stroll as always from elsewhere. Hence, if this was not already assumed, it introduced their presence on the stroll as temporary. That is, their presence was framed as movement, not as identity – as fluid rather than fixed. This safeguarded the johns from definition as immoral and degenerate. *They* did not belong to this place. They were not there by definition. They came here. They moved. And they left. They were the subjects for whom the law worked, granting them the freedom of movement as well as citizenship and individualism. This particular plotting of where the johns lived equipped those imagined as buying sex with a protection from the immoral geography of the city and its various inhabitants.

This symbolic protection is also granted through mainstream and Euro-American conceptions of men's sexuality as embedded in conventions of gender. Of the differential and gendered meaning attached to the sale and consumption of street-level sex work, Razack (1998b, 357) writes:

> [Men's] temporary abandonment of societal norms does not weaken these men's claims of respectability, but, rather, it puts the mark of degeneracy on the women in prostitution and thus reaffirms the men's position within the dominant group. That is, once men leave the space of degeneracy, having survived it unscathed, they return to respectability. In this way, prostitution reaffirms not only the hierarchies of gender but also of class, race, and sexual orientation.

The Edmonton Police Service's maps reiterated a larger cultural narrative, one that allowed for men's consumption of street-level sex work only as a brief hiatus from respectability – a short departure and quick return – but penalized women's involvement (as prostitutes) with the mark of degeneracy and effectively with a refusal of citizenship. Although in recent years there has been more attention to addressing clients' involvement in sex work in Canada and elsewhere, this website recalled an era when men's involvement was historically normalized and ignored by police (Gibbs Van Brunschot 2003).

The use of the term "anatomy" in the title of one of the Edmonton Police Service's webpages anticipated dissection. Indeed, "Anatomy of a Stroll" detailed for the reader the three component parts of a stroll: service areas, arterial routes, and social disorganization. Claiming that these were key parts of Edmonton's stroll repeated a historical association between the urban and the immoral in Western social imaginaries (Hubbard 1999; Walkowitz 1992). Beyond echoing this association, the focus on these features allowed for the inclusion of specific images and maps that give geographical specificity to the places of Edmonton's stroll. As primary tools of nation building, maps are drawn and largely read as objective assertions of territorial control of a region, detailing what is inside and outside (B. Anderson 1991; McClintock 1995; Said 1979). In the daily making of cities, too, the mapping of an area is a technology "of possession, promising that those with the capacity to make such perfect representations must also have the right of territorial control" (McClintock 1995, 27–28). If mapping is read as akin to the right to territorial control, then those imagined to escape or resist such control are likely subject to mappings over and over again, perhaps as an obsessive repetition meant to indicate that those resisting do not actually threaten the "social order" and the "normative" values that the colonial empire represents (McClintock 1995; McManus 2005). It is precisely because, like other heterotopic spaces (Dehaene and De Cauter, 2008),[29] strolls do not actually exist in a stable way in everyday life that a consideration of their mapping in "Anatomy of a Stroll" is crucial. The images and maps of "the stroll" on the website laid claim to a space as though it were stationary, and, I argue, they aimed to produce it as such. However, *if* a stroll existed in the place that the Edmonton Police Service claimed, it would have been as a momentary aspect of the mundane places of parks, parking lots, and alleys. It would have existed more as a series of dynamic negotiations between seller and consumer (Sanchez 1997) than as a stable characteristic of the place. In its mapping, however, the stroll was made into a clearly delineated and static place in the city. This effect perhaps reveals central discursive features of the website: the mapping proclaimed the existence of a stroll and portended to assert territorial control over not only the place but also the people defined as being *of it*.

Visitors to this webpage could click on pictures of parks and parking lots and be informed of their relegation to the status of sex service areas. This interaction had the effect of further conflating some imagined immoral place with the particular places photographed and mapped in "Anatomy of a Stroll." In this way, the representations on this webpage invoked two equally elusive places. What might otherwise be considered everyday public spaces (i.e., parks and parking lots) were represented as clandestine service areas, places to be suspicious of, which effectively proved the existence of a stroll and called for increased surveillance of, if not the total disappearance of, this neighbourhood. But the notion that sex is or should be private is a historical idea, one foundational to the emergence of heteronormative cultures and one that is oriented to contain anxieties about boundaries and borders in Western societies (Berlant and Warner 1998; Sibley 1995). In this context, public sex and the threat that it seems to provoke might be read as having necessitated increased policing in the area, with the effect of casting these places as not the places of the middle-class privilege to play, have a picnic, or visit. Although Canada's prostitution laws actively push those who are most vulnerable to violence in sex work into ever darker corners, strategies such as this webpage seem to concurrently prefigure all public places as potential sites for sex work in precisely those neighbourhoods criminalized as strolls.

Most relevant to the claim that "Anatomy of a Stroll" racialized space is the third anatomical feature of a stroll identified by the Edmonton Police Service: social disorganization. To claim social disorganization is to reify the social as though it existed as a measure on a continuum of organized versus disorganized, the degree of organization being possible to determine. Perhaps it is suitable, then, that "Anatomy of a Stroll" provided further indicators of the degree of disorganization in an area: social mobility,[30] average socio-economic status, and ethnic heterogeneity – or, as the webpage parenthetically inquired, "how racially-mixed is the area." Here, space was made degenerate via the explicit intersections of class and race. This webpage crudely claimed that when the transient (i.e., not property owners), the lower class, and the ethnically diverse share spaces, the outcome is social disorganization. And social disorganization is a feature of a prostitution stroll. Concurrently articulated here was that white, bourgeois (or property-owning) heteronormativity was the embodiment of social order (Peake and Ray 2001). Indeed, this inferred characterization of the embodiment of order corresponds directly to the "sanctioned identity" in modern law (Mitchell 2006; Sanchez 1997); the law confirms and protects the "modern individual as proprietor of his own person and capacity. Similarly, the law confers citizenship through the ownership of property in the form of land and material goods" (Sanchez 1997, 549). Those deemed not to have proprietary rights over their person and not to own property find that they are not protected by the law but rather policed or abandoned by it.

The concept of "social disorganization" has had an enduring place in criminological debate and is still applauded as a context-sensitive approach to understanding levels of neighbourhood crime (Sampson 2002; Sampson and Bean 2006). The notion, however, has also been tied up with naturalized conceptions of racial difference.[31] Although racist typologies may appear more muted in recent academic use of the concept, racial mixing was clearly identified on the Edmonton Police Service's website as a variable that, first, assumed racial difference to be real and, second, reified essentialist associations between people, places, and degrees of their relative humanity. This "race-thinking" (Arendt 1973; Razack 2007) runs directly contrary to recent research that shows that in areas where markers of diversity are high and where various immigrant populations are concentrated, there is no increased likelihood of criminal behaviours. Indeed, these neighbourhoods may even be particularly safe from crime (Sampson and Bean 2006, 9). Further, it appears that much of the research on the artifice of social disorganization ties the concept to violent crime, a category of activity that typically does not include sex work, in part both because sex work is not illegal in Canada and because violence is not necessarily nor inherently a characteristic of all forms of sex work.

"Anatomy of a Stroll" used the terms "ethnic heterogeneity," "racially-mixed," and "racially diverse" to characterize neighbourhoods and used these concepts as an index of social disorganization and thus as predictors of a stroll. In addition to the words used, images supported this idea.

In one image, two men were standing on a street corner as a woman passed behind them. Two features of the image marked the three bodies depicted there as racialized: they each had a different shade of skin colour – one being pinkish and two being different shades of brown – and they each appeared to be in some apparent dishevelment, as indicated by an unbuttoned and partially tucked-in shirt and by wrinkled clothes. Although race is a social and historical construction, in many Western contexts skin colour is read as a signifier of naturalized racial difference. In deploying this naturalized conception of racialized difference through the image of bodies of varying skin tones, this webpage fortified a popular misconception that difference is inherently *of* the body and fused that notion of biologized difference with the degeneracy associated with the stroll. But that was not all. Racialization occurred here through markers of cultural difference as well. Behind the three figures was a run-down and boarded-up shop with a sign apparently in faded Mandarin characters. This image and its specific signification of racial mixing and degeneracy as biological *and/or* cultural contributed to the narrative offered by the Edmonton Police Service that the presence of both or either – really, the presence of mixing of any kind – was a predictor of eventual prostitution. To be clear, this image did not represent the reality of the state of things in a neighbourhood but signified a correspondence between race and degeneracy and by extension tied the two to an imagined geography of "the stroll."

The overall effect of the Edmonton Police Service's website reveals that what was actually under suspicion was difference, or difference as alterity – that is, as defined as divergence from an imagined white, bourgeois moral order that only actually came into existence through the account presented in "Anatomy of a Stroll" and in other media like it (Strega et al. 2014, 18). Assuming some nonracialized, nonethnic normative is a mechanism through which prostitution and place are racialized (Razack 1998b, 2000); the prostitute in "Anatomy of a Stroll" was constituted as an "Other" of sufficient difference to justify the reassertion of the hegemonic colonial order. Presumably, the images also worked to conjure an idea of what moral spaces are made of, signifying against its inverse, where businesses are open and where people own property, have higher income, and are unmarked by biological or ethnic difference. In this way, "Anatomy of a Stroll" came out of and reified an "imaginative geography" where difference and distance were made one and the same (Gregory 2004, 52; Said 1979, 49).

As presented by the Edmonton Police Service's website, racial mixing became a red flag for prostitution. Racial mixing, signified by varied skin tone and non-English language, is enough to mark the beginning of or the potential for a stroll. The contingency of this strategy is of clear importance; racial mixing announces the beginning of a stroll *only* if the reader is imagined as particular. Certain skin tones and languages declare difference *only* for those whose whiteness, language, and cultural identification are invisible and unmarked. For such an imagined viewer, racial mixing is presented as sufficient for one to suspect and thus to survey an area as though it were becoming a stroll. If there was a question regarding who was policed according to this logic, the image of the two men and the passing woman on the Edmonton Police Service's website went to some length to answer this question. Those who come from areas where racial mixing does not occur, where parks are just parks, and where malls are just malls – which can be conceptualized only as some, also imaginary, neighbourhood that is pure white and middle-class – do not endure the symbolic or material appropriation of place. Such places function in imaginations as the organized, and moral, centre against which the racialized and disorganized are made, residing at the other end of a fictitious spectrum in terms of imagined geographies (Said 1979).

An organized society is just as much in the realm of the imaginary as a disorganized one; "the geographies of white Canada set an implicit (and frequently explicit) norm around which belonging is constructed" (Peake and Ray 2001, 180). And the inverse is also true given that, by virtue of the defining of the disorganized, the organized emerges by default as the white, middle-class, suburban space. A white place becomes one of ostensible security and affluence, where bodies are afforded privileges that whiteness invisibly seems to bestow. The identification of those who rent rather than own, of the poor, and of those racialized as inherently criminal and disordered on this webpage, worked to situate owners as wealthy and those who emerge as nonracialized as inherently moral. In the face of socially constructed and exaggerated heterogeneities, "race" as social disorganization is made a constant threat to those who are concurrently nonracialized, and purity as social organization is made the constant (and elusive) goal.

I suggest that visitors to the Edmonton Police Service's website were educated in a certain imaginative geography, one where sexualized and racialized subjects engaged in sex work; this was at once an area where intensified policing was legitimized and an area where those who were not *of it* had a certain freedom from the rule of law there. That is, the website articulated this area as a specified zone of exception – perhaps what Agamben (1995, 19) calls a "camp" – postulating some life as existing as purely biological there and the exercise of law as suspended there (Agamben 1995, 2005; Razack 2000). Life in such camps is "bare life" (Agamben 1995, 2005) – exempt from protection in the law as without political or moral worth. This website framed a particular area and by extension those who inhabited it as degenerate, performing the very relationship that the website appeared simply to express. If operating as an instrument of crime prevention, it was also effective in establishing and maintaining ideas about where violence occurred and to whom. It showed where violence was to be expected, and thus those visitors to the site whose imaginations were open to the geography presented there – those with a naturalized difference and distance from such violence – were primed for a degree of indifference when such violence occurred there. Thus I suggest that the mapping of the neighbourhood on the website marked that place as a space where a kind of socially authorized violence occurred. In short, the website delineated a zone of exception – a place where the law is suspended and murder might occur without retribution (Agamben 1995, 2005; Razack 2014). As a result, if violence occurred there it might be reasonable to consider such violence with the account given by Razack of the freezing deaths of Indigenous men perpetrated by police in Saskatchewan. "With a profound indifference to Aboriginal death as its key feature, spaces of the policing of Aboriginal populations bear a close resemblance to spaces of exception where law authorizes its own suspension. There can be no failure to care, and thus no responsibility for it[,] in such a zone" (Razack 2014, 54). The spaces of exception mapped out through such practices as those found on the Edmonton Police Service's website can be read as having related both to the likelihood of violence in a place without retribution and an inclination toward indifference as the response to that violence.

"Anatomy of a Stroll" exceeded the geographical boundaries of the areas it attempted to map in such a way as to operate in relation to other neighbourhoods of the city, producing the stroll as the internal elsewhere (Taussig 1989) – the place of disorder, violence, and chaos that worked to symbolize order and civility in other places in the city. It was produced as the site of the abject that "Edmonton" and "Canada" cannot actually divest (Kristeva 1982); it offered the image of a space of anxiety and threat, a place where no one with a choice – no choosing subject and thus no liberal humanist subject of Western epistemology – ought to go unless able to realize such status precisely through such an act, exhibiting an apparent right to be there by virtue of having entered and exited the abject space (Razack 1998a, 2000). The Edmonton Police Service's website hence forged the facade of a boundary for those invested in a bourgeois moral order in Edmonton, containing the threat (and possibilities) that "Others" posed to middle-class morality and reinscribing a protective distance from immorality for those who bought services on "the stroll." The website deployed a differentiation that granted security to some and alleviated their blame by inflicting risk and responsibility on others. Among the effects of "Anatomy of a Stroll," then, was a demarcation of the violence that seemed to demand social outrage from the violence that was socially sanctioned, now mapped as inherent to the people in that place. This webpage specifically showcased a particular location while abstracting the stroll as though it were equipped with a singular anatomy – one made up of immoral, impoverished, and racialized parts – and offering the technology for binding spaces beyond that one.

Perhaps it is the overarching metaphor deployed in "Anatomy of a Stroll" that reveals its multiple meanings most clearly. The Edmonton Police Service offered up a version of social space as though that space were itself a body, and in its wake, the website left those living in these places dehumanized. With its dissection, prostitutes became inherent to the place mapped. Racializing processes marked people as indicators of degeneracy. Famously, anti-colonial philosopher and psychoanalyst Frantz Fanon (1963, 1967) has said that it is the colonial practice of turning "the 'native' into a 'thing,' an object of exploitation" (Thobani 2007, 37), that allows for violence against those constituted as Native. Achille Mbembe (2001) also sees this propensity to objectify as a feature of Western thought, identifying such thinking as fundamentally unable to understand difference as variation, taking it up only as nonbeing, only as object. Hence, with the Edmonton Police Service's metaphoric postulate of a place as anatomical, the parameters for the abandonment of particular lives occurred again. The trope also hence postulated ideal life, silently identifying it as particular in its embodied anatomy. If racial difference is a social construct, here was a clear moment of its making. Moreover, just as the body has been employed by colonial powers as *the* essential signifier, here too space was classified, sorted, and moralized according to, and as though it had, essential characteristics that demarcated its value. With this trope, malignant features such as a stroll can be effectively rendered spaces of exception and cut off from the rest of the body of the now healthy and revitalized city.

"Anatomy of a Stroll" existed as an official police webpage with no mention of the ongoing violent disappearances of those working in street-level prostitution in Edmonton. Instead, the page presented "the stroll" as though it emerged through a generic yet racialized and classed body. This stroll, that of the transient, the poor, and the racialized, was presented as though it were not connected to history but only to urbanity, class, and racial mixing. The Edmonton Police Service presented the stroll as though it were a place outside of the present era of sexualized settler colonial relations that have been (and are) harmful, and sometimes life-threatening, to some Indigenous women and girls in Edmonton and elsewhere. The absence of mention of missing and murdered women and girls from the webpage reflected and perhaps reinstalled a gap, or strategic forgetting, in mainstream narratives about the existence and cause of settler colonial violence. Rather than addressing the specific histories tied up in the emergence of this particular space of exception, "Anatomy of a Stroll" abstracted, detached, depoliticized, and dehistoricized the stroll and the violence of some women's and girls' vulnerabilities there.

Each of the projects analyzed in this chapter – one of which claimed to protect those vulnerable to violence, one of which sought the "revitalization" of the city's downtown, and one of which articulated the anatomy of a stroll – offers up a version of social space as though it were a living body. Concurrently, each project, in practice, dehumanized or objectified those living in such a space. In the examples of downtown Edmonton's "revitalization" and the Edmonton Police Service's "Anatomy of a Stroll," we see attention to city spaces as though they were human bodies, and conversely, we see humans rendered mere objects there. The "rejuvenated" city gets treated as though life can actually be breathed into it, as though it were a body in need of resuscitation. Meanwhile, through Project Kare's media and through the Edmonton Police Service's mapping of a stroll, parameters for the abandonment of particular living bodies were set again. What is concealed in these tropes and practices is that the type of life ideally breathed into the city through such campaigns is particular, being exclusively oriented toward a normative order, economic consumption, or "growth." Access to this revived city is prohibited for those who cannot or do not engage it in this formalized way, as well as for those who are postulated as threatening this city's life by their disorganized presence. To apply sociologist Maggie O'Neill and colleagues' (2008) analysis of Western cities to Edmonton, this city space is enacted as white and middle-class. Through notions of social disorganization and racial mixing, the stroll was characterized as though it, too, had a body – an anatomy and pathology.

The boundaries forged in the strategies of state power considered here are not fixed or permanent. If they were, perhaps the present project of overlapping temporally separated contact zones would be unnecessary. The mapping, the boundaries, drawn once would hold, and the abject would be severed permanently from that which it functions to define. However, as philosopher Julia Kristeva (1982, 9) theorizes, "We may call it a border; abjection is above all ambiguity. Because, while releasing a hold, it does not radically cut off the subject from what threatens it – on the contrary, abjection acknowledges it to be in perpetual danger." Thus it is this perpetual danger that will undergird more efforts to "radically cut off the subject" from its abject. Indeed, it is the momentum generated by efforts to secure the subject from past dangers that orients and propels the projects that seem to follow. These attempts, by city administrators and investors and by various police forces, to intervene in the geography and its (supposed) populations were not the first of the interventions into the lands and the bodies of those defined, and required by a white Canadian majority, as the "Other." These projects were about establishing and ensuring distance. They were about binding spaces and then about identifying bodies as indigenous to those spaces, such that specific areas became racialized, degenerate, perhaps already dead, and in need of only particular forms of policing and only particular efforts toward revitalization.

3

"All they could to help" Imaging, Diagnosing, and Transforming Indian Tuberculosis and the City

> *All settler projects are foundationally premised on fantasies of ultimately "cleansing" the settler body politic of its (indigenous and exogenous) alterities.*
>
> – LORENZO VERACINI, *SETTLER COLONIALISM: A THEORETICAL OVERVIEW*

> *I live in a body that is associated with particular kinds of racialized medical "problems" and disciplinary requirements – which is seen as evidence of a significant rupture and decline from the past and a special site of scientific and social-scientific inquiry and intervention.*
>
> – MARY JANE MCCALLUM, "STARVATION, EXPERIMENTATION, SEGREGATION, AND TRAUMA: WORDS FOR READING INDIGENOUS HEALTH HISTORY"

IT SEEMS THAT THE CHARLES Camsell Hospital is haunted (Belanger 2009). In the *Encyclopedia of Haunted Places: Ghostly Locales from around the World*, an Alberta-based "paranormal investigator" describes encounters with ghostly presences during explorations of the old hospital and reports that while the team was investigating the abandoned building, voices were heard crying out "When are they coming to get me?" and "We did not choose to be here" (Belanger 2009, 30). Standing under the now defunct Charles Camsell Hospital, one can almost conjure the voices of those who once were there. An urban mythology has erupted around this now abandoned building, and it seems to be centred on the mysteries concerning what exactly happened there and on how what remains there might speak to these histories.[1]

The derelict building on this site is not the original Charles Camsell Indian Hospital, which opened in 1945 and remained until the mid-1960s. The shell that remains is of the "new" Charles Camsell Hospital, completed in 1967 and closed thirty years later in 1996. Today, some of its windows are broken, its doors are boarded up, and the former hospital stands enclosed by a chain-link fence on which are mounted signs reading "Stop" and "No Trespassing." A private security company guards these ruins. Although not the original Charles Camsell Indian Hospital, this building is near the spot where the old Indian hospital stood. I now read the building for how it stands as a beacon in this neighbourhood, a reminder of events in the mid-twentieth century, and for how these events might linger in the contemporary as absent presences and unanswered questions.

On the northeast corner of this city block, nearly in the shadow of the building itself, stands a memorial pillar that commemorates that first Indian tuberculosis hospital in Edmonton. On each side of the pillar are text and images that situate the original Indian hospital and particular people there as of historical importance. One side of the pillar reads: "The story of the Charles Camsell is one of the treatment and eradication of an epidemic. It is also a human drama – a story of Indian and Inuit patients and about dedicated and caring doctors, nurses and other staff who did all they could to help."[2]

So that perhaps tells of what happened there.

This statement – one that ostensibly summarizes the Indian hospital's story – is an official declaration of history, but it stands in contrast to the mythology around the place and obscures a much more contested version of the past, present, and future in relation to the powers and politics of state-directed health projects in ongoing efforts toward the colonization of Canada.

As the material for the development and maintenance of a particular social and historical imaginary, and for conjuring up a kind of affective identification, the commemorative pillar at the now boarded-up Charles Camsell Hospital might work in a number of complicated ways. Taken alone, and where it stands, perhaps the pillar reads as a straightforward account of the place and its history. There, the history of the Indian hospital is mostly one of benevolence and care. But social anthropologist Eva Mackey (1999) warns of how national identities are formed through such stories and institutions. Read as offering what postcolonial theorist Stuart Hall (1992) calls a "narrative of nationhood," the pillar situates the Indian hospital as meaningful in relation to the nation of Canada. Memorials like this one offer "lessons in history" (Simon 2005, 3), not only invoking an affective attachment to a specific narrative or national history but also affirming what qualifies as normative about the past and what is necessary for a particular present. As a result, among the effects of this pillar is the production both of "Indian and Inuit patients" and of "dedicated and caring doctors, nurses and other staff." This rendering positions some people as sick and vulnerable to an epidemic according to their categorization as "Indian and Inuit." In contrast, their counterparts – the "doctors, nurses and other staff" – are not clearly racialized but are identified according to character (i.e., "dedicated and caring") and vocation (i.e., invested with the authority of Western scientific medicine). This official history, which features Indians and Inuit as well as "dedicated and caring" medical staff, is part of Canada's national narrative and merges with a twentieth-century concern about "health" more generally (Hodgson 1982; Kelm 1998, 2005). The claim that the epidemic was eradicated through the care and concern of good doctors affirms what health consultant Corrine Hodgson (1982) has characterized as the *official* interpretation of what happened in Canadian sanatoria such as the Charles Camsell Indian Hospital in the 1940s and 1950s. Then, as today, what were considered efforts to ensure health, care, or the provision of treatment were framed as benevolent national efforts and thus often considered to be totally separate from more obvious acts of colonial violence or intrusion, although they functioned as effectively in the colonial projects of social regulation, elimination, and control.

The commemorative pillar may soon be all that apparently remains on or near the site of the original hospital. And, I suggest, the memorial is one of a number of on-location commemorative practices that work to depoliticize or disavow histories in and of Alberta. This pillar might work, for example, in ways similar to the Alberta centennial project (see Rosenberg, Dean, and Granzow 2010) to actually establish a particular Albertan history as worthy of celebration and to disavow what is present in the legacy of Europeans' intrusions, treatments, and attempts at the colonization of peoples and lands. The quiet existence of this monument among old trees on the corner of a residential neighbourhood and across from a schoolyard obscures the power of its everyday presence as an active practice of remembrance. But this pillar is like all representations insofar as it "will always show residues and traces of the invisible" (Huyssen 2003, 10). Understood in these terms, this memorial of the Charles Camsell Indian Hospital is haunted by what it does not, yet cannot help but, disclose.

In this case, the humanitarian interpretation of the Indian hospital proffered on the commemorative pillar attempts to obscure how thoroughly steeped the hospital was in the nationalist and racial ideologies that were employed in early colonization efforts and that, I argue, are still required for the continual legitimating of colonial Canada (Hodgson 1982; Lux 2016). Efforts to memorialize the Indian hospital wrap its multitude of operations in a veil of hegemonic nationalism and of responsibility and care, specifically directed toward the sick and vulnerable and, at the time, toward the then supposedly dwindling Indigenous populations. It might be precisely because such efforts are made to cast the Charles Camsell Indian Hospital in the light of humanitarianism, both on the commemorative pillar and in publications about the hospital, that we are compelled to take up this past as present and to seek out the dissimulating aspects of the operations of power in this hospital and in its heritage. Even when publications acknowledge that there was little difference between the sanatorium environment and the residential school environment for Inuit and Aboriginal people (Staples, McConnell, and Oakes 1993, 9),[3] their critiques are diminished by the more general appreciation described for the things done and services offered at places like the Charles Camsell Indian Hospital. Moreover, as evidence against such critiques, the good and caring personal traits of those employed at places like the Indian hospital are often cited; for example, we are told that, "unlike residential schools, the Camsell staff encouraged the use of Aboriginal languages and promoted the production of traditional arts and crafts" (Staples, McConnell, and Oakes 1993, 9). This description is important, in part for how it serves to specifically distinguish the Indian hospital from the Indian residential schools and to position the hospital as the more humane and better place.[4] On the few occasions when the Charles Camsell Indian Hospital is compared to the contemporaneous residential schools and when the shared features of these complementary institutions are considered by those who worked there, it is emphasized that the Indian hospital was itself *not* a residential school. Indeed, it may be that it is only in relation to the Indian residential schools that the history and purpose of the Indian hospitals appear benevolent. The schools and the hospitals, however, were both instrumental institutions in a framework that continues to support a history and a present characterized by efforts to materialize racialized difference and hierarchy in Canada. Segregated institutionalization, whether in residential schools or in Indian hospitals (and often people experienced both), worked to maintain basic tenets of the state's colonial occupations (Lux 2016; Veracini 2010). Although segregated education and healthcare institutions are no longer the formal policy in Canada, a brief look at the local practices and funding structures of these institutions in the past exposes the deep inequities realized through these institutions. My examination here of the Charles Camsell Indian Hospital provides a context for considering its various ties to the present.

Racializing Tuberculosis

According to webpages produced by the Government of Canada and the World Health Organization, tuberculosis (TB) is a serious infectious disease.[5] The infection, usually caused by the bacteria *Mycobacterium tuberculosis,* can occur in many parts of the body but is most commonly associated with the lungs. The infection is spread most easily through coughing, sneezing, spitting, or speaking in places where people live in close proximity. The TB infection can be latent for years, and in most cases people with latent TB never get active TB. When the infection is active, however, TB causes death about 50 percent of the time. Today, Canada has very low and unevenly distributed rates of tuberculosis, with approximately 1,600 cases annually, and the disease is treated with an intensive course of antibiotics.

Throughout the late nineteenth and twentieth centuries, tuberculosis was considered a major threat to the health of Canadians (Northcott and Wilson 2001; Wherrett 1977). In response to this threat, "prominent citizens and volunteer groups" (Lux 2016, 10) opened sanatoria in Canada that resembled those of the upper classes in Europe. Canada's first sanatorium was established in 1897, at Muskoka, Ontario. The Canadian Association for the Prevention of Consumption and Other Forms of Tuberculosis was founded in 1900 (Wherrett 1977, 17–18). Within the next two decades, a number of provincial sanatoria were established, and by the end of the 1930s, Canada had more than sixty dedicated tuberculosis units or sanatoria. In 1953 Canada reached its peak number of beds for patients with TB, which totalled 19,000 (Canadian Lung Association 2019a).

Early forms of sanatoria treatment were based on the premise that the illness was the result of "an abnormal ratio in the size of the lungs and the heart" (Daniel 1997, 178), a condition that was thought to be much improved by the effects of high altitudes (Warren 2006) and by the "rest-cure" – a "regime [of] ... extensive bed rest, particularly while febrile, both in and out of doors, special breathing exercises, and frequent high-calorie feedings" (Humphreys 1989, 159). In Canada a sanatorium stay included a daily routine of bedrest, fresh air, and self-regulation. According to social historian Maureen Lux (2016, 10), these routines were always about more than the physical disease: "Sanatoria treatment required extended stays that focused on improvement and regulation of the self, where the 'soul of the citizen' came under scrutiny." However, initially, a stay at the sanatoria was mostly a luxury accessible only by the upper classes and was generally unavailable to those who could not pay (Wherrett 1977, 12). The provincial sanatoria that eventually opened in Canada were also generally closed to Indigenous peoples, who were "deemed insufficiently advanced to benefit from training in rational citizenship ... [and] not generally accepted for treatment in provincial sanatoria" (Lux 2016, 11). Such exclusionary policies and practices were common at the time and were consistent with myriad other forms of segregation.

In the new province of Alberta, there was concern not only about the number of cases of TB but also about those who might come to the province *with* TB (Wherrett 1977). Because Alberta was considered to have an ideal and curative climate, settlers came to worry that the place was attracting "tuberculosis pilgrims" (Wherrett 1977, 182). Moreover, in the context of a private and segregated healthcare system, there was concern over who was paying for the treatments provided to the poor and to Aboriginal peoples (Lux 2016). This fear of TB and concern over who would pay for its treatment spurred a vigorous anti-tuberculosis movement in the early twentieth century:

> As early as 1907 a petition was made requesting that money be given to set up a system of tuberculosis prevention among the indigent, that competent people be employed to search out all cases of tuberculosis in the province, and that no known sufferer from tuberculosis be allowed to enter the province without special permission and without reporting immediately to the secretary of the Board of Health. (Wherrett 1977, 182)

Little is recorded on the outcomes of the petition cited above, but the Tuberculosis Act of Alberta was passed in 1936, and three years later the Alberta Tuberculosis Association was formed (Wherrett 1977, 183). It seems that early in the history of the province, priority was given to locating known sufferers and preventing their entry into newly defined provincial territory.

Rates of TB were reportedly very high among settlers in the 1800s, but by the 1920s the actual threat of TB had diminished significantly (Northcott and Wilson 2001). It is noteworthy that "this abatement occurred fully twenty years before antibiotics began to be used widely to treat infections, including those arising from the TB bacillus"

(Northcott and Wilson 2001, 33). Although it is reported that the threat that TB posed to white settler populations had largely passed by the early 1900s, there remained considerable fear of TB and of the dangers Indigenous peoples posed given their supposed particular susceptibility (Lux 2006, 2016; Wherrett 1997). As the "white plague" subsided among Europeans, the Canadian government turned its attention to the "Indians" and the "Eskimos" and to the provision of segregated sanatorium time for these populations, framed as particularly "susceptible."[6] These changes were prompted by a shift in thinking that occurred in about the 1930s (Lux 2016). In the early era of European settlement, Aboriginal susceptibility had been framed as a susceptibility that would likely wipe out the less evolved "race," so no treatment or intervention was deemed necessary, but as rates diminished among settler populations, the framing shifted to one in which Aboriginal susceptibility now posed a threat to settlers. This shift was reflected in the emergence of the conception of TB as an "Indian epidemic" and was what prompted newly established settler governments to mobilize resources to strategize for the treatment of TB in Indigenous populations (Lux 2016). There arose at the time "a general fear that the Indians could infect the white settlements" (Wherrett 1977, 14). The "Indian epidemic" now came to be seen as threatening the "white" race and was termed a "national disease" (Wherrett 1977, 12). But the risk of the imagined "Indian epidemic" was not managed through the provision of antibiotics. Indigenous peoples were granted only restricted access to antibiotics, even when antibiotics were otherwise apparently "used widely" to treat settlers and European immigrants (Lux 2006; Northcott and Wilson 2001, 33). Instead of providing antibiotics to all who suffered from TB, the Canadian government established a system of segregated and institutional treatment – a system that could also deliver Indigenous disappearance through various mechanisms, including through the long hospital stay that "curing" TB required. Antibiotics would have delivered only a remedy to the disease, thereby working against Indigenous disappearance, not toward it. Enforced institutionalization was more effective for a settler colonial project invested in long-term legitimacy. Notably, whereas in 1937 only about one hundred of those receiving treatment in Canadian sanatoria were identified as Indigenous, by 1953 this number had jumped to three thousand Indigenous people receiving hospital or sanatoria care for TB (Lux 2001, 222).

It appears that understandings of tuberculosis were flexible. So too was the theory of biological difference. Each of these concerns was employed differently to reinforce and naturalize the idea of an endangered and dangerous "Indian" presence and the idea of a secure colonial presence in the future. Indeed, the construct of race is reified through the establishment of such relationships. The idea of a natural link between TB and race difference emerged as part of the slow process of increased contact between the arriving subjects of the colonizing nations and those who were already residing on the continent. At the time, colonial knowledge already asserted that the Native body harboured a particular susceptibility to TB according to a theory of evolution (Lux 2001). Native peoples were considered to have immature, or less evolved, immune systems and were thought to suffer severely from contact with their urban, mature, and more evolved counterparts (Lux 2001); this was a popular claim and one considered to be scientifically established. At the time, an increasingly authoritative biomedical model proclaimed powerful notions of contagion and evolution, premised on colonial knowledge that was already racist and sexist. This theory of disease justified the numerous prior and concurrent strategies underway toward the assimilation and extermination of Aboriginal peoples. Not only an expression of colonial ideals, this theory also provided the grounds for unabated programs of assimilation framed in terms of uniquely humanitarian justifications that offer an opportunity for the expression of a variation of "settler goodness" (Razack 2013, 353). So how were Indigenous susceptibility, defencelessness, and threat constituted by the newly arrived settler colonial state?

In the early twentieth century in Canada, the rates of TB among Indigenous peoples, particularly "western Indians" (Moore 1961, 1012), were thought to be high and to reflect an innate and particular susceptibility (Ferguson 1955; Grygier 1994; Kelm 2005; Lux 2006, 2016; Moore 1961). However, Lux's (2016) recent history of Indian hospitals suggests not only that the reported rates of TB among Indigenous peoples were inaccurately inflated but also that the rates of TB affliction among white Canadians were under-reported and often hidden. Given the context at the time, we have to consider that if rates were higher for Indigenous peoples, then these rates were just as likely the *embodied effects of such ideas* as their source. After all, it was a social Darwinism that offered the primary framework through which those in the medical establishment and in political power in Canada conceptualized the spread of tuberculosis among Indigenous peoples at the time:

> The ideas of evolutionary theory and survival of the fittest, applied to human societies, were used to explain the Native people's plight. Native people were thus less "evolved" and had to be brought, by force if necessary, to assimilate to the pinnacle of racial evolution, Anglo-Saxon Christian society. Accordingly, they suffered from disease to such an extent, not primarily because of their poverty, but because they were making the necessary but difficult transition from "savagery to civilization." Because civilization was not easily won, disease and death were seen as a sort of penance to be paid. (Lux 1998, 278)

The distinction made between "Indian" TB and "settler" TB was thus understood to reflect degrees of civility realized on and in the body, with reported susceptibility to tuberculosis functioning as "proof" of Native peoples' savagery and conceptualized as a necessary stage in their hard path to "civilization" (Lux 1998, 2001).

The emergence in twentieth-century TB research of a consistent interest in forging and fostering a fundamental difference between Indigenous and settler populations is described by Lux (1998, 2001) as a difference between two versions of TB: "primitive" and "civilized." Lux (2001, 206) showed that, "with the latter, racial immunity was built up in individuals and populations to such an extent that the disease was in the decline." Those situated as "primitive races" were thought to have not yet developed various resistances and thus were considered less evolved than those "races" that had endured particular epidemics. Lux describes the way that succumbing to disease was thought to correlate with civility: "poverty and ill health were seen as an inevitable stage in the struggle for 'Christianity and civilization,' and as further evidence that assimilation was the only path to good health" (Lux 2001, 4). Thus the occurrence of tuberculosis in Native bodies was cited as primary evidence of the need for Indigenous assimilation into white society – again, constructed as a foil against Native societies.[7] This, however, was not a straightforward requirement, as assimilation posed its own threats to the "white" society (e.g., the threat of the invisible Indian), so even though TB treatment may have been offered, it was administered in segregated contexts and did not reflect the forms of care offered in the sanatoria for settlers of the upper classes.

Dr. Robert George Ferguson was a prominent TB researcher in Canada at the time, and Lux (2006) identifies that his research on Indigenous peoples with tuberculosis in Saskatchewan both relied on and gave further credence to a race-based theory of evolution.[8] In *Studies in Tuberculosis,* Ferguson (1955, 8) asserted, "However bad the living conditions, however changed the environment, however distressing the mental factors, the tuberculosis death rate among civilized people has not approximated that among the primitive Indians." With this claim, the idea of a civilized versus a primitive disease was collapsed into the idea of a civilized versus a primitive *people.* Civilized people had civilized TB, and primitive Indians had primitive TB. In addition to this telling collapse, Ferguson's claim disregarded all contextual and social factors that might have helped to explain differential rates of tuberculosis. Instead, he focused on articulating an inherent difference, asserting that there was something about *being an Indian,* something inherent to a population's bodies and to their degrees of embodied evolution, and thus something about race as a central attribute that marked a population as having increased susceptibility to disease.

Social Darwinism, with its assumed distinction between the "civilized" and the "primitive," was part of a system of dualistic infrastructure tied to international medical knowledge at the time and was not simply a peculiar or local development (Lux 2001).[9] The development of such mutually exclusive categories was in fact central to the development of settler colonial knowledges transnationally (Veracini 2010, 32). Lux (2001, 205) illustrates this point nicely when highlighting the remarkable agreement between Dr. Ferguson's assessment of TB among Indigenous peoples in Canada and Dr. Lyle Cummins report on TB among "primitives" in South Africa. Cummins wrote, "The adult 'primitive' in fact reacted to tuberculosis infection just as a 'civilized' child would. But ... the difference between adult 'primitive' and adult 'civilized' was vast. And that difference was not an inherited resistance, although he linked it to the blood, but '*an inherited faculty to develop resistance when brought into contact with infection*'" (quoted in Lux 2001, 205, emphasis in original). Utilizing the same a priori knowledge structure, two researchers, oceans apart, determined immunity from TB to be an evolved and inherited trait. The authority of medical science, coupled with the power of race-based theories, ensured that those who were "civilized" had a certain safety from risk of disease and also made the assimilation of Native peoples a project that was for their own good – a project in which their health and thus their very lives were at stake (Lux 1998, 2006). This form of "hygienic racism" (Swanson 2007, 710), which is practised in many colonial contexts, articulates Indigenous bodies as inherently problematic and contains an imperative that they be dealt with. It is "a racism that pathologizes indigenous bodies as sick, contaminated and dirty," offering up colonial treatment, or assimilation, as the "cure" (Swanson 2007, 710).

While a researcher, superintendent, and doctor at the Fort Qu'Appelle Sanatorium in Saskatchewan, Ferguson claimed that the "introduction of 'white blood'" (i.e., European blood) not only functioned "as a potent factor in civilizing primitive people, altering habits of living, appetites, and desires, but also has a noticeable effect on increasing their resistance to tuberculosis" (quoted in Lux 2001, 206). White blood would, first and foremost, effect an overall improvement, or civilizing, of a people and their practices, but it would also diminish their susceptibility to TB, leading to a dramatic reduction in cases of TB on reserves – tracts of land that Ferguson referred to as "scattered islands of infection throughout Canada" and "a menace to the surrounding population" (quoted in Lux 2001, 212) – an account that tied the system of land reservation to the menace of the Indigenous population itself and its threat to the surrounding nation.

These theories were predicated on the assumption that Indigenous peoples were infantile and of a lesser order, and they ignored the fact that Indigenous peoples had long survived and developed treatment practices for infectious diseases of various types (Lux 2001, 2006). By the time of concentrated contact, some Indigenous communities were already dealing with the problems of TB. Lux warns of the dangers of analyses that propose or assert an inherent defencelessness to "diseases of contact" (Lux 2001, 2006; see also Ferguson 1955; Moore 1961). Theories of Indigenous susceptibility were informed by and also functioned as racist technologies of knowledge and, as such, were effective in the dehumanization of a population (Lux 2001, 2006; Veracini 2010). When authoritative forms of knowledge (e.g., Western medical expertise) organize subjects according to categories of biologically determined susceptibility, when these categories correspond seamlessly and directly to social categories of relative civility, and when this civility is an axis on which the human and the subhuman are defined, then arguably, alongside a determination of biologized health, there is an organizing of subjects according to an invented and relative humanity.

From "Scattered Islands of Infection" to the Indian Hospital

People indigenous to the continent had been legally defined by the newly imposed government as wards of the state since the late nineteenth century, and during the early twentieth century they were considered the formal responsibility of the Indian Health Services Division of Mines and Resources. Within this department, there seems to have been little concern for Indigenous peoples' health and well-being; for example, "[even] the minimal demands of the 'medicine chest' clause in Treaty No. 6 were opposed by many government officials as promoting dependency and laziness among Indians" (Hodgson 1982, 503). Although the government was legally required to provide the medicine chest provisions, it was seen as problematic by those in positions to fulfill this obligation. The Canadian government routinely refused responsibility for the health of Aboriginal peoples in these years (Hodgson 1982), and they did so through these same conceptions of racial and geographical difference. In fact, Lux (1998, 279) writes,

> the Department of Indian Affairs did not accept any responsibility for the medical care of Native people, except for a promise made in Treaty Six to keep medicine chests at each agency. *But it did accept an ad hoc responsibility to keep disease from spilling out from the isolated reserves and posing a danger to business and to the growing immigrant population.* To that end a large medical bureaucracy grew and was fed by the department's need to distribute patronage and its attempt *to protect settlers from contagious disease*. But there was little that physicians could do in light of the economic conditions on reserves. (Emphasis added)

The Department of Indian Affairs seems to have addressed the problem of TB only along lines that were fundamentally about maintaining spatial distances between reserve places and the places of growing immigrant populations. In the government's selective attention to TB, rather than taking responsibility for preventing the spread of tuberculosis generally, it produced a geographical and racialized split that began to look like it corresponded naturally to lines that separated the sick from the well, the threat from the threatened. Not only does such a demarcation have the immediate consequence of prioritizing the protection of one group and space over another, but it also has the longer-term effect of constituting one group as *the source* of the still deadly affliction by virtue of a now racialized and spatialized difference, thus marking that group as needing to be feared by *and separated* from those constituted as well and also threatened.[10] The practices of imposed physical separation used in Indian residential schools and implemented through land reserves were supported by a growing concern, documented since the early 1900s and voiced by medical doctors and scientists internationally, that Native bodies had an inherent susceptibility to infectious disease in general and to tuberculosis in particular (Wherrett 1977, 14). Thus Indigenous bodies became sites for the articulation and reification of innate difference and threat. According to D.A. Stewart of the Manitoba Sanatorium Board, the spread of tuberculosis among Native peoples was "a kind of relentless process of nature, like an earthquake" (quoted in Hodgson 1982, 504), making it a sort of naturally occurring and irrepressible force.

Despite the government's initial rejection of responsibility to provide adequate healthcare to Indigenous peoples and to those on reserve lands, there were doctors who attempted to call attention to the tuberculosis situation on reserves. Dr. Peter Henderson Bryce, for example, took an early interest in the treatment of tuberculosis among Indigenous peoples (Geddes 2017; Wherrett 1977, 103). In 1902 Bryce became the chief medical officer for the Department of Immigration and took up the matter of Aboriginal health as one of federal responsibility despite the British North America Act's allocation of more general responsibility for citizens' health to the provinces (Wherrett 1977).[11] Bryce set up tent sanatoria on Ontario reserves and studied the impact of tuberculosis on Indigenous populations, focusing on children in Indian residential schools (Wherrett 1977, 104). Having found TB to be rampant among children in residential schools in Alberta, with deaths from TB reportedly at rates of 80 per 1,000 students, Bryce suggested that "the schools should be turned over to him, and that most of them should be turned into sanatoria" (Wherrett 1977, 105). Bryce's work showed that the situation was even worse in Manitoba, where reportedly "24 percent of all Native residential school students had died of tuberculosis" (cited in Sproule-Jones 1996, 199). Bryce was, however, relieved of his post in 1912 due perhaps to what has been called the "the hornet's nest of protest from the churches over [Bryce's] suggestion that the administration of the Indian schools be taken out of their hands" (Wherrett 1977, 105).[12] The fallout from Bryce's recommendations suggests that the problem of tuberculosis in Indigenous populations was deemed to be and treated as a problem that was not only, or even necessarily, related to concern about the spread of a disease *within* the population. The high rates of TB in Indian residential schools suggest that the spread of the disease in these contexts hardly registered as a concern, except among very few. Rather, the quality of concern had everything to do with the politically fertile postulate of a kind of "Native threat" to European existence and settlement here. This was a threat that eventually came to be thought of as one that could be mitigated with the maintenance of separate places, a threat that would die out if such boundaries were maintained. It appears that once Bryce was removed from his position, such boundaries were maintained, as Indian residential schools continued to operate into the late twentieth century.

Concern about TB was heightened in the 1930s when scientific research suggested that tuberculosis among First Nations and Inuit peoples would pose a menace to the settler populations (Hodgson 1982; Lux 2006). The following decade brought even greater social anxiety about an impending "Indian epidemic" (Hodgson 1982; Lux 2006). The science framed the epidemic as running a separate course among the Indigenous populations, and the belated and differential care for those Indigenous peoples with TB in Canada reveals that the illness was conceptualized as specifically racialized (Daniel 1997; Lux 2006). The construction and thus the treatment of TB as racialized was, however, masked by terms that addressed TB as a concern for public health (Waldram, Herring, and Young 1995); the racialization of TB is apparent both in the type and in the timing of the provision of TB care for Aboriginal peoples. At the same time, the legal requirement that Indigenous children be institutionalized in Indian residential schools, which were overcrowded and poorly maintained and ventilated, would have had the effect of actually producing much higher rates of TB among these children. The prevalence of TB among children in residential schools was a material effect of colonial categories of racialized difference and segregation.

Not until the 1940s was significant government attention paid to the prevention or treatment of tuberculosis among Aboriginal peoples.[13] In 1945 health services for Indigenous peoples became the responsibility of the department of National Health and Welfare, and sanatorium care, which prior to this time had been dismissed as unacceptable, became a system imposed upon Indigenous peoples (Hodgson 1982, 505; Lux 1996).[14] This system was implemented at the same time that wealthy settler populations were no longer prescribed extended stays in sanatoria when they contracted TB; many were instead treated as outpatients with new and effective drugs (Lux 1996). But when the federal government turned its attention to Aboriginal people with TB in the early 1940s, the strategies utilized were imposed as mandatory and were aggressive (Staples, McConnell, and Oakes 1993).

The Fort Qu'Appelle Indian Hospital in Saskatchewan was one of the first hospitals designated as an Indian hospital in Canada. Built in 1936, Fort Qu'Appelle contained fifty beds (Lux 2017). In 1945 the Charles Camsell Indian Hospital opened in Edmonton. One among a number of what have been called "centralized" tuberculosis treatment centres for Aboriginal patients in Canada, the hospital was the largest of its kind in North America (CCHC 1985; Staples, McConnell, and Oakes 1993). The Charles Camsell Indian Hospital became oriented toward more general care of the population at large in 1973 but claimed to maintain the treatment of First Nations and Inuit populations as a priority.[15] Those treated for tuberculosis during the early days at the Indian hospital were primarily First Nations and Inuit peoples from Alberta, the Yukon, and the Northwest Territories.[16] At the time, sanatoria and the rest cure had been used in North America and Europe for almost a hundred years (Daniel 1997, 178–79) despite the fact that there was little or no specific evidence to indicate that the treatment strategies cured or even diminished incidents of TB (CCHC 1985). Nonetheless, this kind of "centralized" treatment was reportedly "the most effective and cost-efficient way" to manage this particular TB (Staples, McConnell, and Oakes 1993, 6; see also Lux 2016).

The memorial pillar at the corner of the old site of the Charles Camsell Indian Hospital explains that the hospital was a Canadian initiative toward the "eradication" of an "epidemic" and that it was a celebrated success. But it also describes initial local opposition to the hospital, which was framed in terms of fear of a treatment centre and fear of the area becoming a "camp for the natives."[17] These fears were also expressed in local newspapers at the time. While the hospital was still in the proposal stage, some people living in the city expressed concern that if an Indian hospital was opened there, its occupants could not be contained in that space. Reflecting the national concern about the control of "Indian" TB, much of the resistance to the Indian hospital seems to have centred on this problem of containment:

> Mayor John Fry objected to sick Native people being concentrated in his city. The department allayed his fears by pointing out that the proposed hospital would provide employment for about one hundred and fifty staff, and that both the staff and the institution would have considerable purchasing power in the city. The department also noted that the institution would be self-contained and that property values would not be affected. Moreover, the patients would be confined to the institution, and it would be better than having "tuberculous Indians wandering about the streets of Edmonton ... and spreading the disease." (Lux 2001, 222)

From late September through to mid-December 1945, articles and letters expressing resistance to a tuberculosis hospital for Indians at the site of the old Jesuit college appeared almost daily in Edmonton newspapers. Clippings from 1945 headlined local opposition to the establishment of a TB hospital but also recorded the city's inability to block the federal initiative, despite the claim that the hospital would violate city zoning and bylaws and despite a "resolution of the city council that Edmonton exhaust every means possible 'persuasive or legal' to prevent the dominion government converting the Jesuit college into a T.B. hospital" – which included Mayor Harry Dean Ainlay sending a telegram of protest to Prime Minister William Lyon Mackenzie King.[18] A newspaper article of September 28, 1945, reported that a neighbourhood petition against the establishment of the Indian hospital was circulating among homeowners in the area immediately surrounding the Jesuit college.[19] A few days later, on October 3, 1945, another article reported that 425 people had signed a petition against the TB hospital.[20] According to these reports, it was primarily the Canadian Legion and women's groups in Edmonton that led the fight against the opening of a "hospital for tubercular Indians."[21] Mayor Ainlay was quoted in the local news as speaking for *the people:* "The people are not against the college being used temporarily as a tubercular hospital for returned veterans, but definitely don't want the building established as a tubercular hospital for Indians."[22] The threat was posed not by TB but by the "type" that embodied it. Beatrice Calliou, who is identified in the provincial archives as having had Iroquois (Haudenosaunee)[23] ancestry and as having been the great-step-granddaughter of the man who owned and then apparently donated the land upon which the Indian hospital eventually stood, also recalled that local opposition to the hospital was opposition specifically to an "Indian" hospital:

> What a controversial subject it turned out to be ... They said we're sure the Indians would pitch their tents on grounds surrounding the hospital, and try and live in the area. Others said they would be beating the tom-toms and having pow-wows every night and in general making a nuisance of themselves. The Indian hospital would bring down property values![24]

Herself a patient at the Charles Camsell Indian Hospital, Calliou identified the concern about the Indian presence as a concern about a specifically "uncivilized" presence (e.g., tents and tom-toms) and a concern that, having been moved to the hospital, the Indians might then "try and live in the area."

Records in Alberta's provincial archives also indicate opposition to the establishment of the hospital from the local Mountglen Home and School Association: "Mayor Ainlay was asked to check with the city legal department on the resolution that the legal department ask the attorney-general's department to ascertain whether the city council and provincial government can move through the courts to prevent the proposed setting up of the Indian hospital in Edmonton."[25] Even the Government of Alberta was opposed to the federal government's decision, suggesting instead that the Jesuit college's buildings be used to support the city's housing needs.[26] In the end, four of the college's adjoining redwood buildings would go to providing housing, but the Indian hospital would go ahead as well. One newspaper reported that much of the opposition to the hospital was dismissed by federal officials as "racial discrimination," and it questioned why there had been no local opposition when, on two prior occasions, the Jesuit college was proposed for use as a veterans' hospital or as a provincial sanatoria not specifically for Aboriginal people.[27] Although a number of news articles specifically denied that the opposition was motivated by racism, they failed to effectively challenge these multiple observations of racism. City zoning and bylaws were continually changing, and few of the arguments against the hospital seem to have resided on grounds other than racism.

The racist claims on the part of those opposed to a tuberculosis hospital in this location suggest that resistance to the hospital was rooted in particular ways. As Mayor Ainlay stated clearly at the time, the resistance was specifically to an "Indian" hospital, not to a TB hospital. It was the prospect of an "Indian" presence in the neighbourhood that prompted resistance. As another invocation of a land that was imagined as vacant prior to European arrival, this resistance was expressed as though an "Indian" presence did not belong there and as though such a presence was indeed new to the area rather than having already been a part of this place for centuries. The many Inuit who were transported from their northern communities to the Charles Camsell Indian Hospital far to the south had indeed arrived from elsewhere. But the people of many Indigenous nations and communities, including the Cree (Nehiyawak), Saulteaux, Niitsitapi (Blackfoot), Métis, Tsuu T'ina, and Nakota Sioux may have had a longstanding presence in the area, as they and their ancestors may have gathered there or resided in and moved through the area for millennia. Whatever prior or enduring presence First Nations had on these lands, their presence was nonetheless rendered foreign to an emerging urban and institutional place; the presence of the mayor and local homeowners was naturalized, whereas local Indigenous peoples were rendered "Other" within a particular geography. How and why this occurred are explained in terms of the concurrent colonial practices of displacement, transfer (Veracini 2010), and emplacement (Blomley 2004).

"An Operation of Military Proportion"

When the Charles Camsell Indian Hospital opened and accepted its first patients in 1945, there were some challenges. Those considered by the settler authorities to be "the source" of TB were geographically and culturally diverse and were located in rural and often isolated regions of the country, frequently in small communities on treaty land. The Inuit, for example, were among those who were difficult to get to and far from the few "centralized" Indian hospitals.[28] The emergency that this "Indian epidemic" constituted in the 1940s, however, seems to have justified extreme measures on the part of the government. The Government of Canada tackled the problem of TB on what was then still considered the Canadian frontier by mobilizing expeditions to carry out mass X-ray surveys, most of which were organized in coordination with the Charles Camsell Indian Hospital (Grygier 1994, 69). With the travelling X-ray units and owing to the mass marine and air transport that relocated those deemed ill to this southern sanatorium, the hospital became the treatment location for most identified cases of TB among Aboriginal peoples in northwestern Canada until 1965 (Lux 2006). An article in an Edmonton newspaper in 1951 reports organized Indian health surveys as starting in 1946. The object of these X-ray surveys was to "have a chest examination of every Indian once a year."[29] However, Don Harkness (in CCHC 1985, 132), who was in charge of X-ray surveys coming from the Charles Camsell Indian Hospital, wrote that it was not until September 1947 that the hospital sent its first team to X-ray the people of the Ermineskin and Samson Cree nations on reserves around Maskwacis (Hobbema). That day, 350 people were X-rayed, and 9 of them were determined to have active TB (CCHC 1985, 132). From that point on, as one Camsell doctor recounted, "mobile chest X-ray survey teams were sent out to make a massive sweep from the U.S. border to the Arctic Ocean and from Alaska to Hudson Bay" (Barclay in CCHC 1985, 22). Within a couple of years, the Canadian Tuberculosis Association (1950, 4) claimed that "in some remote areas 94% of the population has been X-rayed." Other accounts offer different tallies; for example, one states that "by 1955 it was estimated that about 5,000 Inuit, or half the population, had been x-rayed, some of them more than once" (Grygier 1994, 71). In an audio recording stored in Alberta's provincial archives, a Dr. Falconer speaks generally of the years between 1945 and 1949, and states that in one year 20,000 Indian or Inuit people were X-rayed and that in the following year even more were X-rayed.[30]

In records detailing the numbers of people X-rayed during this time, there is also information regarding how such technologies were effectively imposed. The Canadian Tuberculosis Association (1950, 4) states that compliance "has been made possible by the co-operation of the Indian agents who had insisted that each family pass through the X-ray clinic before receiving their treaty monies." In the case of the Arctic surveys, X-ray teams were scheduled to be there when treaty money came in, as this was the time when the nomadic peoples would gather.[31] Rita (Murphy) Morin, who was a public health nurse and worked in that capacity as a liaison between the hospital and reserve communities, confirms that this was a usual practice (CCHC 1985, 138). In 1948, for example, X-rays were arranged to correspond with payments owed to the Blackfoot (Niitsitapi) peoples by the Canadian nation (and to be paid via the Indian agent) for their contribution to the WWII effort. In this case, because funds were withheld until after X-rays, the whole community (about 1,400 people) was X-rayed within two days. To manage the numbers of people who had arrived to collect the funds they were due, "it was agreed that the head of the household would be X-rayed first and allowed to collect all the money owing to the family, provided that the wife and children would be X-rayed" (Harkness in CCHC 1985, 134). Describing this event, Camsell X-ray technician Don Harkness wrote, "Although it may not have been entirely ethical to use the Indian's own money as a bribe, at the time, the end seemed to justify the means" (CCHC 1985, 134).

The combining of screening for TB with the payment of treaty monies meant that those treaties signed decades earlier functioned in practice in the 1940s and 1950s as a technology of coercion and as a mechanism for the assertion of biological difference and hierarchy through categories of race and gender. Those pathologized as "susceptible" could be lured accordingly. For the family arriving to pick up funds legally due to them, neither option would have been a straightforward one: either give up your money or submit to an X-ray. In the wake of a colonial attack on Indigenous families and cultural practices, giving up treaty funds might have put families in desperate situations, but the consequence of being X-rayed could have meant the legally enforced and immediate separation of family members, with the long-term consequences unknown. In the case Don Harkness describes, it is important to note how the agreed-upon means for the distribution of funds both presumed the existence of patriarchal Eurocentric "households" and positioned women and children to be dependent on (and inferior to) men within this system.

Once X-rays had been taken, people diagnosed with TB were transported to southern sanatoria – usually the Mountain Sanatorium in Hamilton, Ontario, or the Charles Camsell Indian Hospital in Edmonton – by land, air, and/or sea (Grygier 1994). For people living in the North, the trip south was sometimes months long (Grygier 1994). The year 1952 was the hospital's busiest, with an average of 513 patients each day (Bergman in CCHC 1985, 45).[32] By 1956, due primarily to government-sponsored X-ray surveys and efforts to have those diagnosed with TB transported for treatment, "one out of every seven Inuit was in a southern sanatorium" (Grygier 1994, xxi). The number of Inuit people evacuated from the North each year reached its height in 1955, when apparently over 7,000 X-rays were taken and 950 Inuit were sent to southern sanatoria, primarily to the Charles Camsell Indian Hospital (Grygier 1994, 71). Those diagnosed with the disease had little opportunity to avoid a trip south or an often lengthy sanatorium stay.

Those identified as having tuberculosis were not necessarily sick, nor did they necessarily harbour a latent form of TB. Despite the authority invested in and practised through Western medicine, diagnoses of TB were not necessarily accurate or true (Lux 2016). X-ray images produced by mobile imaging units did not actually offer the conclusive evidence for the diagnosis that they were used to issue. Lux (2016, 99) points out that the reliability and validity of a mobile X-ray to determine a diagnosis of TB were highly questionable since "the gains in machine portability and economy" often resulted in diminished accuracy. This problem of accuracy, when combined with the particular conditions under which these mobile X-rays were conducted, the high degree of subjectivity involved in their interpretation, and the already established idea that there were high rates of TB among remote Indigenous populations, would have worked to influence and likely elevate the numbers of TB diagnoses

(Lux 2016). Beyond the questionable accuracy of mobile X-rays, these units were also known to be more damaging to patients than their stationary counterparts (Lux 2016). In some cases, despite these harms, X-rays were given twice a year, as Lux (2016, 98) points out, sometimes over spans of thirty to forty years, but "iatrogenic injury to Aboriginal bodies was the price to be paid to contain tuberculosis infection in Aboriginal communities and, ultimately, to protect an increasingly tuberculin-negative Canadian public."

The operation described here suggests that there was a lot at stake in the diagnosis of TB among Indigenous peoples. In her account of TB among the Plains Indians, Lux (2001, 222) reports, "A Blood elder recalls that when people were sent to Charles Camsell, 'they never came back.'" This view seems to have also been held by Inuit people, given that a journey on the survey boats was thought to be equivalent to "a death sentence" and was likely among the reasons that fear accompanied the arrival of the survey boats in the North (Grygier 1994, 97). In 1954 Bishop Donald B. Marsh reported that

> on his Arctic trip that year he had heard "that the Eskimos fled inland before the arrival of the ship with the medical officers on board, for fear that they would be wrested from their homes and shipped outside never to return, as has happened to so many of their friends and relatives. It is indeed hard to believe that this is the only way that a great nation like Canada can care for a small minority in her midst and who are, after all, our oldest Canadians." (Quoted in Grygier 1994, 76)

From the far northern coast of Canada to its southern prairies, it seems that very early on a trip into treatment was associated with the termination of familial and cultural ties (Grygier 1994). This feature of the treatment strategy was not lost on those involved in issuing the medical attention. Dr. Otto Schaefer (1959, 249) of the Charles Camsell Indian Hospital reported in an article titled "Medical Observations and Problems in the Canadian Arctic: Part I,"

> We must also not forget, that, until a few years ago, discovery of advanced tuberculosis in Northern natives meant, in most cases, parting from their lands and peoples forever to wither away in a strange environment and with a disagreeable type of food. No wonder they fled over the hills in some places when our x-ray equipment was landed. The situation has improved greatly almost everywhere, but many old Indians and Eskimos are still more afraid of evacuation to the white man's land than of death, while they cheerfully accept hospitalization in their own country, where they can talk their own tongue, eat frozen fish, caribou and seal-meat and have visitors.

Imposed travel to the white man's land had developed a reputation. Evacuation meant that geographical boundaries were merging, namely between urban and rural spaces, even as a number of other boundaries were being rigidly enforced, notably between white and Native as biological distinctions and between well and diseased as racial attributes.[33]

Since there are few details available in Edmonton regarding these mass mobilizations, we are left to piece together what these voyages might have been like with little information. In Lux's (2016, 100) history of Indian hospitals in Canada, she writes that during the Arctic surveys, after Inuit peoples were screened and determined to have TB,

> they were kept onboard with no chance to bid goodbye to family and friends. Without proper interpreters and treated as so much cargo, Inuit patients were numbered and stowed aboard, with no opportunity to question their diagnosis or their fate. Their bodies literally inscribed with the colonizers' diagnosis and marked for relocation, patients felt the disciplining power of Western medicine.

Descriptions of the survey boats that transported those diagnosed with TB suggest that they were dismal places and that the voyage itself was difficult to endure. As reported by Robert Williamson, a passenger on an Eastern Arctic Patrol ship in 1953–54,

> The ship was deep in misery. It was terrible because it was the ship which carried the Inuit away from their homes to the sanatoria in the south. And they were herded together in the foc'sle, in the hold of the ship in three-tiered bunks, mass-fed, mass-accommodated. In the stormy seas they were sick, they were terrified, they were demoralized. They were frightened of what was happening to them, of what was likely to happen to them. (Quoted in Grygier 1994, 86)

After what were often very long expeditions by boat, passengers were often then flown to the southern sanatoria. Kathleen Dier, a nurse who helped to transport people south, described the scene at Cambridge Bay for the journal *Canadian Nurse:*

> Getting the patients sent off to Camsell was an operation of military proportion; everyone had to be ready to board the RCAF [Royal Canadian Air Force] flying boxcar the minute it landed on the ice. Each person had a big yellow tag with name, disc number and other particulars filled in at the top and bottom. The bottom part was removed at the Yellowknife hospital where the patients spent the night. The remainder was supposed to remain in place until they reached Camsell, a feat not usually accomplished as the wind kept blowing them away. This of course caused great confusion on their arrival at Camsell, confusion compounded by the fact that in fur parkas it wasn't easy to even sort out the men from the women. For the Inuit the trip south was a bewildering experience but they coped amazingly well. (Quoted in Grygier 1994, 70)

Such reports give a sense of the magnitude and character of the state's task, particularly the difficulty of producing Indian TB, "sorting" those who supposedly harboured it according to Eurocolonial categories, and then transporting and keeping a record of them en route.

It is clear that the emergence of Indian TB hospitals cannot be understood as a government response to taking care of sick people. There are too many details of the practices that leave too many questions unanswered. Beyond these questions, it is also the case that institutions like hospitals worked within a logic that maintained the presence, entitlement, and legitimacy of settler colonialism (Veracini 2010). With the establishment of Indian hospitals also came the establishment of infrastructure for the mass transfer of those defined both as exogenous to the settler colonial population and as a danger to it, and bodies played a key role in this project. Information about bodies was produced and used in this moment as a form of biopower, just as it is in contemporary policing (Foucault 1990), making it a mechanism for the control and regularization of populations. State practices of identifying, testing, diagnosing, and amassing First Nations and Inuit peoples amounted to a kind of massification and control of a type or a "population" (Foucault 2003, 246). Such techniques, in this case, functioned not unlike those that have historically been utilized to delineate populations of supposed inferiority and to mark their inferiority. Lux (2001) describes the aggressive system of imposed collection for transportation to, and treatment in, southern sanatoria as the practical realization of an already prominent theory of "biological invasion." Hence the massification of Indigenous peoples both informed the practice (i.e., as a population, they were already racialized) and emerged as a further outcome of this collection of data (i.e., X-rays) and bodies (i.e., Indigenous peoples). This theory of "biological invasion" functioned in different ways at different times. At one time, the theory informed a colonial governmental retreat from responsibility for the declining populations of Indigenous peoples, which had been recorded ever since contact with colonizing peoples. According to the theory, TB among Native peoples was due to their innate and biological susceptibility. Since TB was understood as a biological manifestation of racial inferiority, the (mostly) European settler population was positioned as unable to do much against such a natural predisposition. At a later time, however, with the opening of the Charles Camsell Indian Hospital and the mass surveying of Indigenous peoples, this theory provided the justification for focusing technologies on specific bodies, defined as evolutionarily and racially distinct. Commemorations of the Indian hospital attest to its history of offering treatment for what was conceived of as a natural marker of racial inferiority. Part of this treatment was based on the idea that through exposure to "white" ways and to the "white" race, those of the inferior race would supposedly evolve accordingly, enhancing their own embodied stature relative to the colonizers.

A break in the historiography offered here is required in order to emphasize the uncanny resemblances between the X-rays taken from Indigenous peoples in the 1940s and '50s and the DNA samples taken from "high-risk" women in the early twenty-first century. In both instances, the body was made to serve a certain utility and was used to enact biopolitical power. In the 1940s and '50s a coerced submission to X-rays and to the techniques and technologies of diagnosis within Western medicine resulted in the potential admission of Indigenous people to an Indian hospital, but it also initiated their potential loss, disappearance, or death. A half-century later, the recording of "tombstone information" and the procurement of bits of hair or slivers of fingernails from women deemed to be at "high risk" signified their arrival on the cusp of danger, disappearance, or death, but it did little to stop such happenings, serving primarily as a record of such anticipation. In both cases, peoples' bodies were turned into sites for the extraction and production of information that became a database upon which certain futures were sought and sometimes secured. When those deemed to be at "high risk" were asked for DNA, their disappearance was anticipated even as no promise of safety was offered. Such DNA served as concrete evidence, first, of a state of high risk and, later, of death, framed as a consequence exclusively of that high risk. After an X-ray and a diagnosis of TB, people were sorted, assigned numbers, and relocated, soon to disappear into a system of rationalized and legally mandated treatment that required their isolation far from friends and family. Although these biopolitical strategies effected different specific outcomes, both used the body (an individual's life) as matter to foster the disappearance of Indigenous peoples (a population) under settler colonial projects and toward settler colonial ends.

Even when such strategies were not tied to a permanent disappearance, as in the case of the Charles Camsell Indian Hospital, the amassing of records was at the crux of rendering Indigenous peoples refugees through their mass transfer (Veracini 2010). The government's efforts brought large numbers of diverse peoples from elsewhere into Edmonton but not as citizens of the city. Rather, Inuit, Dene, Cree (Nehiyawak), Saulteaux, Niitsitapi (Blackfoot), Métis, Tsuu T'ina, and Nakota Sioux were among those brought into the city as wards of the state *for* institutionalization and treatments that offered little or no opportunity for self-determination. Indeed, as Lux (2017) reports, by 1953 it was against the law for "Indigenous people to refuse to see a doctor, to refuse to go to hospital, and to leave hospital before discharge." These laws were enforced by the national police force, the Royal Canadian Mounted Police, which was the same force that would establish Project Kare roughly a half-century later. To enforce the 1953 regulation, the police "arrested patients and returned them to hospital or sent them to jail" (Lux 2017). In either case, the incarceration of Indigenous peoples seems to have been paramount.

This type of enforced movement from the land might be conceptualized as a variation on legal geographer Nicholas Blomley's (2004) "dispossession" or as an additional form of it, exercised specifically in this Canadian context. That is, due to the imposed removal of Indigenous peoples from their home, family, and community, due to their transport to an unknown and institutional place for an indeterminate length of time, and due to their lack of self-determination there, an immediate connection to home was severed, sometimes temporarily but sometimes permanently. People were further dispossessed from the lands they identified as home, lands the Canadian government had already claimed official title to but had not yet generally accessed. The forced movement of people from the places they inhabit as home is a practice that continually colonizes.

Lorenzo Veracini (2010) describes the forced movement of Indigenous peoples, whether to schools or hospitals or to different geographical contexts, as a settler colonial strategy that transforms people indigenous to the land into refugees. Among numerous strategies that are "discursively or practically emptying the indigenous sector of the population system," this forced movement is described by Veracini as an "ethnic transfer," which occurs "when indigenous communities are forcibly deported, either within or without the territory claimed or controlled by the settler entity. Wherever they end up, they cease being indigenous" (Veracini 2010, 34–35). This transfer reflects the settler colonial interest in "turning indigenous peoples into refugees" (Veracini 2010, 35). As "peoples that have been repeatedly forced to abandon their homes, [they] are by definition indigenous to somewhere else – the very opposite of 'Aboriginal'" (Veracini 2010, 35). Veracini's work is helpful for elucidating how the claim to Indigeneity can be thrown into question from the outside, but it is clear that people do not "cease being indigenous," even though through conditions of mass transfer they cease being recognized as Indigenous by those engaged in forging their own naturalized presence in a place. It is less the case that Indigenous people ceased being Indigenous through their forced transfer to the Charles Camsell Indian Hospital and more the case that even local Niitsitapi and Woodland and Plains Cree people were made recognizable as refugees insofar as their displacement to the Indian hospital and subjection to the charity and supposed benevolence of the state meant that they no longer seemed to have a claim to geography or national sovereignty.

Inside the Indian Hospital

Some accounts suggest that those transported to the Charles Camsell Indian Hospital "stayed for an average of two and a half years" (Grygier 1994, xxi). Another source cites an average length of stay at the hospital as twenty-eight months, a period considered sufficient to sever family and community connections (Staples, McConnell, and Oakes 1993, 5). Nurse Rita Morin characterized treatment in the early days of the hospital as long, lasting a minimum of one year and commonly taking three or four years (cited in CCHC 1985, 138). Other sanatoria in Canada kept patients for averages of three to five years, with the Canadian Lung Association (2019b) reporting that some patients spent ten years in a sanatorium. But some patients endured much longer stays at the Indian hospital. In Alberta's provincial archives, one photograph of a woman next to a Christmas tree is captioned, "Elizabeth Beaver Leaving Hospital After 15 Years ... admitted as a little girl, she leaves as a young woman."[34] But few actual records seem to have been kept during the early years of the hospital, so there is little accurate information on who was treated there, for how long, and with what outcomes (CBC 1989; Grygier 1994). A report by the Canadian Broadcasting Corporation (CBC 1989) confirms that as a consequence of enforced transport to southern sanatoria, large numbers of Inuit people permanently lost their families, some never learned the fate of their loved ones, and some were never able to grieve the loss or death of a loved one, as they continued to anticipate the return of those who had been taken (Grygier 1994).[35] There was, then, much more than the cure of TB occurring with the transport of Indigenous peoples and their treatment at places like the Charles Camsell Indian Hospital (Lux 2001).

"After 1944 drugs were developed that made tuberculosis manageable, if not curable" (Lux 2001, 222), and within less than a decade, drug therapy for TB was "extremely effective. The need for sanatoria seems to have been disappearing quickly. Most non-Natives were treated on an outpatient basis with drug therapy. Native patients continued to be hospitalized." Drug treatment was not made generally available to Aboriginal people in Canada until 1964 (Lux 2001). So, whereas white settlers no longer had to see the inside of sanatoria, Aboriginal peoples were increasingly admitted: the numbers rose from only 100 Native patients receiving TB treatment in Canadian sanatoria or hospitals in 1937 to almost 3,000 in 1953 (Lux 2001). Indeed, there appears to be a correlation between the development of antibiotics and drug therapy for settler populations and the concurrent mass institutionalization of Indian and Inuit cases of TB that has, with the exception of the excellent critical scholarship by Maureen Lux (2001, 2006, 2016), received little attention in historical accounts of Canada.[36]

The forced X-ray, examination, diagnosis, and transportation of large numbers of people, the settler opposition to the presence of Indigenous peoples in the city and their forced incarceration there, the existence of an effective vaccine to which Indigenous peoples had no access, and the particular forms of treatment offered at the Charles Camsell Indian Hospital all suggest that the hospital functioned in terms beyond those commonly associated with the provision of care. At places like the Indian hospital, Indigenous peoples faced intensive, long-term, and forced forms of institutionalization, whereas in white hospitals white settlers received outpatient care to such degrees of success that the need for sanatoria treatment was virtually eliminated (Lux 2006). Further, this discrepancy did not function at the time, nor does it even now, as a perceived difference in treatment because Indigenous peoples were seen to require institutional treatment as part of their achieving increased resistance to disease – an increased resistance thought possible for First Nations peoples only through their eventual biological as well as social "evolution" or reform (Lux 2001, 2006). Thus both settler populations and Indigenous populations were paradoxically situated since each "threatened" the other, each being simultaneously the source of the infection and subject to it through proximity to the other. What differed, however, was everything about the treatment, including how such treatment was thought to function for Indigenous people toward their "evolution."

Situating the tubercular "Indian" as a threat to the nation – as a threat to "the rest of Canada" – constituted a crisis that apparently justified the extreme measures taken to cull, control, and confine the "Indian" and by extension the "Indian epidemic." In keeping with Giorgio Agamben's (1995, 2005) notion of a "state of exception," the apprehension and restraint of those situated as threatening the nation were outside of standard legal practice but became nonetheless allowable. Additionally, as I elaborate later, those specifically situated as *threatening* were already ambiguously situated in relation to their recognition as citizens and to the provision of citizenship privileges in the new nation. Under the Indian Act, as wards of the state, Indigenous peoples were not granted the status of a juridical or self-determining legal subject (Thobani 2007). And thus, in regard to legal protections, their circumstances resembled "bare life" (Agamben 1995). As sociologist and feminist Sunera Thobani (2007, 50) observes, "The state commanded that Indians exist officially only in the infantilized capacity of wards, prohibiting their existence as juridical subjects" – a strategy employed by the Canadian state "to empty Native peoples of their human status." Part of such prohibition is tied to the boundaries made in land and space and to practices of forced movement of peoples. Such prohibition also limits who is designated as having full human status, as was demonstrated by the lack of concern for self-determination regarding whether, where, and how the treatment of

Indigenous people might occur. Even when living on lands that were ostensibly set aside for First Nations by virtue of treaty agreements with the Canadian nation, Indigenous people were moved from their homes against their will and with no redress, although never without resistance. The inversion of this relationship to the land such that one's presence on it could be severed through the use of medical and state technologies to produce biological "truths" and knowledge, or biopower (Foucault 1990), effectively functioned in practice to render treaty agreements inconsequential, except as useful tools for the identification of geographies of potential affliction and for coercion of the people there. These areas were mapped as "scattered islands of infection" (Ferguson, quoted in Lux 2001, 212), and the tools of modern medicine, including the construct of "race," were used to locate and bind a geography that corresponded with reserve spaces. Thus an obscured contingency is revealed within treaty agreements. Lands allocated as reserves are also "camps" (Agamben 1995). They are spatial designations whose inhabitants have been identified as a "threatening" presence to the fiction of "national" health and thus have been moved, confined, and treated, sometimes to die (even in a sanatorium), at the will of the state.

In the early years of the Charles Camsell Indian Hospital, Indian tuberculosis was primarily treated through prolonged confinement in southern sanatoria. A vaccine, known commonly as BCG (Bacillus Calmette-Guérin), had been developed against tuberculosis and was proven effective as early as the 1920s, but the Indigenous populations in Canada had little access to the therapy except as test subjects (Lux 2001). Ferguson began to research the effect of BCG on Aboriginal peoples as early as 1927, and between 1933 and 1945 these trials included 609 Aboriginal infants: "306 infants were vaccinated and 303 infants were designated as unvaccinated controls" (Lux 2001, 211). The results showed that "BCG conferred valuable protection in a highly infectious environment" (Lux 2001, 211). Although the vaccination did prevent infants from getting TB, it did not effect a significant reduction in the number of infant deaths because, as Lux points out, "the most obvious finding of the BCG vaccine trial was that poverty, not tuberculosis, was the greatest threat to Native infants" (Lux 2001, 211). This finding is enough to call into question both the government's subsequent reliance on sanatoria to treat TB among Aboriginal peoples and its limited provision of BCG. Treatment through sanatoria, however, allowed the government to deny its implication in the larger social context (e.g., Indigenous poverty), which was a direct consequence of colonialism and the treaty system (Lux 2001). Lux (1996) suggests that, for this reason, in spite of contemporary popular recognition of the federal government's efforts in the 1940s as charitable and responsible initiatives to treat and prevent TB among Indigenous peoples, the provision of segregated institutionalization at poorly funded Indian hospitals was actually a direct *retreat* from the government's responsibility since hospitalization imposed the economic and political factors that were part of colonization and thus caused massive harm to Aboriginal peoples.

The idea that a vaccine might be as effective for First Nations and Inuit peoples as it was for settler populations ran counter to the race-based theory of disease. It omitted the colonial assumption of a link between "civility" and inherent protection from disease. Within a race-based theory, the vaccine would be ineffective as a means for prevention, as it could not address the underlying problem of "race" as a biological fact – that is, the problem of differentially evolved, hierarchically ordered, physical subjects. The prospect of an effective vaccine would have virtually eliminated a basic objective informing the Canadian government's treatment of TB among Aboriginal peoples: social reform (Lux 2001, 5). Inversely, if the government had addressed poverty – which was a direct consequence of, and tool for, colonization – rates of TB would have dropped, and claims about a biological "race" might have faltered as well.

The treatments employed at the Charles Camsell Indian Hospital were not necessarily effective and were sometimes experimental and dangerous (CCHC 1985; Lux 2001, 2016). Like other Indian hospitals in Canada, the Charles Camsell Indian Hospital "provided opportunities for medical experimentation, most often without the patients' consent" (Lux 2017). Drs. William R. Barclay and Margaret Barclay, both of whom began working at the hospital in 1946, reflected on the therapies practised there: "Bed rest, surgical collapse of the lung, and fixation of joints by plaster made up our therapeutic armamentarium," which was based "more on blind faith and trust than on any scientific evidence that they were effective" (quoted in CCHC 1985, 23; see also Geddes 2017). Lux (2001, 222) also suggests that surgeries might not have provided optimal outcomes and describes the surgical collapse of the lung, or thoracoplasties, this way: "A lung was collapsed permanently and ribs were removed. Major surgery created its own dangers, and removal of the ribs resulted in significant blood loss and high mortality. Survivors were badly disfigured; some were given prostheses to keep their chests from collapsing altogether." High mortality and the disfigurement of survivors were characteristics of these procedures. The Barclays listed the other surgeries performed at the Indian hospital – "pneumothorax, pneumoperitoneum and phrenic nerve crush" – and recalled a colleague feeling "troubled by the measures we took to treat patients," reiterating that there was "little or no evidence as to their effectiveness" (quoted in CCHC 1985, 23). Thus, although there is little information to be found in local or provincial archives specifically about the medical interventions utilized in the treatment of TB, there are indications that their use was based more on experiment than on proven success.

Official records suggest that the most common treatment provided at the Charles Camsell Indian Hospital was a regime of bedrest (CCHC 1985, 94). Doctors determined the degree of severity of TB and then decided what level of mobility and activity a patient was allowed. Research on this primary means of treatment has provoked Lux (2001, 223) to characterize patients' time in such Indian hospitals as "unrelieved boredom punctuated by medications." Reporting on bedrest regimes in 1947, the Charles Camsell History Committee (1985, 94) cites six different routines to which patients were assigned depending on doctors' assessments. Those diagnosed with the most severe TB were assigned to Routine One and allowed no movement, subjected to complete bedrest, and bathed only in bed (CCHC 1985, 94). Those assigned to Routine Two were allowed to be out of bed for fifteen minutes each day at a set time but were otherwise totally confined to bed (CCHC 1985, 94). Thus, presumably, as a patient moved progressively through routines, additional freedom of movement was allowed. Arriving at Routine Six meant that one was considered to be recovering from TB, was given significant freedom of movement, and was told that he or she would soon be released (CCHC 1985, 94). Those assigned to Routine Six still participated in mandatory rest periods but were allowed to leave their ward to exercise in strictly designated hospital spaces, such as the canteen or the "park area in front of hospital ONLY" (CCHC 1985, 94). Thus, for all TB patients, the central feature of their treatment was the intensive regulation of the daily movements of their bodies.

Such disciplining of bodies to enforce a routine might have been difficult to implement, particularly for those feeling well despite the diagnosis. And there appear to be some indications of how activity and movement were policed. For example, a major function of the monthly in-hospital newsletter *The Camsell Arrow* seems to have been to maintain an emphasis on obeying doctors' orders for bedrest regimes. The newsletter also cites the practice of placing patients in plaster casts to ensure "cooperative" behaviour (Orford in CCHC 1985, 30). *Lost Songs* (Tourangeau 1999), a National Film Board of Canada documentary about the Charles Camsell Indian Hospital, reports that patients who could not be disciplined to follow the highly regulated bedrest regime were wrapped in casts, partial or full-body, to ensure their cooperation.[37] Casts were apparently put most frequently on children, who, often feeling quite well despite their diagnosis, were not inclined to stay in bed all day. In particular, "rambunctious children were often physically restrained in their beds, or by plaster casts on both legs" (Lux 2017) to "teach the discipline of bed rest" (Lux 2016, 105). Keeping kids in beds was also accomplished through the use of restraints: "A former Camsell orderly explained … hospital policy was to place small children face down at night, their hands tied to the side of the crib to keep them from jumping up and down" (Geddes 2017, 96). Such physical control of children was likely framed as though it were specifically germane to their eventual "cure."

An article in the December 1947 edition of the *The Camsell Arrow* by the Indian hospital's Dr. Thomas J. Orford, titled "Dread Epidemic" (reproduced in CCHC 1985, 30), documents both the threat and the practice of restraint through plaster casts as a method meant to ensure patient "cooperation," and it does so with a deeply disturbing lightness:

> A strange disease, Castitis, has stricken eight known people here, recently. Castitis is caused directly from Cantstayinbeditis – a fever which seems to develop in almost anybody who doesn't realize how serious a disease Tuberculosis is and how necessary bed rest is for cure.
>
> Cantstayinbeditis usually comes on in one person at first but spreads fairly rapidly to others in the same ward and actually it should be listed as a communicable disease ...
>
> The onset of Castitis is usually insidious. As Cantstayinbeditis becomes more acute the case is reported to the Doctor. If symptoms continue despite friendly and then more severe administrations of the medical staff, the patient develops hard, white, stiff, thick casements with cross bars between, on both legs below the knee. As a rule this condition enforces full bed rest although cases have been known in which crusting breaks – by design or otherwise. When this occurs the only known treatment is removal, whereupon, a harder, stronger cast is usually seen to appear which sometimes spreads even to the chest ...
>
> The usual treatment for a person with Castitis is rest and cooperation. The condition seems to improve those cases of tuberculosis which do not voluntarily accept recommended routine. After varying periods of time when the victim is convinced of the necessity for cooperation in the cure of his disease, tuberculosis, the cast suddenly and completely disappears and in the majority of cases does not recur.
>
> The best way to avoid the disease is to keep clear of any symptoms of Cantstayinbeditis.[38]

This text would have worked in ways that both infantilized and threatened patients who were subject to "Castitis." We cannot know the many ways that the text was taken up, and so I consider only the text, not reactions to it. In the same way that "drapetomania" was invented in the 1850s as a diagnosis of madness for the slaves who fled the conditions of slavery

(Bynum 2000, 1615), "Castitis" and "Cantstayinbeditis" were diagnoses that might have reflected the politics and values of the system of their invention. Whereas "the 'cure' for drapetomania was a firm, kindly master, who provided decent necessities and a structured work environment" (Bynum 2000, 1615), it seems that the cure for "Cantstayinbeditis" was the fostering of fear and the threat of plaster casting. In "Dread Epidemic," the responsibility for the appearance of casts was shifted from the medical staff to the noncompliant patient or to the patient who associated with the noncompliant patient. The article naturalized the appearance of patients in casts and framed disciplinary practices as though they were medical practices and thus entirely neutral, exercised without prejudice, and used to treat only those who had caught "Castitis." As "Dread Epidemic" explained, what was to be treated was construed as inherent to the body and therefore as needing to be addressed through intervention in the site of the body.

I argue that Orford's text worked as a technology that targeted the Indian hospital's patients in such a way that – if they understood the English text or had it explained to them – they themselves came to scrutinize their own "symptoms," or behaviours, monitoring their own degree of "cooperation" and needing to demonstrate the seriousness of the affliction. "Dread Epidemic" worked as a mode of regularizing populations (Foucault 1990). It is clear from this account that doctors and nurses were not likely to catch "Castitis." In fact, they likely recognized the text as a humorous, perhaps light-hearted, mode of motivating patient compliance with assigned schedules. The seemingly impartial tone of the text – perhaps employed just enough to be funny to those familiar with reading medical texts – and the fact that this practice of casting actually did occur as a mode of restraint would have made the piece work for doctors differently from how it worked for patients. For those assigned a daily schedule, the piece must have worked as a threat. Those already subject to a racialized version of TB were now required to demonstrate the complicity required to keep "Castitis" away. But for doctors and nurses and anyone familiar with medical texts, the "Dread Epidemic" would have doubled as entertainment, perhaps perceived as clever, precisely because it misconstrued responsibility for the appearance of casts and mimicked the medical authority undergirding the whole operation.

Before considering the practice of casting further, it is important to note that casting was not an entirely successful immobilizing strategy. Its ineffectiveness is clearly invoked not only in "Dread Epidemic" but also in the Charles Camsell Indian Hospital's archives. People moved around despite their casts, the "crusting" broke "by design or otherwise," and people escaped. There are remarkable reports of resistance, with patients slowly but successfully cutting or rubbing through plaster encasements (Fadum in CCHC 1985, 105). A head nurse at the hospital in the early 1950s, Esabelle Middleton, recalls in an interview stored at the provincial archives that "children with leg or body casts would be out of bed at night, hopping or dragging themselves around the room, until staff peeped in and then there was great scurrying back to bed. Many were the notes left on the doctor's desk, 'please see Joe or Peter to repair cracked cast.'"[39] One nurse remembers it taking a young girl three months to slowly cut through her body cast with a razor blade (CCHC 1985, 105). So although casts were intended to restrict and confine – perhaps even *whiten* – subjects entirely, they did so with only limited success. Despite the threat of the dreaded epidemic called "Castitis" and despite the casts themselves, many people physically defied attempts at their immobilization. The "Dread Epidemic" also divulged this resistance and attempted to pre-emptively prevent it with the additional threat of more complete casts: when one cast was broken, a newer, stronger, and even more constraining cast usually appeared, "which sometimes spreads even to the chest" (CCHC 1985, 30).

Casts were a tool used for disciplining movement, but they were also apparently used as treatment for orthopaedic tuberculosis (Barclay in CCHC 1985, 23). Although it is unclear how common the use of casts was for orthopaedic tuberculosis, it is clear that treatments deemed suitable at Indian hospitals were not necessarily considered appropriate in hospitals for settler patients (Lux 2017). This use of casts might complicate a clear-cut understanding of casting as restrictive or punitive, but it actually demonstrates how what can be understood as a benevolent medical practice was also a technology of power. The casting of the body in either case – and there may have been other reasons for casting that have not yet been identified in the data and literature – was specifically meant to immobilize the body defined as ill and Native with the aim of eventually transforming it into the well and civilized white body. Whatever the original intent of the technology, its use would have been discretionary, which is where socially agreed-upon definitions of who is a human become important. There were those suitable to cast for their own good, for their own civility, and even for their "cure," and there were those who decided upon when, for what reasons, and for how long a cast was to be applied. Whether for "Castitis" or orthopaedic tuberculosis, the cast worked in the same ways.

The cast body is more than a marked body. It is a body physically immobilized by the plasters of colonial power. The body cannot be more contained. The fact that the cast body is an effect of biopower is obvious; put to a number of purposes, casting was primarily about taking control of a person's life – its movement, meaning, and quality. Biopower, which Achille Mbembe (2003, 12) defines as being exercised in "that domain of life over which power has taken control," is fully and materially realized through a person's body in such a practice. The internal movement structure – a person's corporeal presence, including skeleton, bones, and muscles – is overpowered and constricted by the external enclosure. The binding and immobilizing of what were defined as "Indian" bodies in white plaster encasements was, in the case of treatment at the Charles Camsell Indian Hospital,[40] a covering-over of skin, that most obvious marker of "race," as well as a covering-over of what was thought to be the barbarity of movement – the physical activity that would aggravate what was now thoroughly and "scientifically" constructed as a racially ascribed affliction. The hard plaster casts can be read as wrapped to forge intentionally enforced cocoons by which colonial powers hoped to birth a newly civilized subject. This interpretation seems to offer something to our understanding of the magnitude of what happened at the Indian hospital even though such practices were and are framed as motivated by benevolent intentions.

There are a number of images of people in casts and of people being wrapped in casts at the Charles Camsell Indian Hospital now available in Alberta's provincial archives. I do not show these images in this book because people's names tended not to be included in the record and because I am not interested in reproducing images that might be read as signifying pure submission to a medical authority – still assumed to be inherently benevolent – in the absence of images that signify the rebellions that occurred there too. Nonetheless, I describe two photographs here for what they tell us about colonial interventions into the lives of Indigenous peoples through their bodies. In one image, dated February 4, 1954, a girl, maybe a young woman, is being wrapped in a cast from chest to knees at the hospital.[41] Only the photographer, the date, and the location of the photo are recorded with this image. In this picture, the girl looks like she is floating on air but is actually laid across three small stools while three men, dressed all in white and presumably white doctors, encase her entire body in a cast. The girl seems to be looking unflinchingly at the camera as the cast is wound around and around her body.

In another picture, a girl lies on her side with a cast encasing her head and neck, while the rest of her body is covered with a blanket; there is no indication of whether the cast extends beyond her neck.[42] This girl smiles as three nurses dressed in white, and presumably socially positioned as "white," stand at the head of her bed and smile down at her.[43]

The use of casts as disciplinary or according to a treatment – or, perhaps most effectively, as both – is called into question by the third representation considered here: two transcripts of an oral interview with a nurse who worked at the Indian hospital from 1949 to 1976, conducted by the Charles Camsell History Committee (1985) for its publication *The Camsell Mosaic*.[44] In one of the transcripts is the following description: "Ward 5A, a little girl was in a body cast. She had TB of the spine. She was in the crib with a cover to keep her in it." In the other transcript, this one marked "original," there is no mention of the girl having TB of the spine as the reason for the cast, although there is mention of a lid. This "original" transcript indicates only that the girl was "in a body cast and in a crib (with a lid on to keep her in)." Apart from this slight exception, the transcripts are identical. Each describes a 1946 visit of the governor general, the Right Honourable Charles Vincent Massey, who saw this particular girl in a cast lying in the crib with a lid and reportedly said, "I'll bet you're a holy terror when I'm not here."[45]

What is the significance of the discrepancy in transcripts? What is the significance of the addition of "TB of the spine" in the second transcript? The "original" transcript does not include any indication of why the girl was in a cast, although it does indicate that the hospital staff had determined that she needed to be contained. The lid was "to keep her in." We cannot know at this point whether this need was due to TB of the spine or because she was indeed "a holy terror" also in the eyes of the staff. I do argue, however, that the discrepancy between texts offers a haunted telling. Not only does the addition indicate the discretionary status of what gets recorded and taken up as history, but it also speaks to the politics of that particular history. Thus I read *The Camsell Mosaic* as a text concerned primarily with producing a history of the Indian hospital that commemorates and celebrates the treatment and apparent care provided to Indigenous peoples by the various governments and individuals working there. Its intent, like the commemorative pillar in the neighbourhood, is to inform readers of the benevolence of the doctors and nurses, "who did all they could to help." Both commemorations erase the fact that incarceration and colonization occurred via the techniques of Western allopathic medicine. They erase the fact that medicine has been used as power over bodies, and they obscure the fact that Indian hospitals – and their doctors, nurses, and all they could do to help – existed among a "carceral archipelago" (Michel Foucault, quoted in Lux 2016, 8) comprised of institutions designed for attempts at colonial control. The use of casts was discretionary and disciplinary and does not fit within efforts to memorialize the Charles Camsell Indian Hospital. Perhaps that is why, in the end, neither version of the interviewed nurse's account made it into the eventually published commemorative book *The Camsell Mosaic.*

As for the description itself, all of the details in the original – the cast, crib, and lid – suggest that this girl must have been a "holy terror" since it is difficult to imagine that a child could otherwise require such restraints. Thus they function in this account as pointing to this "truth" about the child. Yet one cannot help but consider that when the governor general was present, the child was a *child* – a sick child – and was a clearly and fully restrained sick child. She was a thoroughly disciplined subject – docile, passive, caged. He, the white politician, the one whose presence subdued her behaviour – as indicated by the statement "when *I'm* not here" – was the one who embodied this disciplinary and regulatory power. As a patient at the Charles Camsell Indian Hospital, she was an "Indian," she was a girl, and she was a holy terror. That the governor general spoke of a small child in the terms that he did, and under these conditions, suggests that a number of discourses were already in operation here, one of which pertained to the commonly held idea that this kind of treatment must be due to some problem with the girl, a problem that was not only TB, and another of which pertained to the idea that, in relation to the girl in the crib with the lid on it, the hospital staff and the governor general were both disciplinary and benevolent subjects – indeed, perhaps even threatened subjects – who were nonetheless generously oriented in their actions toward her own good.

Massey's claim that the young girl was a "holy terror" is also perplexing because it was likely outside of the terms in which small children were often represented. The statement begs the question of what "holy terror" meant in this context and raises the issue of what else is missing from the text, namely information that would make intelligible the rendering of a little girl sick with TB a "holy terror." For example, that the girl had TB of the spine does not make Massey's claim intelligible. Her casting then would have been undertaken not because she was a holy terror but because she had TB of the spine. Perhaps this distinction, however, was not possible to make at the time and in that context. Since Indigenous people were already defined as heathens and savages and since their inherent susceptibility to disease was evidence of such distance from white civility, the question of whether the cast was applied because of TB of the spine or because the girl was a "holy terror" is irrelevant. The reasons were one and the same. She had TB because she was a holy terror. The two cohered. The cast, the crib, and the lid cured both.

Dangers posed by threats such as a "holy terror" were alleviated not only through physical restraint at the Charles Camsell Indian Hospital but also through treatments for the soul (CCHC 1985, 207). The Indian hospital was a "total institution," of the variety defined as such by sociologist Erving Goffman (1961, xiii) in an era when these institutions were common in North America. It included lengthy treatment according to European norms and a culture of Christianity, making it the perfect model for instigating social reform (Staples, McConnell, and Oakes 1993).[46] The Charles Camsell Indian Hospital had an onsite chapel, and church attendance was available for some patients, depending upon their prescribed schedules. Christian practices were reinforced and fostered during patients' time there, regardless of their spiritual or cultural practices prior to arrival. The cure for TB was not separate from Christianity, and particular attention was given to attending to the "souls" of the patients (CCHC 1985, 207–18). Christmas, for example, seems to have been a major annual celebration at the hospital. There are numerous documents archiving the annual planning of Christmas festivities, the first instance of which took place in 1945, months after the hospital opened.[47] In a box entitled "Christmas Correspondence 1948–65" at Alberta's provincial archives is a collection of photographs, audio recordings, films, letters, menus, and lists that record Christmas at the Indian hospital as a major event that sometimes lasted throughout the month of December.[48] From this archive, it seems that the Christmas of 1948 involved, among other things, a Kinette Christmas party, the Elks Ladies Auxiliary, the St. Andrews Choir, a Gyrettes Christmas party, a staff children's party, the St. Peters Lutheran Choir, the Women's Auxiliary of the Eagles Club, the Junior Red Cross and their girls' choir, carols, a variety show for Indian and Eskimo children and other patients in the recreation hall, and a visit from Santa Claus.[49] *The Camsell Mosaic* reports children would participate in a Christmas play, re-enacting the nativity scene (CCHC 1985, 213–14). There are also records of many gifts given to the hospital and its patients during the season, both from private individuals and social organizations such as the Kinsmen Club and the Imperial Order Daughters of the Empire and Children of the Empire (Junior Branch). It seems that local individuals and organizations supported the hospital and recognized it as a Christian institution.[50]

Former Indian sanatorium patient Alice Ironstar offers an experiential reflection on the kind of transformation that occurred through the biopolitical regimes of the Charles Camsell Indian Hospital. Ironstar was a girl who spent nine years at the Fort Qu'Appelle Sanatorium in Saskatchewan, and whether or not she was ever put in a cast, her description of how she felt upon leaving the sanatorium suggests the assimilating effect of a kind of similar cocooning or transfiguration: "I went to the hospital not knowing English ... I felt I was a white girl when I came out" (quoted in Lux 2001, 218). Regardless of specific practices engaged in at the sanatorium, Ironstar was impacted to such an extent that she felt like she was a "white girl" upon leaving. Feeling like a white girl may have meant that Ironstar no longer felt like she was a member of or belonged in her family or home community. Departing the sanatorium feeling like a white girl might have left Ironstar in the difficult predicament of having no obvious place where she belonged, as she was likely not recognized as white and, given that she was now rehabilitated or "cured," perhaps no longer welcomed in the colonial space of the city despite feeling herself to be a white girl. Linda McDonald of the Liard First Nation in the Yukon, reflecting on the two years of her childhood when she was under treatment for TB at the Charles Camsell Indian Hospital, uses the same language to describe a thorough change: "I went in an Indian girl and came out a white girl" (quoted in Geddes 2017, 96). Here, I want to suggest only that the integration of contact zones discussed thus far seems to demonstrate that this outcome – the rendering of Indigenous peoples perhaps white but also refugees, an effect that I call the *production of the dehumanized without a place or a people* – might be considered a consistent effect of various colonial practices directed toward Indigenous peoples in the Edmonton area since at least 1870.

During the time when the Charles Camsell Indian Hospital was in operation, a national state of emergency was articulated through the particular threat of tuberculosis, and this threat was produced as housed by "Indians" and "Eskimos." I am proposing that the invention of bound spaces of danger and of safety is part of the historical making and remaking of a categorical sense of societal indifference to people in harm. The Charles Camsell Indian Hospital might be recognized in Agamben's (2005) terms as a "camp," a particular and bound place for the treatment of a population isolated according to, and thus reproducing, already established fictions of biologized inferiority and, perhaps paradoxically, threat. Societal indifference is made in part through the spatial separation or allocation of people based on notions of biologized and distinct degeneracy. Like the establishment of reservations of land and residential schools, the Indian hospital functioned to concentrate a number of bodies in and for treatments that were always also micro-processes of discipline and colonization, sometimes death. In this way, the use of the cast worked to bind bodies that were also already bound by the space of the camp.

The Charles Camsell Indian Hospital was a place that from its inception became one of race (Razack 2002). And perhaps it was fear of proximity to such a process that caused early residents in the area to resist an encroaching "camp." The Indian hospital was a place to contain bodies identified as dangerous, diseased, and racialized. Even before the hospital was established, its demarcation as racializing place occurred through this haunting local opposition to the opening of an Indian hospital/camp, and later, during its operation, this demarcation occurred all the way down to the level of the corporeal through practices such as the imposing of X-rays and the dispossession of people, through regimes of coerced confinement under the auspices of "care," and through what must have been a very real fear of being cast – immobilized – in plaster.

Although not the kind of camp feared by local residents, the Charles Camsell Indian Hospital worked as a site for Agamben's (1995, 2005) "state of exception" at least from 1946 to 1955. The state of exception was realized in the institutional and medical treatment of what was articulated as the threatening presence – both in the nation and later in Edmonton – of the racialized, sick, and contagious body. However, in the official history of the Indian hospital, its operation as a camp is obscured, and the place is instead produced as one where those vulnerable and threatened were cared for and saved and where "an epidemic was eradicated."[51] Thus I draw attention to the problem of recognition and suggest that an alternative present demands articulation.[52] This present is one where colonization is understood to be ongoing rather than to have passed, as politically pointed rather than benevolent. This recognition frames the

Charles Camsell Indian Hospital like Lux (2016, 8) does, as, among many things, part of a colonial "carceral archipelago" that was in keeping with other settler colonial projects and one that had effects directly contrary to the national narrative embedded in public memorials.

The forced relocation of Indigenous people to the city of Edmonton for treatment at the Charles Camsell Indian Hospital worked in conjunction with efforts fifty years earlier to dispossess First Nations of the land and to simultaneously keep them out of the city (Razack 2002). The strategy of legally dispossessing First Nations of lands and confining them to tracts of reserve land is one of many that Sherene Razack associates with "overt racist ideologies and their accompanying spatial practices" (Razack 2002, 129). These are practices that city administrators engaged in during the mid-twentieth century in an attempt to keep the wealthy and the racialized poor spatially separated in urban space. Resistance to treating Indians in the Edmonton neighbourhood was in keeping with other efforts in cities to produce distance between the affluent and the impoverished and racialized. I read the confinement of those treated at and visiting the Charles Camsell Indian Hospital to the space that was the hospital as at once a repetition of white settler emplacement, an assertion of settlers' "natural" presence, and an attempt to establish Indigenous people's incompatibility with urban contexts. Recall Mayor Fry's opposition to "tuberculous Indians wandering about the streets of Edmonton ... and spreading the disease" (quoted in Lux 2001, 222). What he expressed was not an anxiety about having people with TB in the neighbourhood but an anxiety about containment. He was not concerned about illness, which was no longer affecting immigrant populations in such high numbers, but about containing some potentially "wandering" population racialized as "Indian." Situating the hospital in the middle of a city – a space already conceptualized in terms of its role in the making of a colonial order – threatened the purity of this space that settlers were attempting to demarcate as "civilized" through their emplacement there, blurred boundaries already concertedly erected, and challenged the imaginative geographies that situated the Indigenous peoples on reserve lands outside of the city as an inherent part of the colonial project.

In concluding this chapter, I recall a question that I posed earlier about the Edmonton neighbourhood now being gentrified, a question whose pertinence across these contact zones is now apparent: how does space both become empty and at the same time become a locale for the state of exception? Or, in light of the examination of the Charles Camsell Indian Hospital, how does a peopled, built place become, in imagination and in practice, a degenerate space? These are arguably endured and enduring processes. Although I claim that they repeat in various ways, such as through an emphasis on "civilization" and on the need to "develop" or "use" particular spaces, they clearly do not repeat to the extent that their utility falters. Rather, they seem to hold strong. Reserve spaces have been the places of abandonment. So too have institutions like the Charles Camsell Indian Hospital and, in a less formalized way, contemporary downtown Edmonton and "the stroll" nearby. All of these places have been enacted through particular practices as though they were in essence empty because the life that has demanded or been worthy of protection has been emptied from them. What is left is "bare life." What is left is life not deemed (by some) to be "ethically significant" (Conrad 1999, 49). Only those socially cast as vulnerable to murder or death still reside there. Juxtaposing these contact zones makes it possible to see the production of particular places as a mechanism or a matrix through which life is made to matter less there. Moreover, the paradox in both the contemporary contact zone and the early years of the Charles Camsell Indian Hospital is that occasions for protection or care are always also occasions for state violence; the prior does not occur without the latter also coming into play. To reference the paradox described by Judith Butler (2009, 26) again, to be subject to protection is at once to be available for violence.

These scenarios, omitted from many published records of the Charles Camsell Indian Hospital and also omitted from published commemorations, tell vivid stories of the way that "race" and disease were produced and treated at the Indian hospital through regimes that disciplined, sometimes disappeared, and sometimes killed the people who were brought there. These accounts differ significantly from the ones told in *The Camsell Mosaic* and on the memorial pillar that stands on the old hospital site. These histories nonetheless inhabit our present and urge further and more concentrated research into the various ways that the Indian hospital functioned, the effects it produced, and the purposes it served. I argue that *The Camsell Mosaic* and the memorial pillar exist for settlers today, articulating a national program and sentiment in the contemporary context that settlers can live with and that settlers *require* both to ensure an affective distance from those "Othered" as indigenous to this place and as refugees within it, to ensure settlers' sense of being benevolent national and belonging subjects. The effects of such practices are not contained by time. A linear conception of time cannot totally delimit the world. Effects reverberate forward, backward, and sideways, and as the juxtaposition of contact zones hopefully demonstrates, these effects are anything but fleeting, anything but momentary. What happened at the Indian hospital bears direct relation to what happens today.

4

"All traces of his footsteps are fast being obliterated"

Fictioning and Controlling Land and Life

MOST OFTEN, INITIAL CONTACT BETWEEN Indigenous peoples and white settler colonialists is thought to have occurred with the landing of Christopher Columbus in North America in 1492, but Norse and early European fishermen had interactions with inhabitants native to the coastal areas even a thousand years prior to that (S. Carter 1999; Lutz 2007).[1] Whatever significance a specific date might hold, the arrival of settlers was slow, and such arrivals were part of Indigenous peoples' experiences and stories likely for much longer than is popularly recognized (Lutz 2007). In what is known as a prolonged protohistoric era, the impacts of contact were multiple and included the exchange of materials and goods, as well as of diseases, which often travelled "along ancient routes" (S. Carter 1999, 23) prior to any face-to-face contact. For hundreds of years, then, there was a circulation of goods, diseases, stories, and knowledges between those taking up residence on these lands and those already living with and moving through these lands. And myths and stories likely circulated in small and large communities of people long before any contact occurred at all. These long eras of stories, myths, and exchanges would have influenced the eventual relationships established between explorers, settlers, and Indigenous people and nations, but always in ways that were local and likely never uniform.

The Dominion of Canada was established in 1867 (Dempsey 2006). Within three years, the new nation was on the brink of an era of expansion and major change; the vast expanse known by European settlers as Rupert's Land would eventually become Manitoba, Saskatchewan, and Alberta, which would become provincial territories in the growing nation of Canada (Fried 1984; Owram 1980). During the 1870s, "present-day central Alberta (Treaty 6) was home to the Nehiyawak, or the Cree, as well as groups of Assiniboine and Nakoda" (S. Carter and Hildebrandt 2006, 238). By this time, relationships between different groups of Indigenous peoples and European explorers, settlers, and fur traders had been initiated, and a European presence had been established in a number of ways in the West. These relationships were mostly affable and cooperative prior to concentrated colonization (Alfred 1999). Even in the middle of the nineteenth century, a marked process of colonization had not yet occurred in what would become the province of Alberta or in the area that would become its capital (S. Carter 1999). Those relatively few Europeans who had set up homes here were able to do so only through a heavy reliance on good relationships with Indigenous peoples and on Indigenous peoples' generous sharing of their knowledge and skills (S. Carter 1999, 33).[2] It was a time during which, if there were sides, "each side was interested in what the other had to offer, and they had to find a means, other than force, to gain cooperation between opposing cultures" (S. Carter 1999, 34). Without the aid offered by those already inhabiting the areas, the combination of scurvy and severe winters would have been too much for the Europeans to withstand (Northcott and Wilson 2001, 21). Yet, even despite the help provided by local peoples, these factors, as well as the presence of other diseases and poor sanitation among settlers, contributed to the extremely high death rates of pioneering European men (Northcott and Wilson 2001, 21).

Whereas Indigenous peoples were largely responsible for the survival of settlers in the West, the impact of the arrival of European people in mass numbers was devastating to Indigenous peoples and communities (S. Carter 1997; Northcott and Wilson 2001). It is estimated that the collective number of Indigenous peoples in what is now commonly called Canada dropped from about 500,000 in the 1500s to only about 23,000 in 1861 (Northcott and Wilson 2001, 19). Among the causes of these high death rates among those indigenous to the continent were the decimation of the buffalo herds by European settlers and the spread of a number of infectious diseases such as smallpox, tuberculosis, cholera, and measles (Northcott and Wilson 2001, 19).

Smallpox has recurred intermittently among Indigenous peoples several times in the past century, killing an estimated one-third of the population in the area of the Saskatchewan River in 1870 (MacGregor 1949, 44) along with half of the Native peoples in Alberta (Fried 1984, 33).[3] Describing the impact of smallpox on Aboriginal people in Alberta in 1870, Cree historian Joe Dion says that the "outbreak of the deadly malady *omikiwin,* the disease of scabs, and the famine that followed, marked the end of the era of independence and plenty for his people" and recalls that "the whole West quickly became a vast grave-yard" (quoted in S. Carter 1999, 38). Some historical research, however, suggests a much more varied and less absolute reality. Infectious disease had long been a part of Indigenous peoples' existence, and different groups responded to disease differently at different times (Lux 1996). Cautious of totalizing histories, Maureen Lux points to the rise in the Cree populations between 1774 and 1839, a time during which in many narrations of the Canadian nation, most Plains peoples were brought to the brink of extinction due to initial exposures to infectious disease. It was not until the era considered here – an era when Indigenous peoples were faced with the loss of the bison, which was the central resource of Plains peoples' trade economy, and with the poverty that accompanied this loss – that infectious disease took such a devastating toll on First Nations populations (Lux 1996; S. Carter and Hildebrandt 2006).[4] Territorial disputes between First Nations and settlers, the displacement of Aboriginal peoples as a consequence of these disputes, and food shortages also contributed significantly to this high death rate (Northcott and Wilson 2001, 20).

Thus it seems that the late nineteenth century brought with it conditions that deeply threatened First Nations in Alberta. The threat was multifaceted and included the deep-felt effects of the impoverishment that accompanied the loss of a primary trade and food source. Various histories suggest that, despite whatever reciprocal relations existed prior to this time, Canadian nationalist projects were now well underway and that the likelihood of much effective resistance to those projects had been greatly diminished by the latter part of the nineteenth century. Historian Hugh Dempsey (2006, 209) notes that the further decimation of Indigenous peoples through famine and the whiskey trade ensured the tractability of Native peoples in their dealings with the North West Mounted Police in Alberta when treaty arrangements were being made.

By the late nineteenth century, European dependency on Indigenous peoples had been replaced by the settlers' expectation that Indigenous peoples would "adjust and adapt to the Euro-Canadian world" (S. Carter 1999, 33). By this point, the possibilities for "progressive partnerships" (S. Carter 1999, 13) had disappeared; a time of "middle ground," with cooperative relationships between Indigenous peoples and Europeans, was over (Richard White, quoted in S. Carter 1999, 34; see also Alfred 1999; Lux 1996). The expansionist movement, the 1900s' explosion in Western wealth, and the change in federal government all led to lost opportunities to develop "common ground" and began a long era of efforts toward colonial domination (S. Carter 1999; Dempsey 2006). In particular, 1870 is considered to have been "a year of violence and change" in Alberta's history (Dempsey 2006, 209). Part of this upheaval was due to the mass settlement that occurred with the opening up of the Canadian West. With the transfer of the massive expanse of Rupert's Land to the Dominion and with the increasingly popular expansionist movement in Canada, very particular ideologies informed primarily European, English-speaking politicians and settlers of a fruitful future for the North West (Dempsey 2006; Owram 1980).[5] Those involved in the expansionist movement in Canada linked the success of the North West directly to the success of building the Canadian nation generally and thus hastened both – primarily through attempts at the rapid settlement of the vast expanse of terrain (Owram 1980). Corporate interests, too, were tied up with expansionist interests and were at the heart of making the West a desirable location for settlement and vacation (Francis 1997). The Canadian Pacific Railway, for example, needed a market for its new cross-country railway and thus promoted the

Canadian West tirelessly and successfully in the East and in Europe (Francis 1997).

The Great Lone Land and *Wanderings of an Artist*

A number of key representations of the Dominion of Canada and its inhabitants emerged with European arrival and exploration of the continent commonly now called North America. These representations, too, were products embedded in and toward colonial practices of nation building, and they were structured as much by social expectations as by the project of nation making both here and there; they were thoroughly ideological. One example is William Francis Butler's book *The Great Lone Land: A Narrative of Travel and Adventure in the North-West of America.* On the first pages, Butler (1872, v) writes,

> There is no other portion of the globe in which travel is possible where loneliness can be said to live so thoroughly. One may wander 500 miles in a direct line without seeing a human being, or an animal larger than a wolf. And if vastness of plain, and magnitude of lake, mountain, and river can mark a land as great, then no region possesses higher claims to that distinction.

Writing of his views on the "existing state of affairs in the Saskatchewan" (Butler 1872, 385), later in the book he continues,

> If I were asked from what point of view I have looked upon this question ... I would answer – From that point which sees a vast country lying, as it were, silently awaiting the approach of the immense wave of human life which rolls unceasingly from Europe to America. Far off as lie the regions of the Saskatchewan from the Atlantic sea-board on which that wave is thrown, remote as are the fertile glades which fringe the eastern slopes of the Rocky Mountains, still that wave of human life is destined to reach those beautiful solitudes, and to convert the wild luxuriance of their now useless vegetation into all the requirements of civilized existence. (W.F. Butler 1872, 385)

Such an articulation is of the kind that postcolonial scholar Edward Said (1993, 5) has in mind when he states, "At some very basic level, imperialism means thinking about, settling on, and controlling land that you do not possess, that is distant, that is lived on and owned by others." Through Butler's romantic contemplation, *terra nullius* was created. Like the Spanish, the British Crown in Canada used the notion of *terra nullius* as a conceptual strategy for colonizing the land now called North America (Thobani 2007; Vowel 2016). Within the European economy and politics of ownership, *terra nullius* described land as unclaimed, "land that belongs to no one" (Vowel 2016, 236), and thus as available for the taking. Discussing the colonial claim to the domination of land, lawyer and author Norman Conrad (1999, 49) writes, "This is discovery. Those lurking in the wood, inhabitants of the lands for millennia – knowers, lovers and users of it all; born, lived and died on it – were 'nothings.' Kings justified this, saying these lands languished empty until their arrival, devoid of ethically significant life, a *terra nullius.* This fillip doctrinally flicked about 100 million Americans from being." *Terra nullius* was tied to a larger "Doctrine of Discovery" rooted in the papal bulls issued in the fifteenth century and still relevant to international law today (Vowel 2016, 235–36). Métis legal scholar Chelsea Vowel (2016) describes how among the effects of these decrees were the legitimation of the transatlantic slave trade and more generally the authorizing of the enslavement of "pagans" or non-Christians worldwide. European notions of ownership embedded in the doctrine of discovery were always also about enslaving non-Christians, which authorized the takeover of both land and peoples as a moral project.

In *The Great Lone Land,* Butler reiterates *terra nullius* repeatedly. Butler's gaze is a settler's gaze and, as such, is "characterized by a tendency to depopulate the country of Indigenous peoples in representations and especially in recollection, [for] settler projects are recurrently born in a perception of 'emptiness'" (Veracini 2010, 82). This recurrent settler project and the "discovery" of emptiness that it requires was made obvious in the contemporary contact zone of the city of Edmonton when its entrepreneurs and planners turned their attentions away from the Boyle Street neighbourhood and toward the newly conceived of "seedy downtown eastside" (Mah 2006) and surrounding area, which they also conjured as fallow land and certainly as being of questionable character. It is clear that this strategy is not a hoary one; it is not one that ceases in effectiveness. Lorenzo Veracini (2010, 82) describes this settler repetition as bordering on "wishful thinking" and as "a mode of perception that informs the whole history of settler colonial endeavours." Such a mode of perception is effectively repeatedly employed toward the contemporary gentrifying of a place and a disregard for people there. The metaphor has not lost its power. The people living in or on this place articulated as *terra nullius,* whether in this century or the last, have been rendered absent via the proclamation, which is at once a declaration of entitlement and a justification for the dehumanization that occurs as part of a version of Christian entitlement.

Another European often considered a significant producer of the Canadian West is Paul Kane, an artist who, beginning in 1846, travelled for over two years through what would be called "Canada" (MacLaren 1989). Kane took notes in a field journal on his journey and sketched and painted the landscape, his accounts gaining him recognition in Europe and internationally. Kane's extensive collection of paintings and writings circled the globe and found acclaim as the initial and most comprehensive representations of Canada in the mid-nineteenth century (MacLaren 1989). His writing and artwork have largely been taken up as objective representations of the western frontier and of those who lived there, and his particular style has become commonly associated with this place (MacLaren 1989). More than a decade after his journey, a book of Kane's field notes was published. It met with huge success and was particularly popular in western Europe (MacLaren 1989). Once I was already immersed in this research, it was this book that I found on my parents' bookshelf. Read as an ethnographic text, this book might have informed their understandings of the Canadian West at some point. Eighty years after it was originally written, historian Ian MacLaren (1989) would reveal that Kane's (1859) book *Wanderings of an Artist among the Indians of North America from Canada to Vancouver's Island and Oregon through the Hudson's Bay Company's Territory and Back Again* differs significantly from the field notes written in Kane's own script.[6] Since according to MacLaren (1989) ghostwriters were often used, such differences were not necessarily unusual for the time, and apparently Kane's writing and spelling skills were weak, but a number of major differences between the popular book and Kane's handwritten journal point to matters that are ideological, not grammatical or editorial. For example, MacLaren (1989) shows that, in Kane's original script, there are references to Aboriginal peoples encountered during his travels and that none of them are derogatory. Pejorative references, however, do appear in the published version of *Wanderings of an Artist.* To demonstrate, MacLaren draws attention to the book's inclusion of an episode of "Indian violence" that, according to historical records, actually occurred at least two months after it is apparently recorded as one of Kane's journal entries. Based in part on this observation, MacLaren suggests that the travel book, translated for popular sale in a number of European countries in the 1860s, was a highly ideological text, adapted from its original form to appeal to European expectations by its various ghostwriters and by its publishers (and perhaps by others) prior to publication. MacLaren argues that the civility of the artist had to be put in sharp contrast to the savagery of the Native so that the tale would be intelligible to the audience. This contrast was necessary because, at the time, those who made up the book's presumed audience were in the process of constituting themselves as the civilized of the "old world" in relation to the Indigenous peoples of this new and pagan world. In *Wanderings of an Artist,* "Kane's persona is quintessentially civilized, and must, therefore, see those who live beyond his civilization as barbaric. Pejorative references to 'savages,' however regrettable one finds them today, were the stock-in-trade of this Victorian persona" (MacLaren 1989, 14). MacLaren's work lends itself to an interpretation of *Wanderings of an Artist* as a report on the terms in which a colonizing nation constituted itself at home in relation to its exploits in a foreign land rather than as anything resembling an objective or ethnographic text. This report worked, as many do, to provide the contours for the recognition of the settler self in an already established Eurocentric binary between "us" and "them," between the civilized and the barbaric. Here again, the construction of difference and distance emerges as central to justifying colonial settlement according to the doctrine of discovery.

In addition, in *Wanderings of an Artist,* Kane (1859) is considered to have authored descriptions of deeply unequal gender relations among the Indigenous peoples he encountered. Since MacLaren (1989) asserts that these descriptions do not appear anywhere in Kane's handwriting, there is support for the suggestion that they too were tailored by an editor for a European society whose civility and whose gender relations required augmenting or indulging. Nonetheless, the following description, appearing in the 1859 version, would have at the time been granted the weight of anthropological evidence:

> It must not be supposed that Indians look upon the softer sex with feelings at all resembling those entertained towards them in civilized life; in fact, they regard them more in the light of slaves than as companionable beings. As might be expected this is most evident in their treatment of aged women, whom they consider as scarcely fit to live. (Kane 1859, 139)

Whether or not such reports specifically informed the development of Canadian law that would distribute human status differently along gender lines through legal doctrine like the Indian Act, they certainly share something with the ideology that underwrites both. Specifically, articulated here is what appears as a common truth both in the arena of travel literature and in the development of colonial laws at the time; Indigenous women were depicted as though both their own communities and their colonizers considered them to be subhuman in relation to their male counterparts. Women's supposedly inferior status among Indigenous peoples appears to be an addition made sometime between Kane's original journaling and the publication of *Wanderings of an Artist* (MacLaren 1989). The irony here, of course, is that the gender relations of the also imagined "civilized life" of European and settler colonialists were deeply unequal. Inequalities that were historically entrenched within the western European social order were being rearticulated as biological in origin and thus not as specific to a context, culture, or people but as transcending these particulars and manifest in inborn sex difference.

The shared presuppositions in Butler's and Kane's accounts of western Canada are significant. Such renditions of the place can be regarded as among those that fed the kind of racist colonial violence that Sherene

Razack (2000) has theorized in the contemporary context. Through Razack's work, a contemporary and urgent connection between texts like *The Great Lone Land* and *Wanderings of an Artist* might be gleaned. This connection does not suggest that these texts are directly predictive of eventual colonial control and violence, but there is an enormous body of colonial work that expresses the assumption of both a kind of enduring emptiness and an appropriateness of annexation, as well as an allocation of Indigenous women to a kind of subhuman status. These expressions appear more than once and as more than mere text, for they gave rise to spatial practices that contained and produced material effects. Thus *The Great Lone Land* and *Wanderings of an Artist* might be understood as elements in a context where the privilege of young white men was described in terms of their contemporary symbolic travel into and return from spaces considered both Native lands and lands to which Indigenous peoples no longer had a right and where this travel was considered to foster colonizing masculine identities as well as to demonstrate Indigenous women's subhuman status, each of which was thoroughly written into the history of the West, as Razack (2000) suggests. These texts might be some of the artifacts with which those in the West remain (pre)occupied. To reiterate an earlier point, what I take from this consideration of the connection between historical representation and contemporary violence is something of the collective and unconscious attachment to historically rooted practices in the ongoing making of place as peopled and in the sanctioning of acts of racialized and sexualized violence such that some lives are made to seem more alive than others.[7]

Yet, prior to the dissemination of the travel books by Butler and Kane, tomes had been written about the Canadian West by those employed by the Government of Canada to assess the prospects there (Pannekoek 2006). The extensive accounts of the West provided by Henry Youle Hind based on an expedition in 1857 and then by Captain John Palliser based on an expedition between 1857 and 1860 are considered to have provoked monumental shifts in the way the West was conceptualized, and indeed treated, by people elsewhere – primarily in eastern Canada and Britain (Pannekoek 2006, 185). These reports reconstituted a West that had been valued mostly for its fur trade as one that offered fertile ground for agriculture and settlement. In particular, the Palliser expedition mapped the territory that would eventually become Alberta, anticipating, as Said (1993) explains, the eventual colonial control of this place (McClintock 1995). Despite the intermittent concern that some members of the expeditions expressed about the impact that settlement would have on those people who already lived on this land (Pannekoek 2006), in general the land was considered empty, fertile, and available for the taking (Thobani 2007). The displacements occurring there were considered justifiable and unavoidable, as they were for the "good" of the expanding British colony (Pannekoek 2006).

Authorizing Land and Life through Reserves and the Indian Act

While an imaginative geography of *terra nullius*, combined with notions of Indigenous paganism and savagery, was being propagated for colonial purposes through art and literature aimed at European consumers, as well as for the purposes of an expanding colonial sovereignty, a real and peopled landscape was under dispute in an emerging nation. In 1870, after much rumour and speculation, the Hudson's Bay Company sold Rupert's Land to the Dominion of Canada for £300,000, and in accordance with the agreement, the company retained lands bordering its trading posts (Dempsey 2006, 211). With the transfer of Rupert's Land, concern grew among Indigenous peoples about colonial appropriation of their lands (Carter and Hildebrandt 2006). People and communities had heard "that their land had been 'sold'" (Carter and Hildebrandt 2006, 242), and so in 1871 "four prominent Plains Cree leaders demanded a meeting with [Fort Edmonton's chief factor,] William J. Christie. They wished to know 'whether their lands had been sold or not, and what was the intention of the Canadian government in relation to them'" (Carter and Hildebrandt 2006, 242). It is reported that "throughout the North West in the early 1870s there was anxiety and anger over the presence and activities of the Boundary Commission, the Geological Survey, a telegraph construction crew and the NWMP [North-West Mounted Police], all in advance of any treaty" (Carter and Hildebrandt 2006, 242). Rumours of the loss of land were substantiated by evidence of land transfer, and the people living in Rupert's Land were given "no special consideration" in the process (Dempsey 2006, 211).[8] Six years later, Treaty 6 was signed, and on September 9, 1876, specific legal control of the area now commonly known as Edmonton was claimed by the Dominion of Canada.[9] Thus, within the six years between 1870 and 1876, a massive area of land was claimed under the jurisdiction of the Dominion, and the Indigenous peoples living there were rather suddenly subject to definition by the newly established nation in terms suitable to its colonial expansion. With both the passing of the Indian Act and the signing of Treaty 6, peoples defined as Indian were considered to belong within particular sections of land, and their use of that land was limited in particular ways. Whereas Indigenous and settler contact had been slow and sporadic until then, the occurrence of three major nationalist events within one decade prompted a radical and unsettling change for the Indigenous peoples who had long lived in these lands, provoking a dramatic increase in the "violence" done to them (Dempsey 2006, 209).

According to the stipulations of Treaty 6, "Aboriginal peoples were given land of their choosing in reserves, six hundred and forty acres for every family of five. Each Indian man, woman and child received $12.00 plus a $5.00 per annum annuity. They were assured food when necessary, medical care, agricultural equipment, cattle and instructors to teach them to farm" (Fried 1984, 33). Apparently, those people under Treaty 6 fared better than some under prior treaties, with Treaty 6 providing more tools and money to aid in the transition to an agriculture-based subsistence (Lux 1996, 35). "The Treaty also promised that in the event of famine or pestilence, the government would, '... grant to the Indians assistance of such character and to such extent ... to relieve the Indians from the calamity that shall have befallen them'" (Alexander Morris, quoted in Lux 1996, 35). To this day, the government has ignored its responsibilities in these matters, and as far as the land is concerned, the signing of treaties left Aboriginal people with practically nothing: "After the signing, the exotic White 1% held 99% of the land. The resident Native people, 99%, were permitted a derivative beneficial interest in the remaining 1% of the land, but even this interest would take over a century of law to establish" (Conrad 1999, 56).

Several theories explain the emergence of a system of land reserve in Canada. Social geographer Evelyn Peters (1998) suggests that the system was implemented after it became apparent to the new Government of Canada that despite the government's assumption and even despite the severe hardship endured by Aboriginal peoples as a consequence of colonial interventions during this time, Native peoples were not going to simply disappear. Peters writes, "When they did not disappear, colonial policies, in conjunction with First Nations people's resistance, resulted in real and imagined geographies which assigned First Nations people to reserves and rural locations and defined urban areas as hostile to First Nation's [sic] cultures and communities" (Peters 1998, 670). Historian Sarah Carter (1990, 24) proposes that the reserve was thought to be "a training ground or laboratory for civilizing the Indian" and claims that the prospect of land reserves "began to take shape in the 1830s with the adoption of the idea that Indians should settle in villages, be weaned from their nomadic life, and be taught to cultivate the land." Vowel (2016, 264) also describes reserves as originally "set up as a civilizing project, forcing First Nations to settle in one place (chosen by the Crown) so they could turn their attention and labour toward whatever the Crown chose – like farming and going to church." Perhaps it is in this early contact zone that the fundamental significance of establishing boundaries and borders becomes most apparent in the European processes of colonization. Since those defined as "Other" would not simply vanish through intensive colonization (e.g., through the depletion of the buffalo), the government had to make direct moves to keep Indigenous peoples geographically separated from the spaces that they were attempting to usurp.

Although the question of the contemporary material and symbolic importance of reserve lands is complex and demands detailed attention, it is not sufficiently addressed in the current work. This book does not adequately examine the importance of the existence of legally protected lands and their ties to Indigenous peoples (see Vowel 2016). In Canada there are now 2,300 Indian reserves (Vowel 2016, 260). These tracts of land are described in the Indian Act in ways that challenge European conventions of property ownership and have become crucial sites of and for resistance among some bands, both symbolically and materially (Peters 1998; Vowel 2016). However, among the government's intended goals for reserves in the 1870s was to spatialize difference in terms of European concepts of race, gender, culture, and civility. Although such processes invariably have numerous, varied, and unpredictable effects, including the production of rich and meaningful sites for resistance, these effects are not sufficiently addressed here. I note only that this is a shortcoming of the approach to temporal analysis taken in this book.

Instead, I focus on the production of reserve spaces by the government in their ideal form – according to the colonial objectives at the time. Implementing a system of reserve lands allowed the government to isolate and to attempt to manage and disappear First Nations peoples; reserves and the pass systems implemented with them simultaneously damaged established economic, governance, and kinship systems in which these peoples were embedded (Vowel 2016, 264). Beyond disrupting crucial cultural elements, these spatially mapped parcels of land are also "quintessential zone[s] of exception" (Thobani 2007, 37). Reserves predated the concentration camps of the Second World War, which Giorgio Agamben (1995) described as the epitome of modern "camps," but this system of land-based reserves is exactly the type of place necessary for the suspension of law (Thobani 2007). Reserves offer the space for the abandonment of life – the place in which the *homo sacer* resides (Thobani 2007). They function in "the relegation of Native peoples to the zones of exclusion organized by the reserve system and the enduring politico-ideological construction of the Indian body as a site of exception to the law" (Thobani 2007, 48). In ways not unlike the Charles Camsell Indian Hospital, by their very establishment, reserve lands function to spatially locate an already racialized population such that, even today, an Indigenous presence in urban contexts is both compelled (see Lawrence 2003) and constituted as problematic and unnatural (G. Pratt 2005). The logic undergirding a perceived need for reserves might be seen as a precursor to the fear that emerged at the prospect of the Indian hospital and at the prospect of teepees in urban spaces.

Since reserve lands were invented, the government of Canada has been shrinking them, and reserves now comprise only about 0.28 percent of Canadian land (Vowel 2016, 264).[10] By the 1890s, with the objectives of the Gradual Civilization Act of 1857 directing their actions, representatives of the federal government subdivided reserve lands in the West. In particular, some of the reserve lands bound by Treaty 4 and Treaty 6 were portioned off for sale (Lux 1996). These land reductions did not happen without resistance: "Bands objected to the surveys of their lands, believing them to be a first step towards surrender. Settlers and land agents became increasingly voluble proponents of land surrenders after the 1890s. Lands held in reserve were considered too large for the people's needs and might be put to more profitable use by 'actual settlers'" (Lux 1996, 258). In part, this usurping of lands that were once promised to various bands was justified by the claim that the land was "unused," empty, or lying "idle" and that the "Indian" "race" was dying (Lux 1996, 258). Recent years had brought a decline in reserve populations, and the idea of the dying or "disappearing" "Indian" seemed to be well established (Lux 1996, 258). Indeed, it was apparently this idea that partly motivated Paul Kane to document Indigenous peoples in his paintings in the mid-1800s, and it was this idea that Kane is commonly thought to have promoted with his (or his ghostwriters') accounts (see Kane 1859, vii–viii).[11] Through their sale, treaty lands were again enacted as empty and unpopulated, even when they had ostensibly been set aside for a particular population less than twenty years earlier. Moreover, with the mass transfer of Indigenous peoples deemed sick with tuberculosis, the lands *were* actually being emptied; if the fictitious "race" was not dying on treaty lands, it was disappearing through loss of legal status and through treatment in Indian hospitals. Contemporary disappearances of Indigenous women and girls are also consistent with this historical colonial project. Each disappearance is tied to larger assertions of colonial nationhood, and taken together they are emblematic of the ongoing contestations not only over land but also over a human presence and relation to that land.

Just as "Canada" was not awaiting the arrival of European settlers, "Indians" were not awaiting their arrival on the shores of the American continents. "Indians" do not predate their "discovery." Instead, the category of "Indian" specifically emerged from, and was reflective of and meaningful to, the European colonial project (Thobani 2007; Vowel

2016). For a reserve system to function according to the colonial logic that it embodies, a mechanism is required for determining who is what and who belongs where – in this case, who was an Indian and who was not and who was subject to treaty restrictions and who was excluded from their domain. To augment the "armed fiction"[12] of Indian-ness, the British colony required and so established a law defining "the Indian" as a category of life in the 1850s (Thobani 2007, 38). The Gradual Civilization Act of 1857 specifically outlined that an "Indian" was not a Canadian and was not entitled to the privileges of citizenship (S. Carter 1990, 194). The Indian Act, created in 1876, was a document that delineated Indian status by outlining who was eligible as a "status Indian," who was ineligible, and who had lost "status." Although this legislation has been modified over time, it continues to provide the Canadian definition of "Indian status" (Vowel 2016, 27). The law implemented a patriarchal system of inheritance and lineage and thus systematically disqualified women, two-spirit people, and children from claiming their rights and status (Vowel 2016). Deemed to be "as racialized and gendered a piece of legislation as one might encounter anywhere under the auspices of the empire, [the Indian Act] has been aptly described as representing the 'Euro-Canadian government's apartheid system' and the 'bureaucratized hatred' of Native peoples" (Thobani 2007, 48). The Indian Act implemented a system that operationalized the fiction of the Indian – as seen in the quasi-anthropological texts analyzed here – in the effort to ensure this same Indian's eventual disappearance (Lawrence 2003). And indeed the legislation has worked in such a way. Recent accounts suggest that, just over a century after the Indian Act was introduced, there were twice as many non-status Indians as status Indians in Canada, effectively leaving "two-thirds of all Native people in Canada landless" (Lawrence 2003, 6). From its inception, the Indian Act functioned as an exclusionary doctrine, and although the criteria for Indian status has changed over time, currently less than half of the Indigenous people in Canada are registered as status Indians (Vowel 2016, 28).

With the Indian Act, "Indians were brought into being as a new category of human life by the 'armed fiction' of the law: the Salish, the Cree, the Mohawk, and the many other indigenous nations pre-existed

European contact with the 'Americas,' while the Indians did not" (Thobani 2007, 38). The invention of the new category that was "Indian" was at once also the invention of the Indian body; it was the imagined realization of an embodied being already known in British colonial culture given that the savage had previously been featured in fiction and ethnography, and it was an invention that authorized and justified the colonial practices at hand, including the takeover of land (Thobani 2007, 38). According to European imaginations, "indigenous peoples were not fully human; they were not Christian; they were not civilized; they had not evolved; they were doomed to extinction by history and progress; they had no recognizable legal systems or concepts of property rights and were thus lawless; and they did not cultivate their lands" (Thobani 2007, 41). In other words, Indians were positioned as contrary to all the ways that European subjects were constituting themselves at the time – that is, as supremely human, Christian, and evolved, as purveyors of the most civilized, rational legal and social order, and as the emissaries of progress. Indians were an imaginary group, cast as the necessary outside, or the "Other," and stipulated as unrecognizable as human both in their presence and in their practices. Recall how Kane's published book worked in this regard.

To become Canadian under the law, some Indian men were eligible to become "enfranchised" if it was established that they were fully "literate, free of debt, and of high moral standing" (Thobani 2007, 25; see also S. Carter 1990). Enfranchisement meant a loss of Indian status and, significantly, a loss of the legal entitlements that such status conferred (Vowel 2016). The legislation implemented a patriarchal system of inclusion and exclusion, allowing, and on occasion obligating, some Aboriginal men, but not women, to become enfranchised (Jacobs and Williams 2008, 122). Further, as Vowel (2016, 28) points out, although enfranchisement was typically thought to be a desirable thing, in the case of those men with Indian status, "it was a concrete way to assimilate Indigenous peoples out of legislative existence, extinguish their rights, and solidify colonial control over lands and resources"; it represented a most profound loss without necessarily securing any equal treatment in Canadian society. In law, Canadian and "Indian" were thus made mutually exclusive categories.

Although an earlier decree, the Royal Proclamation of 1763, had set out that "Canadian governments would treat Aboriginal peoples as 'autonomous and self-governing peoples'" (Mackey 1999, 23), in 1870 Indigenous peoples (excluding the Métis) were officially deemed in law as "wards of the state ... until some date in the distant future when they had met a number of unusual requirements" (Friesen 1987, 129). Laws like the Gradual Civilization Act and the Indian Act were used not only to govern First Nations peoples but also to determine membership in or exclusion from what was becoming a racial category.

Whereas some scholars suggest that relationships between settlers and various Indigenous peoples were, for the sake of the survival of the settlers, often cooperative (S. Carter 1997), former president of the Native Women's Association of Canada Beverly Jacobs and analyst Andrea Williams (2008) claim that already by the 1850s such cooperation was highly unlikely, arguing that the various laws passed at the time were specifically attenuated toward the elimination of Indigenous peoples. The main premise of the Gradual Civilization Act of 1857 "was that by eventually removing all legal distinctions between Indians and non-Indians through the process of enfranchisement, it would be possible in time to absorb Indian people fully into colonial society" (Royal Commission on Aboriginal Peoples 1996, 271). Thus, regardless of the variety of interpersonal relationships in the West – regardless of whether or not they were characterized by respect, cooperation, or dependency – the legal changes in Canada were indisputably intended to achieve the elimination of "Indians." As settler colonial subjects were made citizens, Indigenous peoples lost legal entitlement, both as humans and to their land. Sunera Thobani (2007, 38) explains, "In Canada, sovereign power institutionalized through the law an absolute alterity between different categories of human life, breathing juridical force into the category Canadian while draining it out of the category Indian, solidifying and fixing their identities as different kinds of subjects (and objects) of power." The "Indian," a fiction of the colonizers realized in the colonial encounter, was thus emptied of its potential for status as "human" in the Canadian context and, instead, was produced as a particular object of colonial power.

Essentialisms and Legal Disappearances

Under laws imposed by the Canadian state in the nineteenth century, Indigenous women's legal rights and standings were determined by their relationships to men and by these men's individual choices or situations.[13] Acts passed subsequent to the Gradual Civilization Act of 1857, such as the British North America Act of 1867 and the Act for the Gradual Enfranchisement of Indians of 1869, attempted to entrench government control over Aboriginal peoples and over their lands and kinship relations (Jacobs and Williams 2008). Key to understanding the power of these laws is the recognition that they imposed a patriarchal gender binary (Vowel 2016). Compliance with this hierarchy and binary was both required for the provision of legal rights under subsequent Canadian law and an outcome of these provisions; the various laws required that one be either a man or a woman, and the security of one's status had everything to do with this designation (Vowel 2016). State-appointed rights were contingent on compliance with an essentialist and dichotomous gender order.[14] Regardless of the various other forms of gender (e.g., two-spirit) and social organization (e.g., matriarchal) practised by Indigenous nations and collectivities both prior to and following – and thus despite – colonial state interventions, the state encoded the gender binary and a patriarchal social organization into law. These legal impositions were laid over the established forms of gender and social organization, making relations and kinship networks within communities vulnerable.

Whatever the varied and diverse social positions of women among different Indigenous nations prior to concentrated colonization, within the Canadian nation state Indigenous women were left with little access to legal self-determination by 1870 (Jacobs and Williams 2008; Vowel 2016) as a direct consequence of legislation such as the Act for the Gradual Enfranchisement of Indians, which was "intended to enforce the patriarchy and coerce Aboriginal women to conform to the regiments and edicts demanded by local missionaries and Indian agents" (Winona Stevenson, quoted in Jacobs and Williams 2008, 121–22). Canadian law legislated Aboriginal women's increased subordination both to the settler populations and to Aboriginal men (Vowel 2016). "The process of statutory female subjugation was intensified as regulations were passed which discriminately undermined the traditional roles, authority, and autonomy of Aboriginal women. Almost every aspect of women's lives was directly impacted by the *Indian Act*" (Stevenson, quoted in Vowel 2016, 122). Through the Indian Act,

> the immediate and long-term effect ... was to reduce the number of status Indians the government was responsible for, impose the European patrilineage system, and elevate the power and authority of men at the expense of women ... The result was a major disruption of traditional kinship systems, matrilineal descent patterns, and matrilocal, post-marital residency patterns. Furthermore, it embodied and imposed the principle that Indian women and their children, like European women and their children, would be subject to their fathers and husbands. (Stevenson, quoted in Vowel 2016, 123)

First Nations scholar Sharon McIvor (2004) describes Indigenous women's battles to recover from the legal, social, and economic damages of colonial law, situating such century-old law as instrumental in instilling enduring gendered vulnerabilities and inequalities. Federal laws that advanced colonialist and patriarchal social orders operated to forge alliances between men, Natives and settlers alike:

> Since 1869, colonialist and patriarchal federal laws – most notably the *Indian Act* – have fostered patriarchy in Aboriginal communities and subjected Aboriginal women to loss of Indian status and the benefits of band membership, eviction from reserve homes, and denial of an equal share of matrimonial property. Colonialism and patriarchy have also enabled cooperation between male Aboriginal leadership and Canadian governments to resist the inclusion of Aboriginal women in Aboriginal governance. These denials and exclusions perpetuate the exposure of Aboriginal women and their children to violence and consign many to extreme poverty. (McIvor 2004, 106–7)

The legal and social status of Aboriginal women was thus increasingly defined as outside of the privileges afforded *almost all other people* in the nation. These subordinations occurred on and through the production of the Indian body as a body that was essentially and hierarchically gendered as male or female in colonial terms – that is, through patriarchy (Vowel 2016). Such policies implemented a system of relative power and relative life, according to which being Indian meant being of diminished status, but one's positioning as an Indian man still ensured some grounds for exercising power through the subordination of women. To be an Aboriginal woman, however, was to be denied legal inclusion within your own community as well as to be subject to a colonial and patriarchal power structure – conditions that are tied directly to an increased exposure to embodied vulnerabilities in general (Jacobs and Williams 2008; McIvor 2004; Vowel 2016). Insofar as Indian status was codified in law, it negated the legal standing of two-spirit people and of those whose social position did not map neatly onto the essentialisms embodied by the patriarchal gender binary (Vowel 2016). Although the social standing of such people would not necessarily have been threatened as a result, it is clear that the imposition of such law, when tied with the provision of land rights or material goods, had a real impact on the intimate and kinship relations within communities.

To repeat a refrain of this text, such practices of colonization, although implemented in legislation over a century ago, are not in the past but are ongoing. That these practices are a present concern is reflected in McIvor's (2004) assessment, which is written partly in the present tense. These settler colonial laws and the practices that fall from them did not occur only at one moment but have occurred again and again. Indigenous women's and two-spirit people's positioning as legally, economically, and socially marginalized or disappeared was, and remains, a constitutive feature of the establishment of the Canadian nation, particularly where it is apparent in legal and conceptual designations (Vowel 2016).

The law made the fictionalized Indian woman an object of alterity. Not only were Indigenous women legally defined as subordinate in zrelation to Indian men, but Indian women were also symbolically defined in popular Canadian and British-Canadian representations as subordinate in relation to the European "white women" newly arrived on the Canadian prairies. Carter's (1993, 1997) analyses of colonial representations in the late nineteenth century show that Aboriginal women were depicted as immoral and threatening to arriving Europeans. At least since the late 1800s, Aboriginal women and white women have been situated in relation to each other and defined according to each other (S. Carter 1993, 2006; McIvor 2004). The constructed alterity of Aboriginal women was intimately linked with colonial attempts to instill white women's purity and high moral standing in the European colony (S. Carter 1993, 2006). To make these depictions real, each one required the other. In the West in the late 1800s, white women were, in fact, defined as women who were not Indigenous:

> The white women of Western Canada at that time were overwhelmingly British-Canadian and the "other" women were Aboriginal. White women were cast as the pure, virtuous guardians of the "race," symbols of the future health and wealth of this new corner of Canada and of the British Empire. Aboriginal women were their sinister and dangerous opposite, posing a threat to morality and prosperity. (S. Carter 2006, 44)

The idea of the Aboriginal woman operated as a foil for the idea of the arriving white woman (S. Carter 2006). Each type of woman was defined in contrast to the other, and because these definitions were propagated by and in the interest of the settler colonial empire, they too worked to justify the theft of lands and the nonrecognition of peoples.

Such simplistic and inaccurate representations of white and Aboriginal women effected a national forgetting of the crucial part that Indigenous women had played in the survival of the first arrivals on the continent and in the West (S. Carter 1993, 1997).[15] This forgetting concerned relationships prior to the 1870s, when European settlers needed Aboriginal peoples' skills and resources for their survival and when many of the settler men married and had intimate, loving, long-term relationships with Indigenous women (S. Carter 1993, 1997). By about 1880, this history of relationships was refused:

> The emerging elite in the North-West, as well as the advocates of British settlement, were anxious to establish a society that was not founded on any mingling of European and Aboriginal people and culture. There was a concern to forget the past, to present Aboriginal women as a menace to the emerging community, and to encourage and celebrate the arrival of white women. (S. Carter 1997, 5)

In part, this process required that white women take on special civilizing and race-making responsibilities in relation to the settling of the West and that Aboriginal women accept the denial of their crucial contribution to the survival of settlers and to the success of settlement (S. Carter 1997). The celebration of white women in these roles forged their arrival on the western prairies as an arrival in a place whose peoples were uncivilized, heathen, and inferior. This repetition of ideas around purity, morality, and health in relation to white women aligns with past and present assumptions about pollution, immorality, and disease uttered in relation to Indigenous women, whether today in Edmonton's Boyle Street neighbourhood or previously in the Charles Camsell Indian Hospital. Indeed, there appears to be remarkable consistency in the ways that these colonial fictions find ground and contemporary expression.

Through various forms of legislation, Indian women were constructed in such a way as to exclude them from access to social, legal, and economic power. Two-spirit people were effectively disappeared in such laws. These outcomes were "structural erasures" (Vowel 2016, 112). They were also the legal infrastructure for the dehumanization that they supported through their indifference to violence against particular peoples (J. Butler 2009). With such exclusions and disappearances, the figure of "bare life" (Agamben 1995) appears again as "the quintessential homo sacer of modernity, who, although sacred in the sense described by Agamben, could be, indeed had to be, destroyed on the altar of progress" (Thobani 2007, 40). Indigenous peoples – first defined in essentialist and patriarchal terms and then excluded from rights as well as marginalized in space, both on reserves and in cities (Peters 1998) – came to embody in settler colonial imaginations a position of vulnerability to death; through the

Indian's vulnerability to settler colonialism, a modern Christian and civilized nation could be made. This process required the arrival of white women in Canada as characters in a particular history and present. It enacted a form of racism that was already inherent to Europe's modern settler colonial projects. Such processes were, and remain, instances of the realization of what Michel Foucault has termed "the condition for the acceptability of putting to death" (quoted in Mbembe 2003, 16). Power was in control of life through the production of colonial truths and knowledges about matters like sex, race, and status. The production of such knowledge is not, however, separate from the development of a liberal democracy that claims to put the protection of both the universal human and human rights at the fore. But, as has become clear again, the universal human and their human rights require an outside against which only some lives qualify.

5

"Just bury them and be done with it"

Managing Affect and Producing the Past

It is not a case of dead or missing persons sui generis, but of the ghost as a social figure.

– AVERY GORDON, *GHOSTLY MATTERS: HAUNTING AND THE SOCIOLOGICAL IMAGINATION*

We live, then, in a world of "cinders," which very often act like hauntings, cued to their present purpose by the reminders of particular places. These reminders of remainders may only leave the faintest traces, but they still testify to the fire.

– NIGEL THRIFT, "STEPS TO AN ECOLOGY OF PLACE"

IN 2005 SOME WOMEN IN EDMONTON who were identified as at risk of disappearance were asked to provide "tombstone information" to those whose specific duty it was to guard against their murder, although not to protect them from going missing. A few city blocks from where women have given their tombstone information to police officers, there is a memorial garden at the old Alex Taylor School. It was planted to remember those who "died as a result of their involvement with street prostitution" (Marlow 2005, 3).[1] Women who have been disappeared from the city are likely among those assumed to have died *as a result* of prostitution;

they might also be those whose tombstone information, first solicited in life, was used, belatedly, to identify who they were in death. However, there are no tombstones marking these deaths at the garden. Several kilometres away, in a northwest direction, is the hollowed-out Charles Camsell Indian Hospital. Farther still, beyond the city and near the town of St. Albert, there are tombstones. More accurately, there is a memorial cairn dedicated to those who died during those early years at the Indian hospital. It stands in a lonely cemetery outside of this small neighbouring town. Back near Edmonton's core, another burial ground is commemorated. A new monument officially memorializes a site that was for a long time only a bit of unmarked land between a power plant and a thoroughfare. For much longer, it was an ancient gravesite, and for a while it was the cemetery at Fort Edmonton. This place now supports the EPCOR power plant and a busy road bridging Edmonton's north and south sides, and squeezed between the two is this memorial to those interred in these sacred grounds. Tombstones and graveyards, memorials and monuments – each of these is a record that originated with some intention to mark. Each of these records, at the same time, goes some way toward setting the past in stone. These markers are scattered, and they seem isolated – in geography and in time – each explicitly linked only to a particular place and historical moment. Each seems to indicate nothing of a relationship to the other sites, to the emergence of the city itself, or to the present crisis of missing and murdered Indigenous women and girls in Canada. In this chapter, I frame these marked sites as relevant to each other, to the emergence of the city itself, and to the present crisis. I visit these sites to read against the discrete and linear narrative that they seem to both employ and problematize. I examine these memorial sites as haunted by the pasts they express and by the futures they already work to forge. I ask how the memorial projects commemorating European settlement in Edmonton, the Charles Camsell Indian Hospital, and the disappearance of women and girls from the city's downtown are implicated as social supports for indifference to ongoing practices of dehumanization.

Paul Farmer (2004) reminds us that practices of forgetting might be linked with contexts of ongoing structural violence. For Farmer, as noted in the Introduction, historical memory and those mechanisms for its consolidation (e.g., monuments) work as forms of erasure, effective in enabling structures and conditions that are "both sinful and ostensibly 'nobody's fault" (Farmer 2004, 307). If efforts to memorialize are always pedagogical due to their implication in the regulation of affect, in the erasure of memory, or in the bolstering of nationalist narratives or structural violence, then it is of supreme importance to ask how our commemorative practices work. Thus an analysis of what I claim are patterned forms of racial and gendered violence and of what appears as "societal indifference" to this violence in Canada requires an examination of what practices of remembering or forgetting might be regulating affect in such a way as to support the endurance of this violence in Canada. It is perhaps not a coincidence that each of the contact zones considered here can be associated with a memorial or two erected in or near Edmonton. Memorials are modes through which time is constructed, fortified, and naturalized as linear, and so these memorials exist not as coincidental but as doing the social work of producing this linear sense of reality.

More than direct efforts at communication (Mackey 1999; Simon, Rosenberg, and Eppert 2000), memorials and monuments are always "trials by space" (Burk 2003, 317; Lefebvre 1991, 416); they represent spatially expressed or located struggles over differing social values and ideas. Thus our readings of memorials should not be derived from a single time- and context-specific interpretation but should be ongoing and contested, reflecting complicated and disputed ideas, and they should not be used as mechanisms for the solidification of one story or history (Burk 2003). In her analysis of two monuments to the disappeared women of Vancouver, for example, geographer Adrienne Burk highlights the unique capacities and mutabilities of material productions:

> Unlike rituals, marches, occupations, and riots, which have the power of emphasis, theatre and immediacy in the material world, monuments are conceived in the imagination, slowly framed in the social world, and only lastly fixed in place, largely for strangers. *They thus foil time/space constraints, and present*

> *different opportunities for social visibility. The "trials" they endure, therefore, cannot be assessed solely by their physicality.* (Burk 2003, 318, emphasis added)

Monuments incorporate into their forms the trials, compromises, and changes that have occurred in the process leading up to their physical installation and tenure. Thinking about monuments in this way also allows for an ongoing reconstitution of meanings according to whether and how such physical places change or are used or not used, opening up a means for always engaging with the monuments in our midst in a manner that counters the meanings that they otherwise solidify. It is their inherent transformativity, their foiling of time/space even as they often seem to materially cement meaning in place, that perhaps necessitates continuous returns to these sites in order to engage in the various "trials" that they are themselves part of.

So efforts to mark or memorialize do not work in only direct or straightforward ways (Burk 2003; Dean 2009, 2015; Rosenberg 2000; Simon 2005; Simon, Rosenberg, and Eppert 2000; Young 1993). Indeed, one of the central critiques of remembrance practices is that, among their effects, commemorations might work to obscure an underlying purpose and ultimately provoke a historical forgetting of structural violence (Farmer 2004). Memory studies scholar James Edward Young (1993, 273) warns that this forgetting occurs to some extent with memory's transformation into a memorial: "Once we assign monumental form to memory, we have to some degree divested ourselves of the obligation to remember." This irony exposes the fallacy that the presence of some intended or "original" meaning is sufficient to stabilize signification. As "trials by space" (Burk 2003, 318), as pedagogical practices (Simon, Rosenberg, and Eppert 2000), and as expressions that include and anticipate what is forgotten, memorials communicate, shift, and change, and their effects are thus of contemporary significance.

The mistreatment of the dead is often regarded as reflecting the presumed insignificance of their lives; "Those who were powerless in life have also found their bodies exploited in death" (Highet 2005, 416). Yet it is not only that some people without power in life have historically been misused or ignored once dead but also that other deaths – the deaths of those whose lives have been marked as socially meaningful – have historically been deemed somehow intrinsically worthy of public regard and thus worthy of public mourning (J. Butler 2004). As Judith Butler states, "the funeral is already a certain kind of demonstration, asserting and making collectively known that another valued life has been lost" (quoted in Ahmed 2016, 482). So, whereas some deaths are mourned through demonstrations of loss, others occur quietly, with little or no public ceremony or regard. Public and private practices of commemoration perceive some lives as real and others as unreal, deeming some lives to be worthy of grief and others to be unworthy of grief (J. Butler 2004). Because material markers of death such as tombstones are connected to larger social and cultural contexts and beliefs, they might offer "important clues – and sometimes the only clues – to past forms of rituals which we observe in living context[s] today and to changes which occur in such rituals through time" (Dubisch 1989, 189). In this chapter, I suggest that the appearance of tombstones, in metaphor and literally, points to and produces correspondences between the contact zones considered here. In Avery Gordon's words, tombstones reveal a kind of "haunting" – an entering of the "door of the shocking parallel" (1997, 66). Something haunts how the deaths of some Indigenous peoples in this city, past and present, are coupled with the emergence of a particular narrative of Canadian benevolence and legitimacy. Something haunts how many of these deaths have, for many years, been unmarked by public ceremony even though they were symbolically anticipated precisely through public institutions such as medicine and policing, which used X-rays, tombstone information, and/or DNA to mark certain bodies for death. The idea of the tombstone appears and reappears here again and again, being pivotal to the making of the contemporary colonial space of the city and to the making of the citizenry of Edmonton even when this idea is mobilized in relation to living people. This haunting urges a consideration of the actual appearance of tombstones or other markers of life and death in relation to those described thus far as disappeared from the city's history and its contemporary context.

Death at the Charles Camsell Indian Hospital

> *Many patients were admitted to the hospital in the advanced stages and died. This gave the hospital a bad reputation among the Indian people as it appeared to them as a place to go to die.*
>
> – RITA MORIN, QUOTED IN CHARLES CAMSELL HISTORY COMMITTEE

There are no gravesites or markers, no crosses, and no tombstones for some of those who died at the Charles Camsell Indian Hospital. As is the case with other southern Indian hospitals, there is a dearth of information regarding who died and what happened to those who perished in the first decade of its operation. Among those who were transported to southern Indian hospitals from northern territories, many forever disappeared from their family and communities (CBC 1989; Grygier 1994). The Charles Camsell History Committee's (1985) publication *The Camsell Mosaic* makes only very brief mentions of deaths at the hospital and includes little about how the lives of those who died were commemorated. In *Soapstone and Seed Beads*, a special publication of the Provincial Museum of Alberta that focuses on the handicraft program at the hospital, the authors also fail to describe what happened to those who passed away during their internment. *Soapstone and Seed Beads* does include a photograph of a memorial cairn erected in June 1990 "to memorialize Camsell patients buried in the St. Albert cemetery" (Staples, McConnell, and Oakes 1993, 33). However, no particulars regarding how death was handled at the hospital are available in either of these publications, both of which are oriented more toward celebrating the Indian hospital than toward offering a critical history. Death is for the most part missing from these texts, and it may be death that is part of what is forgotten through them. Given the purposes of remembrance practices (Simon 2005; Simon, Rosenberg, and Eppert 2000), an account of how deaths were handled, particularly among a group of patients who would have had diverse cultural practices, might not have suited the books' designs. It is precisely the absence of these accounts and the effects of this absence that compel their further consideration.

Some of those who died at the Charles Camsell Indian Hospital were buried on the property of the United Church of Canada's Edmonton Indian Residential School just outside of St. Albert. Today, the City of St. Albert is responsible for the site. Its official website claims that, "dating back to the 1940s, the cemetery served as a burial ground for native people who had passed away while at the Charles Camsell Hospital."[2] Since 1990 a memorial cairn has stood at the centre of an area of the cemetery specifically designated as the place where patients from the Indian hospital were buried. Each of the four sides of the cairn faces in the direction of those interred in the corresponding section of the small cemetery, and each side is engraved with the names, home communities, dates of birth, and ages of those buried there. Some names are missing and many of the names listed there clearly reflect a European language and naming tradition. Ages are often missing as well. No specific gravesites are marked.

In the files of Alberta's provincial archives is correspondence between committee members involved in the establishment and dedication of the memorial cairn. This material includes letters appealing for funding, letters from various funding agencies, and letters to and from those invited to attend the dedication of the memorial.[3] The committee responsible for the memorial cairn was the Charles Camsell Historic Society, which was made up of four people who had all worked at the hospital.[4] In this way, the memorial cultural production mimics that of the commemorative book *The Camsell Mosaic* (CCHC 1985) insofar as individuals responsible for the operation and administration of the institution produced each.[5] Consequently, the production of an official written history of the Charles Camsell Indian Hospital has, so far, been in the hands of relatively few people, and these few individuals were employed by the hospital. The written and official history, then, has been produced by "dedicated and caring" staff who describe their conduct in terms of the politically effective colonial dyad of the susceptible and the saviour. Their positioning in this way is reflected in newspaper coverage of the cairn's unveiling in 1990, with one article beginning, "Elva Taylor is still looking out for her patients" (Ellis 1990). Head of nursing at the hospital from 1947–71, Taylor is further quoted as saying that the memorial cairn is "a symbol of our friendship with our patients" (quoted in Ellis 1990). For Taylor and for some individual patients, that is likely true. What is also true is that this framing repeats a certain narrative structure that includes a celebration of heroic settler colonial subjects at the Indian hospital and the rendering of the Indigenous patients there as in dire need of such heroism. This sentiment is repeated again in the engraving at the bottom of the cairn: "This memorial was made possible by the interest and collaboration of the City of St. Albert and former employees of the hospital."[6] The repetition of "settler goodness" that such claims contain is characterized by Sherene Razack (2013, 353) as so common in the national narratives of settler colonial nations in the twenty-first century that it is more a compulsion than a trend. Indeed, this need to assert "settler goodness," with the heroes that its fulfillment quietly produces, is evident in the need of the Edmonton Police Service to assert its goodness in relation to the missing and disappeared from Edmonton's city centre. Crucial to this narrative, in the case of the Indian hospital, is a constituent of *the sick* whose neediness is the critical antecedent to this goodness. I found no indication among materials in the provincial archives that those subjected to the operations of the Indian hospital were also involved in the establishment of the memorial cairn. Although informal or undocumented involvement of past patients or family members may have taken place, the absence of an official record indicating this involvement is also relevant. Participation in establishing the memorial cairn by those who were treated at the Camsell or who had loved ones treated there does not challenge the prior point. A narrative of settler goodness and Indigenous need would have likely been present throughout an institution like the Indian hospital, and variously challenged and accepted. What can be said about the memorial cairn, however, is as a "trial by space," there is much that is inaccessible here and that is nonetheless embedded in its materialization. Today, the site upholds the familiar narrative of "settler goodness," characterized by Razack as a compulsion in settler colonial nations.

There are some records left from the original graveyard of the Charles Camsell Indian Hospital. Provincial archives include a 1962 plot plan, detailed by the brother of the resident supervisor of the school.[7] But like the cairn, these records forge only a partial story; even a quick comparison of the plot plan to the list of names and burial site numbers archived in another file reveals over twenty-two obvious discrepancies.[8] Many more discrepancies are likely hidden beneath the surface. Numerous inaccuracies would likely have been inscribed in the records even before people arrived at the Indian hospital. For example, the names and family origins of people transported from the North were recorded with little concern for or understanding of Indigenous languages, kinship systems, or notions of place. As noted in Chapter 3, nurse Kathleen Dier described the use of a tag system, reminiscent of other camp contexts, as the means by which people were accounted for:

> Each person had a big yellow tag with name, disc number and other particulars filled in at the top and bottom. The bottom part was removed at the Yellowknife hospital where the patients spent the night. The remainder was supposed to remain in place until they reached Camsell, a feat not usually accomplished as the wind kept blowing them away. (Quoted in Grygier 1994, 70)

Whatever records were kept of who was admitted, who was released, and who died in the Indian hospital, today the graves are unmarked except by the memorial cairn in St. Albert. The archival record suggests that the crosses marking individual graves were burned or removed after a fire in the 1970s. Then the City of St. Albert "wanted the federal government to help build a memorial to the people buried in the cemetery. Making no progress, a decision was made to smooth out grave mounds, remove the remaining nameless markers and landscape the area" (Ellis 1990).[9] After attempts to build a monument failed, the alternative was to disappear the markers of graves altogether. Although landscaping the area might seem contrary to the initial impetus to memorialize the site, I propose that this course of action exemplifies the argument made by scholars of memory studies that the building of monuments is less about a full remembering of whole and complex accounts and more about the management of narratives, sentiments, and time (Mackey 1999; Rosenberg, Dean, and Granzow 2010). Thus it makes sense to remove or landscape an area that is unmanaged, wiping away whatever traces might speak for themselves to the present in ways undirected by regimes of settler colonial conquest and time. When an area is landscaped, things are forgotten, removed, absented from the present of the place.

There were of course people who lived and worked at the Charles Camsell Indian Hospital. Whatever was cleared from the landscape at the St. Albert cemetery in the 1970s, the people who were there might be able to address some of the unknowns regarding death at the Indian hospital. The inclusion of patients' stories may also be a necessary step in avoiding key repetitions informing a Canadian national history.[10] However, with every year that passes, the likelihood of the survival of those stories shrinks. At this point, it is important to show that although what happened to those who died at the Indian hospital is not totally unknown, those stories do fail to appear in forms that might be recognizable outside of a narrative of European arrival as the opening of a country and as the eventual civilization and saving of the "savage" indigenous to that country. Much of what happened and to whom it happened has been excluded from official tributes to the Charles Camsell Indian Hospital, just as the markers of individuals' graves are now absent from the St. Albert cemetery.

What is forgotten but embedded in memorials like the cairn might nonetheless seep out. The old Indian residential school outside of St. Albert burned down in 2000. At the time, the property housed the Poundmaker's Lodge[11] and Nechi Institute.[12] These organizations "consulted with elders and organized annual ceremonies to honour former school residents" (Hanon 2008). These ceremonies occurred every year for four years. According to local media, it was during such gatherings that former students exchanged experiences and that "the presence of [additional] graves in several fields on the old school site came to light" (Hanon 2008). Reports indicate that there are many more unmarked graves linked to the Charles Camsell Indian Hospital on the old school property and that there were also additional gravesites outside of the one now officially commemorated with the memorial cairn (Walker 2003).

From the stories that emerged during these gatherings and published in local newspapers, we learn that boys at the Edmonton Indian Residential School were made to dig graves for people who died at the Indian hospital (Hanon 2008). Former student Jackie Williams, for example, remembers that many of the patients who died at the hospital were buried unceremoniously on the school grounds:

> According to several former students, young male students were paid to dig graves in the surrounding fields. The school, run by the United Church of Canada, operated a massive farm to teach agricultural skills. A few miles south, the federal government operated a tuberculosis sanatorium for natives in the now-closed Charles Camsell hospital. Witnesses interviewed by Sun Media said from time to time, the hospital would send deceased patients' bodies to the school, where the boys were paid anywhere from $2 to $10 to dig unmarked graves. "They'd just be boxes," Williams recalls. "No preacher, no service. Just bury them and be done with it." (Hanon 2008)

Williams arrived at the school in 1950, at ten years of age, and "during the next four years he was recruited to help bury dead children and adults. He remembers the bodies being brought to the school from the Charles Camsell hospital ... [and] buried in makeshift coffins that appeared to have been hastily built from scraps of lumber" (Jeffs 2004). In that same article, former student Ray E. Harris also recalls having to dig graves (Jeffs 2004; Walker 2003). Another news story reports the same: young boys burying bodies transported from the Indian hospital in a cemetery of unmarked graves (MacIsaac 2008). *Alberta Sweetgrass: The Aboriginal Newspaper of Alberta* reports, "Some of the students were paid to dig graves there for the Charles Camsell Hospital, and many are still haunted by the experience of seeing the caskets being put in the ground without ceremony or markings" (C. Carter 2004). In light of these accounts, the 1990 memorial cairn at the St. Albert cemetery looks like something of a false tribute – one that perhaps seals (or attempts to seal) the past as settled, offering a final accounting of the dead (Young 1993) as a commemorative effort toward forgetting the violence of hospitalization and tuberculosis treatment at the Indian hospital and toward remembering only the friendship and care of the staff. The experiences of those former students and patients who are still living, however, point to the need for much more work attuned to those who are unaccounted for in the simple listing of names on the memorial cairn.[13]

As was the case with the Indian hospital, some children never returned from residential school, and as a consequence, families and loved ones remain haunted by what is unknown (TRC 2015, 309). In an attempt to find out what happened to children, the Truth and Reconciliation Commission of Canada has established an official death register and has recommended that all chief coroners and provincial vital statistics agencies disclose their records on deaths of Indigenous children in residential schools. The commission's summary of its findings suggests that cemeteries were often abandoned when the residential schools were closed: "In short, throughout the system's history, children who died at school were buried in school or mission cemeteries, often in poorly marked graves. The closing of the schools has led, in many cases, to the abandonment of these cemeteries" (TRC 2015, 103). The commission's recommendations – along with exhibits like *Where Are the Children?*[14] – express a still urgent need to know what happened to people taken into the residential schools, hospitals, and associated facilities. This priority thus reiterates the power of disappearance as described by Gordon (1997), who explains that the absence of the body of a loved one who has died can carry with it a particular burden for those who have lost that person. In the case of disappearance, even when death is thought to be the most likely outcome, without the remains of the body, death remains unconfirmed. The loss remains open. Gordon describes how an absence of knowledge and thus a mystery around what happened to the disappeared can be key to the power of disappearance: "The precise power of disappearance as a system of terror and repression is the other door, being thrust across a menacing threshold and into a somewhere whose whereabouts and coordinates are unknown and threatening" (Gordon 1997, 113). The question of what happened to the disappeared is one of enormous political power. The not knowing is part of the devastation of disappearance as a system of repression and, in this case, of colonization, and conversely, this not knowing is part of the potential to resist this colonization as a political rather than a personal attack (Gordon 1997, 113). This power of the *question* is part of what some efforts at memorialization attempt to manage, sealing off histories where what is unknown is still a "seething presence" in our midst (Gordon 1997, 8). Answers to "what happened" that are too definitive or simplistic put at risk the political power of the question and its present tense (Gordon 1997, 8). What happened cannot be captured in memorial form, yet such forms can seem to resolve questions of ongoing urgency. Gordon demonstrates specifically this potential for resolution when explaining that despite the likelihood that most of Argentina's *desaparecidos* were indeed dead, Las Madres de Plaza de Mayo refused to have their disappeared declared dead. Instead these mothers "wanted to know what happened to the missing ones; they wanted us to know; they wanted those responsible to account for their actions; they wanted to talk with the missing; they wanted the disappeared returned" (Gordon 1997, 112). To declare the disappeared dead was to put the violence to an end, to put it in the past, to remove its potency as a contemporary and social matter. Gordon adds, "The Mothers insisted on keeping the disappeared alive because they opposed the false reconciliation that national-sponsored grieving for the dead and for burying the 'terrible' past promised" (Gordon 1997, 115). Through their avid resistance, they claimed to ensure "a dynamic reintegration of the dead and disappeared into contemporaneity" (Jean Franco, quoted in Gordon 1997, 115). This effort, too, remains ongoing among so many of the people involved in the Annual February 14th Women's Memorial Marches occurring in many cities across Canada on behalf of murdered and missing women and girls. The repetition of the sentiment that "their spirits live within us," so central to this annual march, brings past death and disappearance into the present of our lives.

The multiple political effects of disappearance described above do not address the particular need that people and communities have to mourn those they have lost in specific ways. Instead, they are focused on the political nature of disappearance, highlighting a need to persistently pursue more information and to resist the provision of some answers as definitive by the state implicated in disappearance. In a context where Indigenous children continue to be politically, legally, and economically positioned in ways that make them the most vulnerable to being taken into state custody within a system of child welfare service that discriminates against them, such a question needs to remain open (Blackstock 2007; see also Barrera 2018). The disappearance of Indigenous children and families into Canada's various healthcare and incarceration systems is not only a past occurrence (Balfour and Comack 2006; Blackstock 2007; Comack and Balfour 2004). On first consideration, the work of the Truth and Reconciliation Commission of Canada might appear to be oriented toward settling questions of disappearance in Canada's past. Establishing a death registry and collecting data from provincial offices of vital statistics might go some length toward silencing the question of what happened to the children. But in the context where cemeteries were abandoned, the repetition of these questions secures no definitive answer, only an always partial accounting. The national death registry will remain incomplete because it faces an impossible challenge; too many people have been disappeared through colonial operations of power. In the case of the Charles Camsell Indian Hospital, people disappeared not only after they died but also upon admission to the hospital, and although the demands for an accounting of these people furthers the political project of attending to the role played by the Canadian nation in a history of violence against Indigenous peoples in the colonization of the country, a full accounting is impossible. The question functions today as an effective mechanism toward keeping concern for the national treatment of Indigenous peoples open. In repeatedly asking where the disappeared are, the commission refuses a history that is settled and that positions Indigenous peoples as the recipients of benevolent care at Indian residential schools and at the southern hospitals. The strategy of demanding an accounting is one that keeps the disappeared alive and at work in a political project; it keeps ghosts present, seizing relentlessly upon the question of the disappeared as a contemporary matter.

The memorial cairn also keeps these questions open, despite its offer of a sound narrative about those who died at the Charles Camsell Indian

Hospital. The cairn states that those who died did so of tuberculosis, and it lists a name, age at death, and home community for some of them. And although these lists seem to seal in history so many of the questions contemporaneous to the differential treatment of Indigenous peoples in Canada's healthcare system today, they fail to do so fully. Here, the record falters again. The account provided works only from a distance and only for those who bear no intimate relation to what actually happened at the Indian hospital. For everyone else, there are many discrepancies in the record, mistakes, and missing names. Thus, although some might come here to find and remember those lost to the hospital (Tourangeau 1999), others are left with further questions. What is both explicit and forgotten here is the intimate relation between the celebration of a nation, or those "who did all they could to help," and the disappearance of Indigenous peoples.

On Sacred Grounds

There are many public places in Edmonton where the presence of a history of settler colonialism might be addressed.[15] One in particular is the site of Fort Edmonton and its cemetery. Fort Edmonton operated as a Hudson's Bay Company trading post in various locations on the North Saskatchewan River from 1795 to 1891 (S. Carter and Hildebrandt 2006). Among several historical Fort Edmontons, the one that remains was erected on Papaschase land, along the plains of Edmonton's river valley and adjacent to the river. Also known as Edmonton House, the fort was previously located on the banks of the North Saskatchewan River and was at the very centre of Alberta's fur trade at the time (Dempsey 2006, 211). Stationed at Edmonton House in the 1870s were two representatives of the federal government: William J. Christie, who was the chief factor at the fort, and Richard Hardisty, who was the local justice of the peace (Dempsey 2006, 211). A survey of this fort dated January 1, 1872, conducted as part of the Hudson's Bay Company census, recorded a total of thirty-eight people: eighteen "white" men, four "English halfbreed" men, four "English halfbreed" women, and twelve "English halfbreed" children.[16] This census indicates not only that it was a priority among early government and trade organizations to have an account of who was at the fort but also that this account was rooted in settler colonial notions of novel biologically based sex and racial difference and discreteness. At the same time, this census data points to the presence of relationships between those who had arrived as settlers and those who were indigenous to the area, as well as to a governmental priority and reliance on maintaining a distinction.[17]

Fort Edmonton temporarily existed in this particular place, but this location was also an age-old gathering place for First Nations peoples; archaeological findings from the site suggest that the north bank of the North Saskatchewan River has been a place occupied (if intermittently) by humans for the past 8,000 years (Cunningham 2005, 147). This site is significant not only for its long history of use but also for its specific use as a sacred burial ground prior to the establishment of the trading fort and its cemetery (Zwicker 2004). Although the use of this land – commonly called the Rossdale site – was under dispute for years, this dispute now seems to have been settled somewhat. In 2006 a permanent monument to those interred in the sacred Indigenous burial grounds and in the Fort Edmonton cemetery was erected on this site. Manasc Isaac Architects (2007) designed the memorial, whose construction is estimated to have cost just over $1 million (Rosenberg, Dean, and Granzow 2010, 403). The firm's website provides pictures and a description of the monument, including the various symbols incorporated into the design (Manasc Isaac Architects 2007). But this is only a very recent addition to the site, and for a long time, although it was known that people were buried there, claims over these bodies and this land were anything but settled. Bodies were exhumed in the 1960s when a thoroughfare was built through the river valley connecting south and north Edmonton (Zwicker 2004). At that point, archaeologists from the University of Alberta dug up bodies buried there and took them across the river to the archaeology department. These gravesites were discovered more than once, in 1982 and then again in 2001, prompted by plans to expand the EPCOR power plant: "One of the peculiarities of Edmonton's history is that this graveyard gets discovered over and over again, suggesting that what is buried there is not just physical, but a deeply disturbing psychic relic of settlement" (Zwicker 2004, 5). The repeated discovery of a graveyard, in the absence of tombstones, urges this consideration of a haunting, pointing to the need for more investigation.[18]

In 2001 Blackfoot activist Duane Goodstriker and Métis activist Phillip Coutu had set up a "makeshift memorial" (Zwicker 2004) that consisted of a number of wooden crosses erected overnight on a plot of land around which traffic whizzed. Three features of this memorial made it particularly compelling: "first of all, it's there, a physical reminder that our colonial accounts are not settled. Second, its construction – it just appeared one day – suggests a bold reclamation of public land by the people. Third, its very makeshift nature is productively shocking, especially since it is located directly alongside a major traffic thoroughfare" (Zwicker 2004, 8). Now this memorial is gone. Although I am not sure when or how or by whom the crosses were removed from the site, they are no longer there. As was the case with the Charles Camsell Indian Hospital's cemetery at St. Albert, the markers disappeared, the wood was replaced with stone and steel, and the ambiguity around the relationship between the dead and the land was replaced with an official memorial – a production that makes an assertion rather than putting forth a question about this particular relationship. At both the St. Albert cemetery and the Rossdale site, a contemporary effort to permanently memorialize – in stone and steel – was initiated that replaced the rough, temporary, and politically ambiguous means of marking the significance of the dead and their relation to a place.

So what is forged in steel and stone at the Rossdale site's 2006 memorial? This memorial is more formal in its claim and it reflects a kind of certainty or concreteness in the present. Although this memorial will provoke its own ambiguities and questions, if those who pass by are perplexed by the symbolism on display, there are information panels onsite that describe and explain the symbols utilized. Among the components of this monument are eight granite markers, or headstones, laid into the ground, none of which bear the names of those buried there. Not all of the names of those buried at this site are known. But something about the eight represented by these markers is known, perhaps because they were exhumed and examined by archaeologists and researchers in the 1960s. The resting place of each of the eight is engraved with a general descriptor such as "adult male," "infant," or "adult female." A Traditional Burial Ground and Fort Edmonton Cemetery Commemorative Site information panel tells visitors that these markers indicate the location of eight caskets reinterred on this site in August 2005. About the specific conditions for the unearthing of the remains in the first place and of their study and storage (for an unstated amount of time), the memorial's information panels say nothing, reporting only that the remains had been "previously removed and kept at the University of Alberta and the Medical Examiner's office."[19] Information about who removed these remains, for what purposes, and with what right is missing. The memorial thus reports on and takes responsibility *only for the keeping and returning* of the dead, conceived of as a *just* return: "[the remains] were returned in a ceremony respecting their cultural and religious tradition."[20] The information provided onsite forgets and erases very recent history, when some human remains were dug up, removed, and studied without consultation with community or family, without ceremony, and with little apparent consequence.

I have questions about what these eight gravestones do at this memorial site. Are they read as marking some generic version of *the human* to visitors of the site or to passersby? If so, how (well) can they work as social reminders of a particular history of settler colonial and Indigenous relationships here? What do the markers do other than depersonalize what might otherwise be pursued as some present connection to those buried here through such basic descriptors? These seemingly generic descriptors, however, are not universal; rather, these bodies may have been submitted to classification according to Eurocolonial conceptions of sex and time. And so the gendering and aging of those once buried and now reinterred here does do something to our sense of who and what they were – of their significance – in life. The things that have happened here are particular. And what might get read as nondescript engravings hide these complex happenings. It is not only "adult males," "adult females," and an "infant" who are buried here but also 8,000 years of Indigenous inhabitation, which seethes into a present where the deaths of Indigenous peoples are again naturalized by already established understandings of what constitutes a human life. The apparent lack of specificity in these still specific categories allows dominant narratives free reign, feeds assumptions of respect for human equality, and misrepresents the complexity of the site both historically and in the contemporary context, where it is a contested but nonetheless actively utilized site of human exchange and inequality – a contact zone – and thus a place where the relative value of human life was once struggled over and is now made manifest.

Another part of the monument is "The Memory Wall." It is described onsite as listing "the names of First Nations, French Canadian, English, Métis and Scottish ancestors buried on the site, or who are believed to have been buried in the immediate area" (Manasc Isaac Architects 2007). Thus the memorial includes both the names of the buried listed on "The Memory Wall" and eight markers of spaces set to look like individual graves, which bear no names but only an indication of the age and sex of the dead reinterred here. The listing of names is a feature that might seem to work against the kind of claims that I suggest are made by the nonspecific tombstones given that the names are specific and identify the loss of individual and valued people, but the list is not comprehensive. For example, among "the names" of the dead are those identified only as a freeman, an infant, a Norwegian, a woman about 100 years old, an old Indian wife, and a Catholic infant. Moreover, in addition to providing an account of those recorded to be buried at this particular site, the memorial lists others who died in the Edmonton area between 1809 and 1886. Significantly, at the time of this analysis, one panel in the memory wall remained blank.

One reading of this coupling of a naming of the dead with the provision of an empty panel is that the past has not been settled and that "The Memory Wall" thus fosters an open orientation to what happened and is happening here. This feature of the structure is arguably consistent with the political project of decolonization, which in part struggles to keep the colonial past open for examination in the present rather than allowing it to be represented as settled. Indeed, the empty panel could easily be filled if the scope of the memorial were a "reckoning" (Gordon 1997, 202) with a colonial present rather than a consignment of colonialism to the past.[21] Instead, as a memorial associated with Alberta's

2005 centennial celebrations, the larger project memorializes the past's dead as an important part of the city's bright future (Rosenberg, Dean, and Granzow 2010). This settled past was exactly what was required for the kind of future imagined by the organizers of the provincial centennial celebrations in Edmonton (Rosenberg, Dean, and Granzow 2010).

A feature of this commemorative structure that further removes a history of colonization from the deaths of those buried here, and indeed from the usurping of land that occurred in the establishment of Fort Edmonton and from the present, is the melding of Aboriginal design with iconic Christian symbolism. Although those peoples indigenous to the area held a variety of belief systems, the uniting of disparate iconography suggests that the Indigenous and settler colonial systems of thought came together in an unproblematic union upon contact between First Nations peoples and those who were new to the area. This of course was decidedly not the case by about the 1870s in Canada, when the church and state took up specific strategies toward the disappearance of First Nations, Métis, and Inuit peoples. Thus, regardless of an individual's or community's beliefs or faiths, the combination of Indigenous religious motifs and Euro-Christian iconography effectively disavows the colonization that has occurred in this spot for over a century. Like the text of one of the memorial's information panels – "The success of the fur trade was dependent on many groups. Fort Edmonton was built and thrived thanks to the First Nations, French Canadians, Métis, Scottish and English" – the project as a whole forgets the legacy of colonial violence in Edmonton's past and, indeed, its reverberations in Edmonton's present.

Memorializing Disappearance and Murder

Among the peculiar repetitions that this consideration of contact zones has exposed is the settler colonial strategy of defining and deeming collectivities of people as removable. For example, a number of those who were murdered during the course of this research were taken out of the city to more remote and rural locations. This feature of a number of the murders had local and national newspapers reporting it as a "trend," one that they highlighted by publishing maps of what they callously called the "dumping grounds" where women's bodies were found (Kleiss and Farrell 2004; Mahoney 2004). This expulsion and its reporting seem to be something of an obsessive repetition, paralleling expulsions that run throughout the operation of the Charles Camsell Indian Hospital and attempts at the settler colonial takeover of peoples and lands. Early in the operation of the Indian hospital, those who perished were also disappeared and either received no burial or were moved away from the city and buried in unmarked graves near the Edmonton Indian Residential School, open from 1924 to 1966 (Hanon 2008; Jeffs 2004). Instead of graves for those who died at the Indian hospital, a memorial cairn was installed. Remains of the dead were dug up from their sacred burial plots in the city's river valley, and after being held by the University of Alberta's archaeology department for over forty years, they were reinterred on the grounds outside of the EPCOR power plant (Rosenberg, Dean, and Granzow 2010; Zwicker 2004). Although the removal of bodies seems significant here – a haunting recurrence – it is the return of bodies to this sacred site that has been a celebrated aspect of the site's memorialization. Their prior unearthing is not accounted for in the present memorializing of the place. Individual markers for graves at the Rossdale site work in multiple ways but never seem to touch on the conditions central to attempts at settler colonial conquest of the site and the people here (e.g., the importance of the bison is stated on the information board, but the conditions and effects of the animal's elimination are not). The omission of information about the site's colonial past is clearly of material and symbolic contemporary importance. When the bodies of those removed were no longer here, no claim could be made to their mattering in the present or to their having a claim on the present. Symbolically, movements through spaces such as the Rossdale site can be meaningful and powerful enough to offer an apparent realization of settler colonial and masculine subjectivity, if only temporarily (Razack 2000). If this is the case, then the significance of removals from such a site is their assertion of rights over land and peoples that no longer exist in the contemporary urban context.

As is seen at the Rossdale site, some of the symbolism of such removals is managed by the presence of a memorial or monument. Each of the contact zones is linked to relevant memorial sites, and there are several memorials to murdered women in Edmonton. But at the time of this research, there were no permanent public spaces specifically dedicated to remembering the growing number of Indigenous women and girls being disappeared from Canadian cities. In 2009 Remember Our Sisters Everywhere (ROSE), a collective of activists, scholars, and researchers, provided an online list of memorials to murdered women across the country and identified four in Edmonton: a memorial garden, the February 14th march, a bench entitled *Fourteen Not Forgotten*, and a sculpture entitled *Vision of Hope* (ROSE 2009).[22] Although each of these memorials is identified as a means of remembering murdered women, one is specifically dedicated to women who died due to their involvement in prostitution, and two are tied to a specific event that occurred far away from Edmonton in 1989. Both officially and in their text and symbolism, *Fourteen Not Forgotten* and *Vision of Hope* commemorate the violence of December 6, 1989, when a gunman entered Montreal's École Polytechnique and killed fourteen women.

The connection between the contemporary disappearance and murder of Indigenous women and girls from Canadian cities and the 1989 massacre has been made by activists and scholars, and it now forms part of "Canadian cultural memory" (McNeill 2008, 382; see also Cultural Memory Group 2006). Of this connection, McNeill (2008, 382) writes,

> Since the victims were, in both cases, killed because they were women, their deaths bookend a problematic, enduring, and largely unaddressed history of femicide in Canada. They suggest a history that's not being included in the official/ dominant stories of the nation. Paired together, they are meant to remind Canadians of the omissions of collective memory and, through the memorials [sic] acts these events inspire, seek to insert this history into that official record.

Despite the very significant differences between the murders of Indigenous women and girls and the mass shooting of women attending a Canadian university, McNeill highlights their coupling toward a strategic end, that of inserting into the official record the "history of femicide in Canada." Yet, even with efforts to include these events as part of the official record in Canada, the Cultural Memory Group (2006)[23] has shown that when memorials are designed to remember murdered women in Canada, they have the shared fate of often going unseen. This is the case despite what the group calls a Canadian "landscape ... dotted with memorials to women murdered" (Cultural Memory Group 2006, 13). The Cultural Memory Group argues that the unseen existence of monuments to murdered women in Canada is not an accidental consistency characterizing these efforts (Cultural Memory Group 2006, 13). The ways that monuments are realized in spatial locations are part of their "trials by space" (Burk 2003, 318) and are as important as their production. Of how monuments to women murdered in Canada conventionally turn out, the Cultural Memory Group (2006, 14) notes, "City councils tuck them into marginal locations, funding bodies shunt them to the bottom of the agendas, plaque-writers dedicate them in codes that wedge words between silences. Memorials protesting a central scandal of our society occupy the most tentative positions in our public space."[24] As "trials by space," monuments materialize – they literally gain *ground* – as negotiations and negotiated sites. As city planners, interest groups, friends, families, and various logistical considerations (e.g., the weather) play into the production of such monuments, the ideas and values (i.e., the theoretical *ground*) upon which the monument stands (e.g., as a provocation or call to action) are ultimately transformed (see Rosenberg 2000 for a good example). The memorial garden at the Alex Taylor building is one example of a site likely to go unnoticed unless specifically sought out, tucked as it is into the corner of the old schoolyard. As the single monument in Edmonton dedicated to local women whose deaths are related to involvement in prostitution, the remote location of the garden does little to draw public attention to the fact that women and girls are being murdered and disappeared from the city.

But the location of these monuments is not their only difficulty. Without arguing against the strategic possibilities for reading several monuments together, Sharon Rosenberg (2000, 78) considers the problem of the collapse of specific event-oriented memorials into more general kinds of communicative acts to be part of a kind of "emblematic memorial practice." Writing of memorials and the 1989 shooting at École Polytechnique, Rosenberg argues that emblematic practice effectively "stabilizes *resemblance* (between the fourteen women murdered and all women subject to violence at the hands of men), *continuity* (between the past, present, and future), and *a definitive separation between grieving and activism* (first mourn, then work for change)" (Rosenberg 2000, 78, emphasis in original). In the case of the Indigenous women and girls disappeared from Edmonton, as has hopefully been demonstrated in reading three contact zones through each other, there is much about the specific violence occurring in Edmonton that is disavowed by a collapse into femicide. In these cases, emblematic representation does not do enough, perhaps in part because the rendering of women and girls as victims is already too familiar. Forgotten in a collapse into emblematic reading are the makings of societal indifference here in relation to peoples specifically situated not only in a national narrative, history, and present but also in proximity to violence. There are specific practices toward the production of spatial distance – such as naturalized displacement, transfer, and emplacement – and affective distance from Indigenous women and girls, who excessively bear the effects of socially orchestrated historic deprivations as well as of histories of colonial violence and conquest, and these effects are refused and perhaps even bolstered by such an emblematic reading. Although *Fourteen Not Forgotten* and *Vision of Hope* might attend to a historic trend of femicide in Canada (Cultural Memory Group 2006), I suggest that by virtue of their overt referencing of a very specific and traumatic national event, the *Fourteen Not Forgotten* and *Vision of Hope* memorials are likely not commonly read as provocations for present-day action or as a critique of present-day forms of racialized and spatialized violence and murder in Edmonton.

The Annual February 14th Women's Memorial March is another memorial to the women who have been disappeared, and who may continue to disappear, while working in Edmonton's outdoor sex trade.[25] This march is organized in conjunction with marches across the country in cities like Vancouver, Toronto, Winnipeg, and Calgary, each of which is concerned specifically with drawing attention to the incidents of missing and murdered women in Canada. The march was first organized in 1991 when "Aboriginal and non-Aboriginal women's organizations in inner-city Vancouver declared February 14 a day of remembrance to honor neighborhood women who have been murdered or who have disappeared" (Culhane 2003, 594). Since then, the march has become an annual event in numerous Canadian cities and has become "an occasion to protest against racism, poverty, and violence against women, and to celebrate resistance, solidarity, and survival" (Culhane 2003, 594–95).[26] The march has been considered a powerful site for addressing the current unjust conditions and social contexts for disappearance. According to Amber Dean (2015), the march provides opportunities for the "difficult return" of the past (Simon, Rosenberg, Eppert 2000, 4) by forging opportunities to "expose how we are ourselves implicated in the injustices that contribute to the losses being remembered by evoking the social and psychic legacies of the past in the present" (Dean 2015, 120).

When this research was completed, no public material memorial existed in Edmonton to specifically address the relevance of colonization, racialization, and sexualization in the disappearance of particular women and girls from the city.[27] Coarsely put, although living women provide their "tombstone information" to police officers in Edmonton and are positioned as subjects at risk by such "protective measures," there seems to have been little opportunity to direct their literal individual vulnerability into collective recognition or action. Visited as separate sites, these memorials do not set us up for a reckoning (Gordon 1997, 202); they do not encourage a grappling with the various ways that we are implicated in a past that reverberates in the present (Simon, Rosenberg, Eppert 2000, 4). Perhaps when these memorials are read together for a sense of what they compel into the present and beyond, such a "difficult return," in which our own implications in the present are at stake, is made more likely?

Each of the monuments examined stands in for the mysteries around those disappearances that they concurrently memorialize. I consider them markers "of the doubt that remains" (Mair 2016, 274); they do not speak explicitly of what is unrecoverable, tending instead to settle something by naming or stabilizing what is thought to be known (e.g., names, ages, and genders) and to obscure much of what is not or cannot be comfortably known (e.g., the fact that such categories might have been imposed and details about where people are buried, how they died, and toward what ends). Discussing her own visit to gravesites as informal archives, social theorist Kimberly Mair (2016, 274) asks, "What actually *rests* there?" (emphasis in original). She argues,

> They both present [us with] the problem of the undead, with what cannot be fully buried, with (what) *remains*. The marker is a trace of the doubt that remains. Perhaps the gravesite – as, arguably, the most obvious and most reverent formation of the practice of public memorialization – articulates a desire to divide up and banish such significances from our everyday spaces out of an unspoken fear of being consumed by an ever-present accumulation of multiple and shifting memory that will be there, in place, waiting for you. (Mair 2016, 274, emphasis in original)

Among what is significant and is banished might be an unsettling inkling that colonial practices linked to these memorials live on. Again, Michael Taussig's (1999, 2) notion of the "public secret" addressed earlier seems apropos here too. Memory of what happened at the Charles Camsell Indian Hospital is not singular but multiple and includes violence, care, assimilation, resistance, cure, death, and "all they could to help." These outcomes are not disconnected. And they are not distinct from the treatment of Indigenous peoples in hospitals today (e.g., see Lett 2013). Everyday practices of the present that render some lives worthy of protection in life or of memorialization after death might also be among these significant banishments. The particular memorialization of (some of) those who died in Edmonton and across contact zones suggests not only that bodies and their treatments matter but also that they matter beyond the realm of the momentarily living and thus function as features that might bridge the past and the present to posit some things – like a relative valuing of life – as continuous even if expressed differently. And thus far, it appears there can be no full reckoning with the disappearance of Indigenous women and girls today, with the loss of those Indigenous people who were never heard from again after they were shipped to southern hospitals, or with the difficulties of those Indigenous people who remain subject to legal dehumanization through the Indian Act and other forms of colonial legislation.

Conclusion

What interests me is not so much the state of things but the relations between them ... Relations come before being ... When our relations to death, the body, the world, other people and knowledge change, humanity itself is transformed.

– MICHEL SERRES, IN "THE ART OF LIVING"

By reading through the contact zones discussed in this book, I have aimed to respond to literary scholar and cultural critic Homi Bhabha's (1990) provocations used to open this work. Bhabha asks how we might "encounter the past as an anteriority that continually introduces an otherness or alterity within the present" and goes on to question how we might "narrate the present as a form of contemporaneity that is always belated" (Bhabha 1990, 308). Taken together, the texts and memorials of early settlement and the Charles Camsell Indian Hospital as well as the texts of contemporary policing and gentrification processes enable a consideration of some of the varied ways that difference is first made and then made to operate as power according to authoritative Eurocentric understandings, institutions, and practices. In the preceding chapters, I have examined the violence enacted through targeted and specific aggressions against particular people, or rendered bodies, in particular places and through the sometimes impalpable and nearly impossible to study damages of historical objectification and erasure. Read through each other, these contact zones suggest the endured heritage and the promised future of the incidents of disappearance and violence in Edmonton. Positioned as transcending an immediate time and place, these contact zones expose repetitions that occur in temporally separated moments and in spatially separated (yet always) local places to haunt and indeed (pre)occupy the city and those who live there. When positioned in relation to each other, these contact zones reveal that what has been called "societal indifference" to violence looks more like various small (sometimes big) and specifically dehumanizing practices that might be considered to effect not a passive indifference but an active and affective authorization of violence on a larger social scale. Acts of violence are bolstered by the social affect embedded in particular practices (J. Butler 2009, 50), including in the claim itself of an expectation of indifference, which not only names but also, I think, prepares and instructs. The notion of societal indifference toward some deaths references the production of both citizen and noncitizen subjects – the former of whom are considered human and internal to the settler colonial nation and the latter of whom are considered exogenous or even threatening to the nation and are thus *dehumanized.*

I understand the practices examined in this book as maintaining a Euro-American metaphysics across contact zones through their adherence to and repetition of (1) an implicit acceptance of violent racist and sexist acts when they are specifically based on constructed categories of biological distinction that function to effectively determine one's relative safety from (and others' proximity to) violence; (2) ahistorical, event-oriented readings of the past, present, and future; (3) a spatialized, and thus naturalized, separation from or proximity to violence; and (4) a progressive social mythology, which, in this case, amounts to a national colonial narrative that offers a benevolent or morally "good" interpretation of a history of events and relationships. Whether framed as social indifference to violence or as a social authorization of violence, the violence that accompanies such dehumanizing practices occurs in conjunction with private, local, institutional, and national practices of the past and present that, indeed, seem either to feed into the future or to repeat. They are practices that make and remake territories, binding and reifying Edmonton as a natural municipal entity and Canada as a natural national one. An examination of such practices suggests that the postulate of any kind of sustained "indifference" on the part of "society" in general or an individual in particular – defined as nonconcern or, when used as the characterization of something, as neither good nor bad – is wholly inadequate. The lives and deaths of Indigenous people, most notably women and girls, make *a considerable difference,* and thus matter very much, to the processes of constructing a city, its constituents, a nation, and the bodies of lawful and unlawful citizens. Operative in the development and prospering of colonial narratives of civilization, humanity, progress, health, and illness and sustained in contemporary constructions of who belongs where (e.g., in the city), ideas about the Indigenous woman and her fate have mattered greatly in attempts to make and remake Canadian colonial society. Use of the term "indifference," then, is not even close to accurate but instead functions as concealment. When taken as a general admonishment, the term berates without a specific object or recipient and concurrently disappears those subject to violence as well as those actually committing these acts of violence from "society" at large.[1] With this critique, I nonetheless urge continued efforts toward finding more apt and complicated means of addressing settler colonial violence in Canada. Such measures are not only those that attempt to elude the conventional individualization of what are phenomena with clearly shared, produced, and contested investments (e.g., in health, progress, and the nation) – investments that, to some degree, are often considered to be shared by the "majority" – but also those that attempt to address these various investments in violence without resorting to the too abstract and exclusive notion of a grand-scale "social," one that is intended to easily carry the implication of violence.

I have postulated that many of the practices described in the previous pages are oriented, first, toward constituting a populace through difference and, second, toward constituting its members as life less valuable and less valued. I have not given sufficient attention to *those lives made (i.e., situated in time and place) to matter* in the current socio-political context through such practices. I have not sufficiently described those citizens deemed internal to the settler colonial nation. If the disappeared have been rendered the subjects of "bare life" (Agamben 1995), there are also those who are cast as *the indifferent* (Amnesty International 2004, 2). In *Powers of Horror: An Essay on Abjection,* Julia Kristeva (1982) demonstrates the primary importance of the abject *to the subject.* Kristeva names the abject as the corpse and states that the corpse is effective in *determining* those on the other side of the abject – those still alive. Those defined as dead and the ways that they are treated point us directly to what constitutes the living. As Kristeva writes, "refuse and corpses *show me* what I permanently thrust aside in order to live ... There, I am at the border of my condition as a living being. My body extricates itself, as being alive, from that border. Such wastes drop so that I might live" (Kristeva 1982, 3, emphasis in original). Both Kristeva and Judith Butler (2004) attribute the affirmation of the living, of the mattering subject, as occurring according to practices and meanings that rule out the non-living, the nonsubjects, the unreal. For Kristeva, *dead* is part of the living's primary structure because a confrontation with the body, with its fluids, and with its inherent dying is what makes the living. Death and bodily defilement provide the living with the lines, borders, or boundaries from which the living turn away and according to which life is affirmed so that the living might more surely live (Kristeva 1982, 3). According to Kristeva, the corpse works as "death infecting life" (1982, 4). Such a postulate perhaps goes some way toward explaining the function of a callousness or even cruelty apparent in representations addressing disappeared and murdered women and girls.

But for the living, not all deaths work as uniform confrontations or affirmations. In the case of Edmonton's disappeared women and girls, the deaths through which some Canadians are (more or less) constituted as living always seem to be specified (yet not always obviously) as the deaths of the "Othered," as the deaths of the already nearly dead, as the deaths of those deemed to be abject, to be located elsewhere, or not to belong here, and as the deaths of the unrecognizable and unrecognized. Through practices of racialization, engaged in throughout the development of Western science and imported with European knowledge systems, and through settler colonial practices of occupation and territorialization, in which geographical and myriad other boundaries are made to be of utmost and defining importance, people are posited as though they differed in their proximity to death and as though this difference warranted differential protections in life from death as well as distinct kinds of remembrance in death. It is important to recognize, however, that those who are deemed worthy to live are only provisionally – temporarily – so positioned and are always dependent upon an "Other" for their status as other-than. Distance from the "Other" is not a state of being but a series of *activities engaged in* and thus made in the moment through daily practices (J. Butler 2004). Through what are often perceived as mundane engagements, but are also always relative engagements, life is made to be real or unreal, and only the *real* life is deemed to matter (J. Butler 2004). For this reason, it goes without stating that if there are those contingently rendered as constituting bare life, there are also those concurrently positioned as *living,* but this status, too, is always contingent.

Positing two positions might strike readers as sidestepping the aforementioned imperative to address what I have tried to conceive of as exceedingly complicated relations to violence and to its harms and benefits (e.g., righteous belonging). What I hope might be somewhat redeeming about this momentary oversimplification is its potential to highlight that there are actually no secure or innocent positions within ongoing practices of state-sponsored violence and that, although each position may be habitual, it is also essentially temporary and relational. Even if flawed, this proposal seeks both to leave no one out and to escape any individualization of implication.[2] For this reason, I want to focus a bit more on those whose presence is naturalized and protected through the kinds of alterity described here. Lorenzo Veracini (2010, 20) refers to this group as "the settler collective."

To address the contingent relation between those supposedly rendered at risk and those rendered safe, we need only to think again about the practices whereby Indigenous peoples are transformed into refugees (Veracini 2010, 35). There are complementary practices whereby the presence of members of a so-called settler collective are naturalized or seem to be made indigenous to the place now commonly called Canada, perhaps as nurses, doctors, lawmakers, police, and johns. Settler belonging, too, is enacted in various and contrary ways; for example, the settler collective is both "coming from elsewhere *and* ... sees itself as permanently situated" (Veracini 2010, 20, emphasis in original). If anything, what the previous pages have perhaps highlighted most clearly is that making the presence of a settler colonial collective requires ongoing and guarded practices of naturalization. But as Veracini points out, a settler collective is only ambiguously made and in ways that conflict; the pull for a settler collective to assert a natural, autonomous, and even indigenous presence is at odds with the necessity of replicating all that is "European" and the "civility" that such replication promises (Veracini 2010, 99). As "fundamental features of settler projects" (Veracini 2010, 22–23), these two contrary pulls to indigenize and Europeanize are never resolved; the effect is that a settled settler state remains forever just out of reach, or in Veracini's use of the work of French poststructuralist Jacques Derrida, a promise of the society "to come" (Veracini 2010, 23). Moreover, because these are practices and languages, there is always slippage between who is rendered naturally internal to the nation and who is made exogenous to it, and within this structure, a persistent effort is required to attempt to keep the promise of eventual settlement coming. The blasting of contact zones laid out in the previous chapters suggests that efforts toward some eventual full settlement persist, shifting in guise, language, and practice but continuing to require our attention for the damages they do. This point has been clearly made by Indigenous scholars, communities, and activists, who highlight that multiple and enduring forms of resistance have continually impaired ongoing attempts to fully settle a nation called Canada (see Hunt 2017; Lawrence and Dua 2005; Palmater and McAdam 2018; A. Simpson 2014; L.B. Simpson 2017; L.B. Simpson, Nanibush, and Williams 2012).

For a means to think through how such efforts to finally settle a nation shift in guise, language, and practice, it seems appropriate to return to Achille Mbembe's (2001) classification of the various forms of colonial violence as both inherent to and disavowed in contexts of Western liberalism. Mbembe also explains that the European obsession with the "Other" is such that the "Other" poses to the European not only a *different* form of being but also a form that cannot *be* at all. According to Mbembe, alterity is in this context nonexistence, not simply difference. Within such a system of thought, the "Other" cannot be accorded the value or respect of human life. Rather, the "Other" is eliminated through violence. Bringing the development of law and the development of a sovereign state to an understanding of European colonization on the continent of Africa, Mbembe explains that colonial sovereignty has been achieved and maintained by three types of colonial violence exercised toward the elimination of the "Other": "the founding violence of conquest; the legitimating violence of transforming conquest into moral authority; and the ordinary and banal violence necessary for the maintenance of colonial sovereignty" (Mbembe 2001, 25). As I close this work, I consider how the practices identified through each of the contact zones can be described according to Mbembe's three forms of colonial violence. Does Mbembe's work allow a notion of those rendered contingently living to be included in each of these forms of violence?

On the "instituting role" of "the founding violence of conquest," Mbembe (2001, 25) writes, "It helped to create the space over which [the right to conquest] was exercised," and "it regarded itself as the sole power to judge its laws – whence its once-sidedness." In each of the contact zones considered, a clear imperative was at work in establishing the matter of place – that is, *the places* of and for settler colonial practices. Although boundaries were identified differently in each historical moment, an overlapping analysis shows a repeated concern with *spatially* locating and rooting the exercises of colonial power. Such spatial boundaries or territorializations are part of what marks proximity to violence; some are rendered distant from and thus secure from not only violence but also a concern about violence. The farther a subject is from a particular (always mythological) place, the less likely a subject is to be confronted with corpses or other indications of the abject, all of which have the capacity to reveal to the subject a disavowed tenuousness of life. Thus the indifferent, or the contingently living, or the settler collective are those for whom distance from violence is secured through such temporary creations of places. Only with the continual forging of such boundaries can indifference become a believable postulate.[3] In the early era of European arrival, these boundaries were achieved through the imposition of the reserve and treaty systems and through the federal and provincial theft and control of lands. In the mid-twentieth century, the Charles Camsell Indian Hospital also functioned to bind spaces and bodies as well as to illustrate through its discourses of benevolence the colonial fitness and right to govern both. And most recently, in discourses and images used by the City of Edmonton, the Edmonton Police Service, and the federal task force Project Kare, some spaces have been rendered both empty and degenerate through their identification with places and bodies of violence to be cleared and policed.

The second form of violence identified by Mbembe (2001, 25) occurs with those legitimations that give the colonial order meaning – those features that "help produce an imaginary capacity converting the founding violence into authorizing authority." Monuments contain just such an authority in their iterations of the past as prior and democratic. So too do decrees determining citizenship and exception from it. So too do the technologies and practices of Western medicine that justify the examination, diagnosis, relocation, treatment, and detainment of numerous people of distant lands (places) "for their own good." Each of these modes of authority can be witnessed as intended *for* the production of a settler collective whose members are seemingly natural to this place but who might be considered contingently living given that the valuation of their lives is dependent on the production of a provisional set of people to be removed through, and without a stake in, colonization. That is, not only do these legitimations work best for those subjects who are situated as though they existed without an experienced and direct relationship to founding violences or for those involved in exercising violence on behalf of an already legitimated authority, but they also work *for* the production of such kinds of subjects. Notably, in declaring Canada to be without a colonial history, former prime minister Stephen Harper, too, converted violence into highly legitimate authority (Ljunggren 2009).

Within these foundational and legitimating practices, the violence itself is often obscured. Mbembe (2001) describes the third form of violence as the kind of brute violence that, in other settings, would be easily recognized and would/should be intolerable. However, in a settler colonial context, the everydayness, the usualness, of this violence loses its potency *as violence* and becomes consistent with the "central cultural *imaginary*," thus enabling the foundational and legitimating forms of violence to maintain their course:

> Falling well short of what is properly called "war," it recurred again and again in the most banal and ordinary situations. It then crystallized, through a gradual accumulation of numerous

> acts and rituals – in short, played so important a role in everyday life that it ended up constituting the central cultural *imaginary* that the state shared with society, and thus had an authenticating and reiterating function. (Mbembe 2001, 25, emphasis in original)

One of the central aims of this book is to understand the dynamic that Mbembe describes – to unpack the dynamics of how violence can play such multiple and pivotal roles yet can be perceived so thoroughly as an everyday occurrence as to provoke the declaration of societal indifference. But given the preceding analysis, and Mbembe's own insights, indifference is not what is operating here. The reiteration of particular and ordinary violence is a constituent factor in the development of a particular shared cultural imaginary, and those who benefit from it cannot be imagined as indifferent to such repetitions.

Mbembe (2001) returns us to the contemporary context of the disappearance of Indigenous women and girls from Edmonton and to societal indifference reported as both reason and response (Amnesty International 2004). The preceding work prompts me to counter the claim of indifference with the argument that a conception of these events as banal is particular, purposive, and not at all general. These acts of violence have become ordinary only to specific populations, those that I conceptualize as belonging to the contingently living settler collective. The members of these populations, Kristeva (1982, 3) asserts, "hardly and with difficulty" seek ways to endure what is also their intimate knowledge of their own proximity to death and thus attempt to distance themselves from it. The result is the emergence of collective efforts not merely to achieve some kind of affective distancing from particularly targeted violence but also to ensure this separation through numerous historical, political, geographical, and social processes – including in large part by propagating and protecting accounts of history that effectively dissolve the means for an endured and situated critique of settler colonialism.[4] It is those most deeply invested in this separation who share *with the state* a "central cultural *imaginary*" that amounts to a continual disavowal of Indigenous presence, lands, knowledges, rights, and histories, and it is through this disavowal that the humanity of Indigenous peoples is also disavowed. Perhaps this conclusion is too large a leap, but I argue that one of the consequences of settler colonialism is that in the place now commonly called Edmonton, some lives are deemed in daily practices in particular places to matter more than others and in multiple ways.

However, these daily practices commonly occur in obscured ways in these places and, when examined, seem to point to how the contemporary city is haunted. These places are haunted, most clearly, by the repetition and reproduction of mechanisms toward maintaining what operates in effect as "societal indifference" to the well-being and life prospects of those indigenous to the place. By describing these practices, mechanisms, and specific engagements, I have attempted to facilitate their further identification and detection. Moreover, I have aimed to show that the repetitions made apparent in this fabrication function to dispel suspicion around them, my hope being to demonstrate that when made discernible, the repetitions themselves attest to the saliency of their effects. One of my basic contentions is that the repetitions described here give credence to the claim that colonization is a continual, incomplete, and dynamic set of *practices* through which differentially privileged subjects have been provisionally but not randomly made. These enacted subject positions thus seem to carry within them a specific defining of the value(s) of human life. This form of colonization *is* a present-tense occurrence.

I began this book with the stipulation that what I put forth in these pages is a kind of fiction – a strategy that has allowed me to explore some ideas while (supposedly) shrugging off the weight of transcendent authority that so much scholarly work assumes. Situating my work in this way, however, does nothing to diminish those aspects of the book that have performative powers. And in my attempt to examine Canada's violence as it occurs against those situated in practice, in time, and in place to matter *less,* I have not escaped the problem of producing my own arguably simplistic constructions. In describing some of the specific practices through which the relative value of life is asserted in historical and present-day Edmonton, I have thus addressed the making of devalued positions subject to bare life (Agamben 1995, 2005) and of valued positions relative to that positioning. And regardless of what this binary does to offer a language for how we are structurally positioned either to benefit from colonialist projects of the past and present or to be endangered by them, it is clearly a problematic place to stop. Without further interrogation, it begins to look too much like the dichotomy "separating the coloniser and the colonised" (Veracini 2010, 16), which is so pivotal to settler colonialism in the first place. A key difference between these dichotomies is that colonial practices make settler colonial separations appear to be and to operate as stable and natural (e.g., in the form of biological race, sex, or illness), whereas notions of bare life and the contingently living are explicitly relational, being tied not to bodies but to positionings effected through social processes and practices in the always incomplete production of human subjects. Although novelist Toni Morrison's (1987) *Beloved* is set in a different place and time – Ohio just after the American Civil War – in its pages, Morrison powerfully illuminates for me several aspects of key significance to this idea: an innate relationality; the trouble that such constitution through alterity poses for provisionally made subjects; and the necessity of scrutinizing the insidious effects of this relation.

Crucial to Morrison's understanding is that this disavowal of a relational stance continually requires a war, one waged not only against the supposed "Other" but also eventually against and through the construct of the self as one guards ever more closely against one's implication in the violence that underpins the relational dynamics of human life. Michel Foucault (2003) wrote about this idea, too, in his lectures on racism. The concepts that I suggest here are ones that I hope display this relationality. I concede that by using them, I am at the same time releasing them for use in other ways, including perhaps their too easy reduction and utilization to express and perform some "truth" that may be inconsistent with the political orientation of my project.

I want to frame my use of these concepts as a sort of deterritorialization (Deleuze and Guattari 1994)[5] or redescription (Patton 2003), one that provides an interpretation of the commonly unacknowledged practices effective in constructing categories of human worth in a specific place, differently across time, and toward the eventual destruction of those who are devalued. However, in the attempt to discern how life has been differentially valued through spatial accomplishments in Edmonton's presently felt past, I have arguably created new categories without doing enough to ensure the present or future elimination of these categories. That is, if in my research I state that those who constitute *bare life* are made vulnerable or positioned closer to death and that those who are positioned as *contingently living* participate in maintaining the shared production of such proximities, I risk a literal (or otherwise) appropriation of the false dichotomy that I set up. Being clear about this danger, I speculate nonetheless on the productive capacities of the present description. Again, I hope that – as a particular expression – it begins a process of deterritorialization, one that works not only as an assemblage of some features of Edmonton as a place in its contemporary context but also as a "complex movement or process by which something escapes or departs" (Patton 2003, 168) from what is already known or inscribed as Edmonton. I intend for it to function as the beginning of an "unpacking [of] the ways ... subjects had previously been treated as containerized units" (Sparke 2005, xi), one that works "to challenge essentialized understandings of knowledge and truth" (Jones 2009, 178). I am inspired by the suggestion that it is through the deterritorializing impact of new and provisional concepts that thinking is moved to imagine another future: "The creation of concepts in itself calls for a future form, for a new earth and people that do not yet exist" (Deleuze and Guattari 1994, 108). For this reason, the concepts with which I work here provide only a beginning; the trick is to seek and create social positions, places, people, and a present that exist outside of the constraints that bound categories presuppose and repeat.

I conclude this book with just a gesture to the significant work being done toward decolonial and anti-colonial futures. The limitations embedded in the use of provisional concepts can be addressed by drawing on writing by Judith Butler (2009; J. Butler and Athanasiou 2013; see also Ahmed 2016). This work pushes through the tendency to stop at the notion of a relational definition in order to offer the beginning of a framework for living differently. In *Frames of War,* Butler (2009) outlines a way of thinking about the earth, about people, and about their innate relationality. Butler proposes that rather than remaining constrained by inherently violent institutions and structures (e.g., nation, religion, and identity) that are indebted to relations of categorical opposition, we invent ones that foreground our only truly essential characteristic: our shared precarity and dependency. This would require that we detach notions of the value of human life from concepts like citizenship or status within a specific nation-state and instead allow a more general ethic toward human precarity to guide social organization and collective concern. This undertaking would provoke a shift away from a commitment to ensuring that individual citizens have a good quality of life or access to human rights and toward an ethical commitment to ensuring that the collective conditions for equitable and just human life are met. Doing so would include acknowledging that our survival is not a matter of individual bodies securing limited resources but a matter of inventing and maintaining socially supported life-sustaining practices because life is precarious for all of us. Accordingly, those practices that produce and protect only the boundaries of valued life fall away and are reframed as acts that threaten rather than sustain human existence more generally. We would no longer dedicate efforts to boundary maintenance but to the inherently *social nature* of survival and the necessity of collective thriving. As a guiding principle, such a commitment to innate relationality would prohibit the abandonment of people according to the dictates of constructs like nation-states and would instead recognize the constant precariousness of human existence (Butler 2009). The myth of the humanist neoliberal subject, with his independent and autonomous existence, necessarily disappears here and is replaced with a conception of mutual dependence and precarity. The solitary subject dies as an idea and as the ideal, and what survives instead is the recognition of our lives as contingent on social networks, relations, and practices.[6]

In an interview with feminist writer and independent scholar Sara Ahmed (2016, 491), Butler directs us to focus our attention on the question of what kind of life we want to live together: "What if we shift the question from 'who do I want to be?' to the question, 'what kind of life do I want to live with others?' … If the I who wants this name or seeks to live a certain kind of life is bound up with a 'you' and a 'they' then we are already involved in a social struggle when we ask how best any of us are to live." A focus on the features of the life one lives with others might have us attend to our shared precarity and to our mutual need for each other in order to sustain our lives. Like Butler, I see this shifting of the questions that preoccupy us as a crucial undertaking.

The ideas outlined above, through the work of the various poststructural scholars addressed, are not novel or even radical – unless one remains exclusively and firmly entrenched within the training and norms of a Euro-American ontology and epistemology.[7] These insights are radically disruptive only to common-sense notions of reality based on a humanist theory of the subject and only within Euro-American contexts where subjects, time, and space have been emptied of their relational and fluid characteristics and endowed with a teleology tied to exploitation and accumulation in capitalist economies and knowledges. It is perhaps, then, not surprising that university contexts might be among those places where there is the most adamant adherence to settler colonial ontology and epistemology. These are the places where knowledge is made according to such assumptions. However, scholars like Paula Gunn Allen (1992), Jodi Byrd (2011), Glen Coulthard (2014), Vine Deloria (1995), Sarah Hunt (2014), Audra Simpson (2016), Audra Simpson and Andrea Smith (2014), Leanne Simpson (2016, 2017), Linda Tuhiwai Smith (1999), Zoe Todd (2016), and Vanessa Watts (2013) are among the many who have done much to demonstrate the specificity of the ontology and epistemology that inform Eurocentric understandings of the world and that provide for and naturalize relations of domination. Indigenous ontologies and epistemologies do not ground the same assumptions, nor do they proclaim universal truth. And although some Indigenous worldviews might prove immensely useful in enabling us to imagine different persons and places, unless we work against the specific features of settler colonial foundations on a daily basis, incorporation of Indigenous knowledge and ontologies is perhaps neither enough nor actually possible.

Irreducible Lives

In each chapter of this book I have examined discourses employed by those who (would) likely see themselves as having done (only) "good" in the city of Edmonton. I have also referred indirectly and overly generally to people who have suffered harm, violence, and death here. That is particularly true of my accounts of treatment at the Charles Camsell Indian Hospital in the mid-twentieth century and of the disappearance and murder of women and girls over the past decades. The detachment that this analysis expresses, like the distancing of those accounts that I critique, obscures the magnitude of the pain and loss suffered by those who were hurt or who were violently disappeared. It also does nothing to address the pain and loss experienced by those loved ones who have been left behind.

Upon a critical reflection on the crisis of disappeared women and girls in Edmonton, scholars like Amber Dean (2009, 2015) and Sharon Rosenberg (2013) rightly identify the delicacy and complexity required in any attempt to address these human experiences. It is the case that the people whose experiences I have touched on in this book have had vastly different lives and will be mourned and missed differently. In the case of the recent loss of Indigenous women and girls, disappearances in Edmonton have been articulated by social advocates, sometimes by their friends and families, and now by researchers "in relation to the deaths of more than 20 women involved in sex work in Edmonton who have disappeared or been murdered since the mid-1980s" (Rosenberg, Dean, and Granzow 2010, 401). Thus, although one cannot overstate the loss that each woman entailed, one also cannot understate the significance of the number of these particular women who have suffered violence, either abduction or murder, due to their racialization and marginalization through poverty and in turn through involvement in street-level sex work. I hope that this work has not shrouded this crucial point.

In her insightful analysis of representations of the mostly Indigenous women who were disappeared from Vancouver's now notorious Downtown Eastside, Geraldine Pratt (2005) shows how even the efforts of families and friends to deliberately draw attention to the particulars of the people whose subjects and lives had been dehumanized and abandoned – often first through conditions of poverty and later in media reports as the victims of violence – were able to do so only by effectively erasing the terms of these women's specific experiences, thus effecting another kind of dehumanization. According to Pratt, this process, engaged in by those who had personal relationships with the disappeared, most often assumed the following course: "re-incorporating the missing women into the social body by assimilating them within the space of the white middle-class family ... establish[ing] the family as the criterion by which their life is grieveable, and ... resituat[ing] the missing women – not as citizens within the city – but within the private sphere of prepolitical life" (Pratt 2005, 1064). In their analyses of representations of women who were disappeared from Vancouver's city centre, Amber Dean (2015) and Shawna Ferris (2015) repeat these concerns. It is not a simple matter of refusing the conventional terms of dehumanization used in media representations or state institutions of women impoverished or involved in street or survival prostitution. Rather, the matter is much more complex, involving a continuous asking after the always inadequate and variously power-laden effects of any attempts at representation of a life (J. Butler 2004).

In writing about violence against women, many academics have not been able to avoid objectifying those whose experiences they necessarily address. Criminologist Gail Mason (2002, 251) claims that, as academics, "we tread a fine line between the need to maintain the integrity of these experiences and our desire to employ them so as to resist the social conditions that make them possible in the first place," and she goes on to indicate that in treading this fine line, there is no alternative to making "the experience of violence into an object of study."[8] In this work, I have not addressed the experience of violence, but I have always been writing about a particular violence – about violence against particular people – mostly against people I have not known. I have not addressed the individual women and girls who have been disappeared; I have mentioned that some of the disappeared women also identified as Indigenous. I have written that some of the disappeared were said to be involved in sex-for-money exchanges. These are dangerous but, I still think, necessary things to write. Some of the women who disappeared were not Indigenous. And some were never engaged in prostitution. Of these complex people and specific situations, I know nothing. What I know of the actual women and girls whose disappearances have prompted my writing is only in relation to claims of brutalities against them and a national indifference to that violence. And so I would rather have known nothing about them at all.

But I have heard their names in conjunction with the cruel, inappropriate, condemning inadequacies that have characterized many media accounts. I stress that this problem of representation is a major deficiency in this project, too, although it is at the same time a shortfall central to the project: it is in fact the issue. Through the process of this research and writing, I have asked how the disappearances of particular people are related to their (prior) recognition or recognizability as lives that matter in a particular social time and place. I must therefore continually attempt to reflect on how this work plays into producing the limits of such recognizability and to consider how it might actually prevent the recognition that certain lives matter. But I can also ask how it might, more ideally, change the prospects such that recognition is not the precondition for granting a life value.

It should not be necessary to assert the following, but given the postulates of this book, it matters very much that I do: those whose lives were violently ended are not at all reducible to the terms in which I have described them here. At the same time, the particular features of their lives – that they might have engaged in street-level exchanges of sex for money or that they were often Indigenous – cannot and should not be ignored as features related to their violent deaths and, importantly, to what I have been describing as a social reaction to these murders. Indeed, I have argued that the very opposite is true. Even at the end of this work, I continue to struggle over the difficulties of acknowledging the complexities of lives and of tapping something of those features that seem to somehow crucially cut across lives.

Complex subjects cannot be reduced to categories such as occupation, life circumstances, or sets of relationships. Avery Gordon (1997, 4) addresses this specifically and "reminds us that even those who live in the most dire circumstances possess a complex and oftentimes contradictory humanity and subjectivity that is never adequately glimpsed by viewing them as victims or, on the other hand, as superhuman agents." Gordon insists instead on recognizing our "complex personhood" (Gordon 1997, 4) and then elaborates on the various ways that such a notion escapes easy assessment: "At the very least, complex personhood is about conferring the respect on others that comes from presuming that life and people's lives are simultaneously straightforward and full of enormous subtle meaning" (Gordon 1997, 5). Complex personhood cannot be reduced in any capacity. At the same time, we rarely see or endure its elaboration, and I argue that it does not conform easily or perhaps even at all with representation in language. The effort to represent our common complexity should necessarily slow down and encumber all sociological analysis and all of our quests to know what happened. It should prompt us to ceaselessly interrogate for further complexities rather than to seek out simplistic explanations, and it should force careful and thoughtful representation, as Butler (2004) argues, with detailed attention to the failures of representation and to the recognition that much more than we know is always at stake. For this reason, both of the postulates set out in this work – the bare life and the contingently living – fail terribly and demand reconfiguration and challenge even immediately upon their proposal. Butler's work takes us some way toward resolving the limits of this relative positioning. And those writing and working against the truths of a Euro-American ontology and toward Indigenous ontologies and epistemologies deepen our thinking on this even more (Allen 1992; Byrd 2011; Coulthard 2014; Deloria 1995; Hunt (2014); A. Simpson 2016; L.B. Simpson 2016, 2017; A. Smith 2003, 2005, 2014; L.Tuhiwai Smith 1999; Watts 2013). These writings urge a refusal of those everyday practices that augment and re-enact Euro-American metaphysics, including the assumption of a humanist subject and the espousal of a concept of history that renders us free from responsibility for the present.

Finally, I cannot close this work without addressing what is often unacknowledged in writing such as I have done here. Literary critic Patricia Yaeger (2002, 46) warns that when writing about the dead in particular, "the writer needs to stutter" in order "to explore the possibility" that the dead

> might experience their "texting" as posthumous harm, might not consent to the critic's own figurations. Without this discursive doubt, the critical ecstasy and self-certainty that spins off these spectral bodies tells us too much. It creates the

> possibility that these ... bodies tell us more about the cultural critic's own investments, and still more about the easy commodification of the dead in the face of a critic's own desire.

I think Yaeger is right. Doubt is supremely important. Dean (2009) addresses this issue as well: "There is some degree of pleasure in theory making about the dead, and to deny this is to do a kind of injustice to those missing or dead persons who occupy one's thinking" (49) – and so we ought always to stutter. Questions that Yaeger (2002, 29) poses have occupied me since I began with this work, and I continue to keep them at the fore: "What are our responsibilities when we write about the dead? ... What happens when we 'textualize' bodies, when we write about other people's deaths ... as something one 'reads'?" What does this writing say about my own investments, about the "easy commodification of the dead" (Yaeger 2002, 46) or disappeared? These remain open questions for me. So I worry about writing about the contexts of the disappearances and deaths of Indigenous women and girls. I also worry about what it would mean not to write about them. Neither option is without difficulty. Neither frees me from implication in settler colonial violence.

Notes

INTRODUCTION

1 See Bourgeois (2014b); K. Anderson and Lawrence (2003); Beads and Kuokkanen (2007); McGillivray and Comaskey (2004); and Silman et al. (1987) for more on Indigenous women's experience of violence and modes of resistance to violence. The Native Women's Association of Canada (2015) identifies some problems with government statistics on violence against Aboriginal people, as does Cree activist, academic, and author Robyn Bourgeois's (2014a) response to the RCMP's report. Despite these limitations, it is worth noting that Statistics Canada reports Aboriginal women are three times more likely than non-Aboriginal women to experience violent victimization (this includes spousal violence) (Perreault 2011).

2 Funding for the NWAC's Sisters in Spirit initiative was cut dramatically in 2006 by the Conservative government.

3 The Institute for the Advancement of Aboriginal Women (2019), a non-profit organization in Alberta, also received federal funding through Status of Women Canada for a project titled "We Have Cried Enough." As stated on its website at the time, "The objectives of the project are: To develop an Edmonton-specific action plan to implement applicable recommendations of the Stolen Sisters Report; To develop close relationships with natural allies to lobby for changes; To lobby for policy change within government and city based agencies." Retrieved November 11, 2009, from http://www.iaaw.ca/pdf/WHCEIndex2.pdf.

4 The NWAC website further described the Sisters in Spirit research plan: "The initiative will be undertaking qualitative (life histories) and quantitative research on racialized, sexualized violence against Aboriginal women with cooperating families who have female family members that are missing or murdered, in order to gain a better understanding of circumstances, root causes and trends. The initiative will develop community education/action kits for use by community organizations, as well as host some workshops and conferences. NWAC will work with participating families and the community to develop a policy agenda in order to influence required changes with government and community." Retrieved September 26, 2009, from http://www.nwac-hq.org/en/background.html.

5 I relegate Amnesty International's (2004) second and third factors to effects of the first factor and thus suspend their consideration for the time being.

6 This list is not definitive and was compiled using the map created by the nonprofit society Native Land Digital (2019) and the *CAUT Guide to Acknowledging First Peoples & Traditional Territories* (Canadian Association of University Teachers 2017). The names used are sometimes contested and are not necessarily universally accepted as appropriate. None of the names as written here use proper Canadian Aboriginal syllabic characters. Today, more than 600 First Nations exist in Canada (Vowel 2016, 260).

7 "The *Sisters in Spirit* initiative is beginning to identify 'clusters of activities' across the country where Aboriginal women are at extremely high risk of violence, disappearance, and death. These include Regina, Saskatoon, Edmonton, Winnipeg, Vancouver, and communities in northern British Columbia on Highway 16, centering on Prince George. Other clusters have been identified in northern Ontario, the Northwest Territories, New Brunswick, Newfoundland, and Quebec" (Jacobs and Williams 2008, 134).

8 A crucial element of my own situation at the outset of this work was that my encounters with this problem occurred through radio and newspaper reports of incidents of violence, not through interactions with people who were disappeared or whose loved ones were disappeared. This issue is considered at greater length in later chapters.

9 Thanks to Dr. Amy Kaler for pointing out this important possibility for interpreting societal indifference.

10 This type of theorizing also works to question the violences that occur against groups of people determined to be "less-than" according to other "biological" distinctions as well, such as gender, ability, and age. This is a very broad notion of racism that is supported by the work of Michel Foucault (2003) and that does not obscure, but specifically demonstrates, that although articulated differently in the social world, much of what functions to oppress in various ways relies on the construct of a biologized structure for the making of an "inferior-superior" hierarchy.

11 Rather than invoking a notion of biological race, I rely on the notion of racialization as a social process that has the effect of making biological race real: "Once 'races' are reified as real differences among and between individuals, these differences become naturalized and normalized" (Armstrong and Ng 2005, 43). A process of racialization, then, is "the act and effect" of "race," the outcome of which is racism, defined as "the ideology *and* practice of inferiorizing and excluding groups of people by virtue of their 'race,' bearing in mind that racial differences are socially constructed" (Armstrong and Ng 2005, 43, emphasis in original). Sara Ahmed's (2002, 46) essay "Racialized Bodies" describes "racialization as a process that takes place in time and space: 'race' is an effect of this process, rather than its origin or cause."

12 There must be a language or concept for violence – since it has meaning. This is a claim that has been made repeatedly by sociologists. For example, scholars concerned with gendered violence expose the commonly obscured links between experiences of violence and patriarchy (Kimmel and Holler 2011; Sanday 1996).

13 I am making use of Evelyn Peters's (1998, 670) distinction between imperialism and colonialism as articulated by Edward Said (1993, 9), who defines imperialism as "the practice, the theory, and the attitudes of a dominating metropolitan centre ruling a distant territory" and colonialism, more specifically, as "the implanting of settlements on distant territory."

CHAPTER 1: A HISTORY OF THE PRESENT

1 The insights on this notion were developed while working in 2006–07 with Dr. Sharon Rosenberg and Dr. Amber Dean in a theory reading and writing group organized as part of Rosenberg's research project "Opening the Present to the Violently Dead," funded by the Social Sciences and Humanities Research Council of Canada. I am also indebted to Wendy Brown's (2001) insights, developed thoroughly in her book *Politics out of History*. Most recently, my thinking on this issue has been informed by Elizabeth Povinelli's (2011, xi) notion of "tense, eventfulness, and ethical substance" and in upcoming work, I consider how disappearance is rendered a non-event, whereas official inquiries into such violence are produced as national events.

2 Sara Ahmed (2000, 12) has suggested that the concept of contact zones assumes a problematic linear movement from distance to proximity between peoples otherwise separated. In this work, I assume no coming to *know* the "Other" through contact zones. I assume only that contact zones are zones of transformation and struggle, and I continually question the degree to which proximity is what is pursued or even allowed for in a colonial encounter within a contact zone. One of Ahmed's (2000) most compelling and useful points is that distance is exactly what is maintained in colonial relations, even within a contact zone, and it is this distance that is required for the continual recognition of an "Other" as a stranger deemed foreign and to be feared. Ahmed's work is significant here, a major contribution to a still small body of work that does not assume an eventual integration between subjects in modern colonial states but instead asserts the opposite – arguing that the state has social investments in maintaining the "Other" as a stranger in colonialism, as this undertaking is a primary method for ensuring the perpetuation of the racism inherent to empires. Thus, although scholar Mary Louise Pratt's (1992) notion of the contact zone is helpful as a means of first extracting seemingly disparate moments and then drawing these moments together, I utilize the notion without the assumption of a resolution. Ahmed's contribution is recognized, and the term "contact zone" is used here to refer to ongoing and contemporary engagements. It is not a reference only to early exchanges

between Indigenous peoples and immigrants on this land but refers also in particular ways to engagements in Edmonton in the mid-twentieth century and in the early twenty-first century. I use Pratt's concept with regard to present contact zones and without some imagined resolution on the horizon. That is not to suggest that a resolution would not be welcome, but in the continual production and spatialization of racialized difference, understood as a national commitment of sorts, contact zones are continually made.

3 I use the term "righteousness" here as a means to address the particular dynamics in a very conservative and highly religious setting, in which membership in dominant groups seems to equip one with a divine right to various revered aspects of life, land, and morality. In his analysis of the "settler collective," Lorenzo Veracini (2010, 21) describes the collective as "invariably represent[ing] itself as virtuous."

CHAPTER 2: "IT IN NO WAY MAKES YOU SAFER"

1 Retrieved September 28, 2009, from http://www.kare.ca.

2 Retrieved January 28, 2008, from http://www.rcmp.ca/ab/prog_serv/hrmpp-kare_e.htm.

3 A serial offender is, according to RCMP constable Tamara Bellamy, "someone who is responsible for more than one murder with a cooling-off period in between those murders" (quoted in Harding 2005b).

4 At the time, considerable media attention was paid to the arrest and charging of Robert Pickton for murders linked to the disappearance of numerous women from Vancouver's Downtown Eastside (Dean 2015).

5 In one case, this indication of a serial perpetrator was accomplished by mention of Robert Pickton, a now notorious convicted serial killer in Vancouver, and by the statement that Edmonton law enforcement could learn from the Vancouver cases.

6 Former Canadian prime minister Stephen Harper is on record as having done both when in office.

7 I am aware that there are important subsequent critiques of the applicability of Giorgio Agamben's work in settler colonial contexts, and I intend to take them up in later work.

8 This question is of key importance in relation to the National Inquiry on Missing and Murdered Indigenous Women and Girls. For a critique of the inquiry, see the special issue of the *Canadian Journal of Women and the Law* 28, 2 (2016).

9 Retrieved November 12, 2006, from http://www.kare.ca/content/view/2/.

10 Retrieved September 19, 2009, from http://www.kare.ca/.

11 My wording here is intentional: one might pursue an escape from the oppressions and confines of the bureaucracies of white, Eurocentric, bourgeois existence. The pursuit of this freedom was expressed explicitly to me by an acquaintance who preferred street-level sex work to working for the state

within the legitimized economy and assigned to "processing" Indigenous peoples through that very system.

12 I am deeply indebted to Shawna Hohendorf whose brilliance, experience, generosity, and deep insight has impacted my work as it is developed here.

13 This quotation is taken from Michel Foucault's lecture on racism on March 17, 1976, and published posthumously in *Society Must Be Defended.*

14 This argument is developed to some extent through the organization of this book but will also be the topic of forthcoming research.

15 Retrieved November 13, 2007, from http://www.kare.ca/. Each of the quotations in this paragraph is from the *Ride Along with Project Kare* video.

16 These four objectives are "1. Prepare and Implement strategies to minimize the risk of having any further 'High Risk Missing Persons' murdered; 2. Pursue investigational strategies to investigate all leads, capture and prosecute the offender(s) responsible for these crimes; 3. Establish an integrated homicide unit that enables the province of Alberta to have the capacity to investigate High Risk Missing Persons, unsolved historic homicides, and serial offenders; 4. Create a template of 'best practices' for utilization in other similar projects nationally." Retrieved November 12, 2006, from http://www.kare.ca/content/view/2/.

17 The Treasury Board of Canada Secretariat considers "tombstone information" to be "a cluster of personal information [that] consists of a number of data elements that are collected, used and/or disclosed in a similar manner. For example, tombstone information might typically consist of a name, address and telephone number." Retrieved September 28, 2009, from http://www.tbs-sct.gc.ca/pgol-pged/piatp-pfefvp/assistant/mod9/mod9-1_e.asp.

18 Retrieved November 12, 2007, from http://www.kare.ca/content/view/6/. Particular thanks are due to my copy editor Robert Lewis, whose curiosity and thorough attention to this manuscript revealed that the Project Kare "philosophy" comes from the FBI moral code and that this moral code was penned by J. Edgar Hoover. This connection reveals important and shared international practices in an era of "modern" and scientific policing, in which, as Foucault (2003, 255) has described, there exists a relationship between the power to let die, or to kill, and the power to live more or better. This I see as another haunting aspect of the analysis and one I hope to address more thoroughly in the future.

19 Portions of this section were previously published in Granzow and Dean (2007).

20 According to Statistics Canada, Indigenous populations made up 4.4 percent of Edmonton's residents in 2000 (cited in Heisz and McLeod 2004, 35), but among the city's low-income population, 11.1 percent were members of an Indigenous group in 2000 (cited in Heisz and McLeod 2004, 36). These statistics demonstrate the overrepresentation of Aboriginal peoples among low-income residents in the city. Because of the number of services provided

to those with low or no income in the area, the neighbourhood set for "revitalization" is an area of the city likely used more often by those with low or no income than by those of the middle and upper classes in Edmonton.

21 Although in 2006 this was explicitly the case, in 2007 a flyer was circulated around the neighbourhood (a year and a half after the "revitalization" began) announcing a call to "hear the experiences and ideas of those who now live in this area or use this area as 'home.'" The flyer states, "The City is seeking this input and we want to find some people who could work over the next few weeks to sit with people and listen to them talk about these things." Although it is implied that this call was issued by the City of Edmonton, the flyer bears no names or contact numbers for city representatives and seems instead to have emerged from a large church-based social service organization in Edmonton known as the Edmonton City Centre Church Corporation (E4C). Further, it is significant that this initiative was undertaken a year after City Council had already accepted "The Vision" for the area.

22 For example, after decades of being overlooked by the city, rooming houses that for years have offered only substandard housing options to those with few alternatives are now conveniently receiving inspections that deem them unfit for human occupancy. If such inspections had occurred earlier, prior to investor interest in what the city hopes will become prime real estate, the outcome might have involved repairs rather than increased homelessness. Inspections of these premises occurred only once the gentrification process had begun; prior upkeep of the buildings would have run contrary to the capital-oriented processes of disinvestment in urban areas, which are a critical antecedent to gentrification and are processes from which landowners and eventual investors stand to substantially profit (N. Smith 1996). A prior disinvestment in inner-city neighbourhoods such as this one makes the business of urban reinvestment (i.e., gentrification) possible and profitable (N. Smith 1996). The terms "reinvestment," "revitalization," and "urban renewal" all obscure, depoliticize, and rationalize the continual and violent appropriation of land and the actual dispossession of people.

23 On February 2, 2006, architect Don Stastny referred to the neighbourhood as "fallow, fertile ground" during the first public meeting on the Downtown East revitalization project, and city representatives called it an "open palette" (Phillips 2006). Stastny later apologized for his assessment of the space in which upward of 2,500 people live.

24 Such spatial separations are in keeping with those implemented well over a century ago through the Canadian government's imposition of the reserve system (Ferris 2015; Silver et al. 2006). Professor of urban and inner city studies Jim Silver and colleagues (2006, 15) describe the contemporary "spatial location of more aboriginal persons within specific inner-city areas in Vancouver, Edmonton and Saskatoon [as] effectively reproduce[ing] the reserve system." Although not explicitly embedded in state policy, state techniques like

gentrification and, as discussed in the next section, crime prevention materials online work to nonetheless repeat this enduring state dedication to producing and maintaining distance in the interest of producing and maintaining vital differences between a legitimate Canadian citizenry and those constituting bare life (Ferris 2015).

25 Retrieved May 21, 2006, from http://www.police.edmonton.ab.ca/Pages/Prostitution/InEdmonton/InEdmontonMain.htm. "Anatomy of a Stroll" and "The Prostitution in Edmonton Resource Centre" webpages are now defunct. I have nonetheless included the URL for each of the sites analyzed and their retrieval dates. Since this analysis was conducted, the Edmonton Police Service has radically revised the webpages relating to what it now calls the sex trade or sexual services industry.

26 Thanks to an anonymous reviewer for pointing out this very significant change in the legal classification of sex work as well as remnants of the former definition on the Edmonton Police Service's website.

27 Retrieved January 16, 2016, from http://www.edmontonpolice.ca/communitypolicing/familyprotection/prostitution/legalitiesofprostitution.aspx.

28 The website did not describe the assorted stakes in what is a very culturally broad sex industry. It avoided acknowledging, for example, the more socially acceptable forms of trade in sex (e.g., off-street, in massage parlours, through escort services, and informal sex work).

29 Drawing on the work of Michel Foucault, urban studies scholar Michiel Dehaene and philosopher Lieven De Cauter (2008, 4) define heterotopic spaces as "other places" and refer to "various institutions and places that interrupt the apparent continuity and normality of ordinary everyday space."

30 Social mobility was defined on the website in terms of questions such as "how permanent is the population – is there high turnover? Do they own their own homes? How many renters? Etc."

31 Much social disorganization research relies on dichotomous racial constructs, such as black and white (see Sampson and Bean 2006).

CHAPTER 3: "ALL THEY COULD TO HELP"

1 YouTube has several videos taken at the now defunct Charles Camsell Hospital.

2 This quotation and much of the descriptive information provided about the Charles Camsell Indian Hospital appear on the commemorative pillar on the northeastern corner of the property.

3 Like attending residential school, a stay at the Indian hospital meant separation from family and community for extended periods of time. For children, in particular, such extended absences led to "loss of identity" (Staples, McConnell, and Oaks 1993, 9).

4 Yet there are occasions when such distinctions evaporate. One nurse, asked to recall her time working at the Indian hospital, first as an aide in 1950, reports that experiences at the hospital might have had effects on the patients similar

to those suffered by residential school students, observing that "most of the patients demonstrated that sense of despairing resignation so evident at a residential school" (Steinhauer-Anderson in CCHC 1985, 101).

5 The basic information on tuberculosis that informs this paragraph is from Government of Canada (2019) and World Health Organization (2019).

6 Provincial Archives of Alberta, PR1991.0443/26.

7 Indeed, readings suggest there was no plurality here. Research at the time was interested in the Native versus the white, not in determining differences between the variety of people conceptualized as "Indian."

8 Ferguson's early work on the evolutionary theory of disease continues to be used by Canadian researchers seeking to show a genetic link between tuberculosis and Indigenous populations.

9 The larger question concerns the role of colonial conquest in the development of western European forms of medical knowledge and practice.

10 This racialization of TB has taken a new form in recent years, such that TB appears to be a racialized disease in relation to settlers' fear of immigrants (see Reitmanova and Gustafson 2012).

11 This division between health as a provincial responsibility and Indian Affairs as a federal responsibility is indicative of the separation that legislation had in the allocation of rights. Although addressed later, it seems there was a time when no single governing body was responsible for the health of Indigenous peoples.

12 Bryce's position as chief medical officer was not reassigned for another seventeen years (Wherrett 1977, 105).

13 This claim is made despite some attention to First Nations peoples with TB in the Fort Qu'Appelle Sanatorium in Saskatchewan. In the 1920s forty beds were "available for Native patients in order to repay debts to the federal government" (Lux 1998, 280). In addition to these beds, medical experimentation with the BCG (Bacillus Calmette-Guérin) vaccine was conducted on Aboriginal infants during Ferguson's tenure at the sanatorium (Lux 1998). This experimentation, which demonstrated the effectiveness of the vaccine, also demonstrated that the primary threat to Aboriginal infants was not TB but the abject living conditions created by an unjustly adjudicated treaty system (Lux 1998).

14 The end of the Depression in the 1930s, the end of the Second World War, the development of drugs to treat TB, and finally the emergence of a Canadian welfare state are all reported as factors that prompted the Government of Canada to turn its attention to treating TB among First Nations peoples (Hodgson 1982). Lux (1996, 343) reports an additional factor: "Only after drugs for non-Native tuberculosis patients had emptied sanatoriums did hospital beds become widely available to Native people."

15 Provincial Archives of Alberta PR1991.0443/12

16 The hospital also served a limited number of war veterans for the first few years of its operation.

17 It is perhaps an indication of an ongoing haunting that I propose over a half-century later that this place was indeed "a camp," although not the kind of camp the local residents seemed to fear. I propose the exact inverse – that it was a camp that allowed for treatment outside of the bounds of legal convention, offering a kind of site of exception where medical containment, experiment, and treatment might have taken precedent over the fostering and protection of human life.

18 Articles titled "King Gets Protest on T.B. Hospital," November 22, 1945, and "Finds City Unable to Block Hospital," November 29, 1945, are at the Provincial Archives of Alberta PR1991.0443/18. These clippings were originally accumulated at the Alberta Legislative Library and did not include the names of the newspapers. However, all articles after 1951 would have appeared in the *Edmonton Journal*, and all articles prior to 1951 would have appeared either in the *Edmonton Journal* or in the *Edmonton Bulletin*.

19 Article titled "Circulate Petition on T.B. Hospital," September 28, 1945, in file "Charles Camsell Hospital," City of Edmonton Archives.

20 Article titled "City to Support Hospital Protest," October 3, 1945, in file "Charles Camsell Hospital," City of Edmonton Archives.

21 Article titled "Ask for Backing Hospital Protest," October 2, 1945, in file "Charles Camsell Hospital," City of Edmonton Archives.

22 Article titled "Conducting Survey of T.B. Indians," November 20, 1945, in file "Charles Camsell Hospital," City of Edmonton Archives.

23 The name Iroquois was used by the French, whereas the British used the name League of Five Nations. The Haudenosaunee Confederacy is now considered the appropriate name and is used by member nations to describe their union (Haudenosaunee Confederacy 2019).

24 Provincial Archives of Alberta, PR1991.0443/21

25 Quoted in newspaper article in Provincial Archives of Alberta, PR1991.0443/18

26 Article titled "Dominion Rejects Hospital Request," November 16, 1945, in file "Charles Camsell Hospital," City of Edmonton Archives.

27 Article titled "Ottawa Refuses to Change Plans for Jesuit College," November 23, 1945, Provincial Archives of Alberta, PR1991.0443/18.

28 It is perhaps obvious that the definition of these TB hospitals as "centralized" reflected the position of the majority of the settler colonial settlements, which were concentrated along the southern corridor of the country.

29 Article titled "Indians Tuberculosis Drops by Half," January 3, 1951, in file "Charles Camsell Hospital," City of Edmonton Archives.

30 Provincial Archives of Alberta, phonotape 86.424/50.

31 Ibid.

32 In 1952 about 67 of these 513 patients were not tuberculosis patients (CCHC 1985, 45).

33 One source provides a radically contrary assessment of the X-ray teams and of the transportation of the Inuit to southern sanatoria. In a pamphlet

reprinted from the *Canadian Geographic Journal*, June 1954, is the following description: "Yet, such is the confidence these teams have inspired that there is seldom any difficulty in persuading the sick native to climb into a plane, say good-bye to friends and family, and set off for the great unknown 'civilization' outside for an indefinite length of time." Provincial Archives of Alberta PR1991.0443/19. Although integrating these conflicting assessments seems problematic, a likely conclusion is that each was politically motivated and that experiences were not uniform. Notably, as indicated by its glowing report of this Canadian initiative, the *Canadian Geographic Journal* was in strong support of the mass mobilization campaigns.

34 Provincial Archives of Alberta, PR1991.0443/18.

35 Understood through Judith Butler's (2004) notion of dehumanization, the disappearance of a loved one and the lost opportunity to grieve the loss of a loved one may factor into the making of the unreal life. The appeals made by family members to find those lost to and in the southern sanatoria system are appeals that resound, although differently, across the country.

36 Alongside praises written of the Indian hospital's first years, some work also questions the overt purposes and practices in the establishment and operation of the Charles Camsell Indian Hospital. Hodgson (1982, 506) suggests that although government motives for the new level of care imposed on Aboriginal peoples in the 1940s were generally thought of as humanitarian, alternative interpretations revealed such "care" to be "a threat to [Aboriginal peoples'] social and cultural autonomy." Even in 1944, Dr. Ross Millar, who was then "the medical assistant to the Department of Pensions and National Health" (Grygier, 1994, 62), recognized that the new system of treatment was also a threat to Aboriginal peoples. He wrote to R.A. Gibson, the director of Northwest Territories and Yukon affairs, to argue for the local treatment of Inuit people with tuberculosis and against their transport to southern sanatoria: "The removal of northern natives to southern institutions is not good practice, but almost invariably the patients ... become lonesome, decline, and sometimes die" (quoted in Grygier 1994, 62). Although Millar's recommendations generated little attention, they indicate the presence of alternative perspectives at the time. Thus the history of the Charles Camsell Indian Hospital cannot be excused with a mythology of pure and good intentions. There was dissension among government officials and likely among the doctors, nurses, and technicians involved in the targeted campaign to attempt to control TB and/or Aboriginal peoples this way. Arguments in support of the hospital resonated more with the Canadian government's position. For example, Brooke Claxton, the minister of health and welfare, reported in 1946 to the Senate and House of Commons, "For humanitarian reasons and as a very necessary protection to the rest of the population of Canada, it is essential to do everything possible to stamp out disease at its source wherever it may be within the confines of the country" (quoted in Lux 2001, 221–22). Casting

Native populations as the source of TB, despite the prior rates of the disease among the new settlers, effectively justified the use of extreme and enforced measures to "stamp out" its existence.

37 Casts were also used as treatment for orthopaedic cases of TB. Drs. William R. Barclay and Margaret Barclay report that there were so many of these cases that they "spent most of our afternoons applying plaster casts." They go on to report on the unpleasantness of this task: "The old casts that we first had to remove were filled with [the] stench of suppurating fistulae. The children resented being immobilized and did their best to prevent us from applying a cast from which they couldn't subsequently wiggle free" (quoted in CCHC 1985, 23–24). What we can ascertain is that the practice and threat of casting (whether therapeutic or punitive) worked in a number of ways as a technology for immobilizing particular bodies. Moreover, the variety of its "usefulness" as a technology meant perhaps that its utility – medical, disciplinary, and practical – may rarely, if ever, have been questioned.

38 Upon its reproduction in *The Camsell Mosaic* (Orford in CCHC 1985, 29–30), the article received no critical attention.

39 Provincial Archives of Alberta, PR1991.0443/26.

40 This caveat is important, for I argue that this treatment performed on white bodies elsewhere, as was the case, had a different meaning.

41 Provincial Archives of Alberta, Bl.2152/6.

42 Provincial Archives of Alberta, Bl.2213/8.

43 These photographs are not contained in any commemorative text but are filed away separately, the first under the heading "Charles Camsell Hospital" and the second amid other photos from the hospital but with no record in the card catalogue. As is now apparent, much has been left out of the official public historical record on the Indian hospital and on the people treated and working there.

44 Provincial Archives of Alberta, PR1991.0443/26.

45 Ibid.

46 Total institutions are defined by Goffman (1961, xiii) as "a place of residence and work where a large number of like-situated individuals, cut off from the wider society for an appreciable period of time, together lead an enclosed, formally administered round of life." Total institutions have long been recognized as a highly effective means of eliminating Indigenous peoples and practices and have been used in many settler colonial contexts (Veracini 2010).

47 Provincial Archives of Alberta, phonotape PR1986.0424/50.

48 Provincial Archives of Alberta, PR1991.0443/25.

49 Ibid.

50 Among letters of thanks sent in January 1953 are two from nurse F.E. Taylor to the English Cocker Spaniel Club of Alberta and to the Canadian Daughters League No. 37, each of which gave $25.00 to the Indian hospital. Provincial Archives of Alberta, PR1991.0443/25.

51 Quotation taken from the memorial pillar on the old site of the Charles Camsell Indian Hospital at the corner of 127th Street and 115th Avenue in Edmonton.

52 I think such revised accounts are heard more and more often now. I expect that the outcome of a recently initiated class-action lawsuit filed on behalf of those treated at Canada's Indian Hospitals will have significant consequences in this regard.

CHAPTER 4: "ALL TRACES OF HIS FOOTSTEPS ARE FAST BEING OBLITERATED"

1 In *Myth and Memory: Stories of Indigenous-European Contact,* John Sutton Lutz (2007) describes "contact" itself as a problematic term for suggesting one moment of coming together between two unfamiliar groups. In my use of the term "contact" and indeed in my appropriation of the phrase "contact zones" (M.L. Pratt 1992), I want to stress the ongoing nature of contact and the multitude of sites in which it occurs. Thus I see my work as moving along the same lines as that of Lutz by contesting the term "contact" as definitive. I employ the term precisely toward its reconceptualization as denoting more enduring and transcending occurrences.

2 By 1872 there were still apparently fewer than 15,000 people living in Alberta, of whom a mere "twenty-seven men, seven women and seven children" were white (Dempsey 2006, 209).

3 Popular historian James G. MacGregor (1949, 44) reports that the 1870 smallpox epidemic and those of the prior hundred years reduced the Aboriginal population in Canada by 90 percent. That is, nine out of ten Aboriginal people were killed by smallpox.

4 The poverty that befell Native peoples following the eradication of the bison was made worse with the introduction of alcohol. "In addition to coping with the problems of smallpox, the Blackfoot tribes were also beset with whisky traders in 1869–70 who invaded their hunting grounds and completely decimated and demoralized the tribes" (Dempsey 2006, 227). Like other Hudson's Bay Company posts, Fort Edmonton had its "share of violent incidents fuelled by alcohol. In his 1870 tour of the West, William F. Butler said that a state of 'lawlessness' existed at Edmonton House, Victoria and Fort Pitt, and that 'robbery and murder for years have gone unpunished in the region of the Saskatchewan" (S. Carter and Hildebrandt 2006, 241).

5 Historian Doug Owram (1980) provides a more nuanced account of the expansionist movement in Canada, identifying its priorities as largely those of a particular segment of the population, whose agenda was initially challenged by a number of diverse groups, including many groups among the French Canadian population. Owram also suggests that despite considerable argument and controversy about how and whether the North West should be so rapidly opened for agricultural settlement, the historical record seems

to indicate that the *ideals* put forth by the mainstream of the expansionist movement were those that were put into practice through strategies used to settle the West. Indeed, Owram states that most people who went west were English speakers.

6 Significantly, MacLaren (1989) has published the handwritten version of Paul Kane's journal in the *American Art Journal,* thus enabling readers to compare it to the popular edited publication *Wanderings of an Artist.* The only version that is verified to be in Kane's original script, this much shorter account is largely without the "romance" of the western frontier prevalent throughout the original publication. *Wanderings of an Artist* was published prior in 1872, just prior to the era under consideration as a contact zone examined in this section of the work, but it is a text that has informed the colonial imaginary of Canada, of Rupert's Land, and of the various people encountered there.

7 Cree artist Kent Monkman's painting exhibition *The Triumph of Mischief,* shown in Hamilton, Toronto, Halifax, Calgary, and Victoria from June 2007 to September 2010, offers a magnificent contemporary rebuttal to the now iconic paintings by Paul Kane as well as to works by other nineteenth-century artists of the western frontier. Monkman's adaptations of Kane's paintings are a means of "reclaiming the land, and of exploring themes of racial and sexual oppression through alternative narratives of the art and mythology of the frontier" (Timm 2007). Monkman states that "the artwork of the 19th century was really about freezing Aboriginal people in time and setting us backward. A lot of my work is about deconstructing the authority of these paintings – because they continue to hold authority over how First Nations are perceived" (quoted in Timm 2007). My thanks to Tanya Harnett in the Department of Fine Arts at the University of Alberta for pointing me to Monkman's work.

8 Dempsey (2006, 211–12) writes, "The Rupert's Land agreement gave the HBC £300,000 along with one-twentieth of lands in the 'Fertile belt,' land surrounding their trading posts, and other concessions as well. In exchange, the Dominion took over the entire western prairies, including what is now Alberta. William McDougall was appointed the first lieutenant governor, and he travelled west through the United States in anticipation of the transfer. However, when he arrived at Pembina in late October he was refused admittance to the territory by Riel and his followers."

9 Although most often assumed to be a strategy of colonization and primarily established between the federal government and individual Aboriginal bands, treaties themselves have a much longer history on this continent; many Aboriginal groups crafted treaties with each other prior to those imposed by European settlers, even though these Aboriginal treaties were informal and seem to have lacked the rigid immutability of those made with the queen of England (S. Carter and Hildebrandt 2006). A corporate interest in the making of treaties was also new. Treaty No. 6, like other treaties made between Indigenous groups and the federal government, was forged in part as a

consequence of the prior deal made between the Canadian Pacific Railway and the Government of Canada, in which the government indicated it was committed to "extinguish[ing] Indian titles to the land" (Fried 1984, 32; see also Francis 1997).

10 The Conservative government under Stephen Harper continued to expedite the settler colonial exploitation of Indigenous land and water rights with the introduction of Bill C-45 in 2012 (Palmater and McAdam 2018). Despite the passing of this bill, the *Idle No More* movement emerged as a massive and international grassroots Indigenous movement in opposition to government attempts to further infringe on innate and legally protected Indigenous rights (Palmater and McAdam 2018).

11 "All traces of his footsteps are fast being obliterated from his once favourite haunts, and those who would see the aborigines of this country in their original state, or seek to study their native manners and customs, must travel far through the pathless forest to find them" (Kane 1859, vii).

12 Sunera Thobani (2007, 38) credits Dara Culhane (1998) for the term "armed fiction."

13 This would remain the case for over a century until, in 1985, the Canadian government passed Bill C-31 in an attempt to amend the Indian Act such that it no longer violated the Canadian Charter of Rights and Freedoms (Jacobs and Williams 2008; McIvor 2004). Analyses of Bill C-31 suggest that it still has a multitude of problems regarding passing on Indian status to children and the registering of children, both of which call for identification of paternity as a prerequisite for children's status (Jacobs and Williams 2008; Vowel 2016).

14 I am not suggesting that gender binaries were nonexistent within the varied forms of Indigenous social organization across the "Americas." There was and there remains great diversity among different Indigenous communities and traditions. Yet the passing of laws tying legal rights to Eurocentric and normative gender schemes in the process of colonizing Canada marked a significant point of intervention for those who were in turn regulated, through the same laws, by the colonizing state.

15 Carter (1997) discusses such representations as primarily about forgetting a national history in which Indigenous people, including women, played crucial and cooperative roles. Scholars of social memory and history, however, suggest that history cannot be remembered without a forgetting since historical narrative is always an interpretation and is thus made in particular ways. Remembering is forgetting; the two cannot be separated. The version of history with which Carter takes issue effects an eclipsing in addition to a forgetting.

CHAPTER 5: "JUST BURY THEM AND BE DONE WITH IT"

1 The Alex Taylor School building recently belonged to one of the city's church corporations and stands a stone's throw from places where sexual services are available for sale on the street.

2 Information for this section was taken from the St. Albert cemetery's website. Retrieved August 10, 2008, and August 17, 2009, respectively from http://www.stalbert.ca/admin/contentx/default.cfm?PageId=104 and http://www.stalbert.ca/cemetery.

3 Provincial Archives of Alberta, PR1997.0726.

4 These four people were Elva Taylor, the director of nursing; Maxine LeClair, a nurse; Don McBride, a teacher at the Indian hospital and an administrator at the Edmonton Indian Residential School; and Dr. Otto Schaefer, a medical researcher based out of the Indian hospital (Ellis 1990).

5 Note that the title is the same as that of the onsite commemorative pillar, also called *The Camsell Mosaic.*

6 Although I do not doubt that some of those who worked at the Indian hospital did so with the most sincere intentions to provide their patients with the best care and support, they did so under conditions I have analyzed as instrumentally about maintaining colonial relations that were fundamentally about ensuring racialized and gendered definitions of life and of access to land.

7 Provincial Archives of Alberta, PR1997.0726.

8 The plot plan is located in the Provincial Archives of Alberta, PR1993.0243 and the list of names with burial site numbers is located in Provincial Archives of Alberta, PR1984.0425.

9 Provincial Archives of Alberta, PR1997.0726.

10 Maureen Lux's (2016) work on Indian hospitals goes a long way toward filling in the stories of what happened there.

11 Poundmaker's Lodge (2019) "is an Indigenous addiction treatment centre near Edmonton, Alberta. Established in 1973, Poundmaker's Lodge has been a leader in the provincial, national and global addiction treatment community. Poundmaker's Lodge accepts all peoples from all walks of life as outlined in its mission statement. Through concepts based in the cultural and spiritual beliefs of traditional First Nations, Metis and Inuit peoples in combination with 12-Step, abstinence based recovery, Poundmaker's Lodge offers an Indigenous holistic treatment experience that focuses on the root causes of addiction and empowers people in their recovery from addiction." The lodge is located at the site of the old residential school.

12 Nechi Institute (2017) "is recognized as one of the finest Indigenous training, research, and health promotions centres in the world." The institute is located at the site of the old residential school.

13 A 1990 newspaper article reporting on the dedication ceremony suggests that some patients who perished at the Charles Camsell Indian Hospital in its early years were sent to the Stony Plain Indian Reserve (Enoch Cree Nation) for burial (Ellis 1990), but there is little to no other mention of this practice among city and provincial archives. Further research is needed.

14 The mystery around those who were disappeared appears in projects like the archival, documentary, and photo exhibition *Where Are the Children?* curated

by "urban Iroquois" artist Jeff Thomas and produced by the Aboriginal Healing Foundation in partnership with Heritage Canada and Library and Archives Canada. This exhibition focuses on children who were disappeared through the Indian residential schools operating in Canada between 1831 and as late as the 1990s (Legacy of Hope Foundation 2001a, 2001b). Considerable work has now gone into collecting information about what happened in residential schools, but much more remains to be done, and a number of civil and criminal cases are as of yet unresolved.

15 Research for this section was conducted with Sharon Rosenberg and Amber Dean and was supported by a research grant from the Social Sciences and Humanities Research Council of Canada. For a more fully developed description and analysis of this site and its significance in Edmonton's present, see Rosenberg, Dean, and Granzow (2010).

16 Provincial Archives of Alberta, PR1980.0284. In 1870 smallpox hit Edmonton House (S. Carter and Hildebrandt 2006; Dempsey 2006, 223).

17 However, this accounting is not to be mistaken for an objective one; it was conducted at one moment in time using methods that cannot be confirmed as reliable, and the account does little to inform us about the number of temporary residents or about those who passed through Fort Edmonton. To be certain, there were times when the fort would have been quite busy, such as during a migration of over 200 through Fort Edmonton to the Cariboo Gold Fields in 1862 (MacGregor 1949, 175). Although the numbers suggest the predominant presence of those called "whites," it is not the numbers that are of most importance here but the system of counting and dividing according to "race."

18 Rosenberg, Dean, and Granzow (2010) consider this psychic relic further, pursuing it as a particular type of haunting presence in the city, one that revises Alberta's provincial narrative of pride.

19 Quotation taken from the information panel onsite entitled "Traditional Burial Ground and Fort Edmonton Cemetery Commemorative Site."

20 It is questionable whether this ceremony could actually have respected the traditions of specific people given that the number of people represented by the remains reinterred cannot even be known.

21 I use Avery Gordon's (1997, 202) notion of reckoning as "about knowing what kind of effort is required to change ourselves and the conditions that make us who we are, that set limits on what is acceptable and unacceptable, on what is possible and impossible." Whether any information panel might open up such a reckoning is questionable, but at minimum it would require a consideration of the site/land in the present and of how we are constituted as subjects or not in relation to it.

22 The *Vision of Hope* sculpture was unveiled in 1999 at Mary Burlie Park in Edmonton. Note that in the years since this time specific memorials have dropped off of this webpage and new ones have appeared. In November 2019,

the memorial garden no longer appeared on this list. A *Trinity Sculpture* at the University of Alberta has since appeared on this list.

23 As of 2006 the Cultural Memory Group included scholars and activists, namely Christine Bold, Sly Castaldi, Ric Knowles, Jodie McConnell, and Lisa Schincariol.

24 For an abridged excerpt from the Cultural Memory Group's (2006) book *Remembering Women Murdered by Men: Memorials across Canada,* see Cultural Memory Group (2016).

25 What was previously the Prostitution Awareness and Action Foundation of Edmonton (PAAFE) is now the Centre to End All Sexual Exploitation (CEASE) (2019). PAAFE had been involved in holding an annual memorial on August 14 since 2000. This memorial is not exclusively for women who have been murdered but also for women involved in sex work who have died of addiction, health problems, and suicide. More recently, it seems that the march has turned primarily into a march to remember and protest the deaths of Edmonton's missing and murdered women.

26 Returning to Burk's (2003, 317) characterization of physical monuments as "trials by space" (Lefebvre 1991, 416) and recognizing that the act of the memorial march is unique in its own ways, I do not address the Edmonton marches. I do, however, point to the Edmonton and Vancouver February 14th marches to show that in both cases the meaning of the march has shifted in time, indicating that it, too, might hold or even surpass the complexity that Burk grants the material memorial as a "trial in space." For example, the Vancouver march was initiated to address the local disappeared women but has become a more general forum for protesting things like systemic racism, inadequate housing, and high rates of poverty in the area (Culhane 2003).

27 Since its completion, however, such a memorial may have been made. In July 2007 an article in the *Edmonton Sun* described a plaque inscribed with the names of Edmonton's missing women and reported that the plaque was out of date by the time it was given to Carol-Lynn Strachan, a local sex trade activist, so that she could "find a place to put it where the women would be honoured." Chris Dowding, a man living at a shelter in the Boyle Street area of Edmonton, had asked his step-son to make the engraving, which is entitled "Dedicated to the Missing Women" and lists twenty-nine names, the year of each woman's disappearance, and her age (Hanon 2007).

CONCLUSION

1 With its attention to case studies, Amnesty International (2004) is specifically working to generate concern for missing and murdered Indigenous women and girls. Amnesty International's approach is to be applauded for its unique attempt to escape individualistic strategies of blame. Its specific attention to the social context for harm against Aboriginal women should be recognized as an attempt to address a heritage of violence that must be understood in

terms that extend beyond individuals. Although the notion of societal indifference is critiqued here, the larger goal of Amnesty International's initiative is recognized.

2 See Mi'kmaw equity studies scholar Bonita Lawrence and sociologist Enakshi Dua (2005) for a discussion of implication in colonization and decolonization.

3 To regard the places of Edmonton's Downtown East, the stroll, and the old Charles Camsell Indian Hospital as spaces of colonialism is not to say that colonization does not occur or is not witnessed in other spaces, even ones that are not at all delineated as racialized or sexualized in particular ways as spaces for particular relations. Indeed, the entire city of Edmonton can, has, and does operate as a colonial space. However, I suggest that each of the places examined here is specific for the various forms of violence it has authorized.

4 Again, only in this context can Stephen Harper's claim that Canada is without a colonial history (Ljunggren 2009) make sense to a national citizenry.

5 "Deterritorialization" is defined and described in numerous ways (Patton 2003). It is in keeping with philosophers Gilles Deleuze and Felix Guattari's (1987) project that the term escapes solidification.

6 Indigenous writers, activists, scholars, and storytellers have been engaged in cosmologies that elaborate and enact alternative worlds and relations (e.g., see Little Bear 1998; L.B. Simpson 2016, 2017; and Watts 2013).

7 Which I was, for the duration of my formal academic training.

8 See critical race and Indigenous studies scholar Eve Tuck (2009) for a consideration of the limitations of this position.

References

Agamben, Giorgio. 1995. *Homo Sacer: Sovereign Power and Bare Life*. Trans. Daniel Heller-Roazen. Stanford, CA: Stanford University Press.

–. 2005. *State of Exception*. Trans. Kevin Attell. Chicago: University of Chicago Press.

Ahmed, Sara. 2000. *Strange Encounters: Embodied Others in Post-Coloniality*. London: Routledge.

–. 2002. "Racialized Bodies." In *Real Bodies: A Sociological Introduction*, ed. Mary Evans and Ellie Lee, 46–63. Basingstoke: Palgrave.

–. 2016. "Interview with Judith Butler." *Sexualities* 19 (4): 482–92.

Alfred, Taiaiake. 1999. *Peace, Power, Righteousness: An Indigenous Manifesto*. Don Mills, ON: Oxford University Press Canada.

Allen, Paula Gunn. 1992. *The Sacred Hoop*. Boston: Beacon.

Amnesty International. 2004. *Stolen Sisters: A Human Rights Response to Discrimination and Violence against Indigenous Women in Canada*. https://www.amnesty.ca/sites/default/files/amr200032004enstolensisters.pdf.

Anderson, Benedict. 1991. *Imagined Communities*. London: Verso.

Anderson, Kim, and Bonita Lawrence. 2003. *Strong Women Stories: Native Vision and Community Survival*. Toronto: Sumach Press.

Arendt, Hannah. 1973. *The Origins of Totalitarianism*. New York: Harcourt, Brace, Jovanovich.

Armstrong, Jeanette. 1998. "The Disempowerment of First North American Native Peoples and Empowerment through Their Writing." In *An Anthology of Canadian Native Literature in English*, ed. Daniel David Moses and Terry Goldie, 239–42. Toronto: Oxford University Press.

Armstrong, Jeanette, and Roxana Ng. 2005. "Deconstructing Race, Deconstructing Racism (with Postscript 2004): A Conversation between Jeannette Armstrong and Roxana Ng." In *Situating "Race" and Racisms in Space, Time, and Theory: Critical Essays for Activists and Scholars*, ed. Jo-Anne Lee and John Lutz, 30–45. Montreal and Kingston: McGill-Queen's University Press.

Audette, Trish. 2005. "Another Sex Worker Declared Missing: Métis Woman Tried but Failed to Get off the Street." *Edmonton Journal*, October 21, B1.

Backhouse, Constance B. 1985. "Nineteenth-Century Canadian Prostitution Law: Reflection of a Discriminatory Society." *Social History/Histoire sociale* 18 (36): 387–423.

Balfour, Gillian, and Elizabeth Comack, eds. 2006. *Criminalizing Women: Gender and (In)Justice in Neo-Liberal Times.* Halifax: Fernwood.

Barrera, Jorge. 2018. "Ottawa to Increase Funding for First Nations Child Welfare Services." *CBC News,* February 1. http://www.cbc.ca/news/indigenous/ottawa-fnchildwelfare-tribunal-1.4513951.

Beads, Tina, and Rauna Kuokkanen. 2007. "Aboriginal Feminist Action on Violence against Women." In *Making Space for Indigenous Feminism,* ed. Joyce Green, 221–32. Halifax: Fernwood.

Belanger, Jeff, ed. 2009. *Encyclopedia of Haunted Places: Ghostly Locales from around the World.* Rev. ed. Franklin Lakes, NJ: Career.

Benjamin, Walter. 1968. *Illuminations.* Edited and with an introduction by Hannah Arendt. Translated by Harry Zohn. New York: Schocken Books.

–. 2002. *The Arcades Project.* Trans. Howard Eiland and Kevin McLaughlin. New York: Belknap.

Berlant, Lauren, and Michael Warner. 1998. "Sex in Public." *Critical Inquiry* 24 (2): 547–66.

Bhabha, Homi K. 1990. "DissemiNation: Time, Narrative, and the Margins of the Modern Nation." In *Nation and Narration,* ed. Homi K. Bhabha, 291–322. London: Routledge.

Biehl, João Guilherme. 2001. "Vita: Life in a Zone of Social Abandonment." *Social Text* 19 (3): 131–49.

Blackstock, Cindy. 2007. "Residential Schools: Did They Really Close or Just Morph into Child Welfare?" *Indigenous Law Journal* 6 (1): 71–78.

Blackwell, Adrian. 2005. "The Gentrification of Gentrification and Other Strategies of Toronto's Creative Class." *Fuse Magazine* 29 (1): 28–37.

Blomley, Nicholas. 2004. *Unsettling the City: Urban Land and the Politics of Property.* New York: Taylor and Francis.

Bourdieu, Pierre. 1999. "Site Effects." In *The Weight of the World: Social Suffering in Contemporary Society,* ed. Pierre Bourdieu, 123–29. Stanford, CA: Stanford University Press.

Bourgeois, Robyn S. 2014a. "An RCMP Report Won't End Violence against Aboriginal Women." *Huffington Post,* May 18. http://www.huffingtonpost.ca/robyn-bourgeois/rcmp-aboriginal-women_b_5345651.html.

–. 2014b. *Warrior Women: Indigenous Women's Anti-Violence Engagement with the Canadian State.* University of Toronto.

Brown, Wendy. 2001. *Politics out of History.* Princeton, NJ: Princeton University Press.

Burk, Adrienne L. 2003. "Private Griefs, Public Places." *Political Geography* 22 (3): 317–33.

Butler, Judith. 2004. *Precarious Life: The Powers of Mourning and Violence.* London: Verso.

–. 2009. *Frames of War: When Is Life Grievable?* London: Verso.

Butler, Judith, and Athena Athanasiou. 2013. *Dispossession: The Performative in the Political.* Cambridge: Polity.

Butler, William Francis. 1872. *The Great Lone Land: A Narrative of Travel and Adventure in the North-West of America.* London: Sampson Low, Marston, Low, and Searle.

Bynum, Bill. 2000. "Discarded Diagnoses: Drapetomania." *Lancet* 356 (9241): 1615.

Byrd, Jodi A. 2011. *The Transit of Empire: Indigenous Critiques of Colonialism.* Minneapolis: University of Minnesota Press.

Canadian Association of University Teachers. 2017. *CAUT Guide to Acknowledging First Peoples & Traditional Territory.* September. https://www.caut.ca/sites/default/files/caut-guide-to-acknowledging-first-peoples-and-traditional-territory-2017-09.pdf.

Canadian Lung Association. 2019a. "The Sanatorium Age: Introduction." http://tb.lung.ca/tbhistory/sanatoriums/index.html.

–. 2019b. "The Sanatorium Age: Life." http://tb.lung.ca/tbhistory/sanatoriums/life.html.

Canadian Press. 2017a. "Families Call for 'Hard Reset' of MMIWG Inquiry." *CTV News,* August 8. https://www.ctvnews.ca/politics/families-call-for-hard-reset-of-mmiwg-inquiry-1.3537010.

–. 2017b. "Missing, Murdered Indigenous Women Inquiry in 'Serious Trouble': Advocates." *CTV News,* May 15. https://www.ctvnews.ca/canada/missing-murdered-indigenous-women-inquiry-in-serious-trouble-advocates-1.3414529.

Canadian Tuberculosis Association. 1950. "Indians Are Winning Battle with TB." *Canadian Tuberculosis Association Bulletin* 28 (4): 4.

Carter, Carl. 2004. "Journey Continues to Heal School Trauma." *Alberta Sweetgrass: The Aboriginal Newspaper of Alberta* 11 (10). https://ammsa.com/publications/alberta-sweetgrass/journey-continues-heal-school-trauma.

Carter, Sarah. 1990. *Lost Harvests: Prairie Indian Reserve Farmers and Government Policy.* Montreal and Kingston: McGill-Queen's University Press.

–. 1993. "Categories and Terrains of Exclusion: Constructing the 'Indian Woman' in the Early Settlement Era in Western Canada." *Great Plains Quarterly* 13 (3): 147–61. http://digitalcommons.unl.edu/greatplainsquarterly/764.

–. 1997. *Capturing Women: The Manipulation of Cultural Imagery in Canada's Prairie West.* Montreal and Kingston: McGill-Queen's University Press.

–. 1999. *Aboriginal People and Colonizers of Western Canada to 1900.* Toronto: University of Toronto Press.

–. 2006. "Britishness, 'Foreignness,' Women and Land in Western Canada, 1890s–1920s." *Humanities Research* 13 (1): 43–60.

Carter, Sarah, and Walter Hildebrandt. 2006. "'A better life with honour': Treaty 6 (1876) and Treaty 7 (1877) with Alberta First Nations." In *Alberta Formed Alberta Transformed,* vol. 1, ed. Michael Payne, Donald Wetherell, and Catherine Cavanaugh, 235–68. Edmonton/Calgary: University of Alberta Press/University of Calgary Press.

CBC (Canadian Broadcasting Corporation). 1989. *Seeking Treatment, Losing Family.* Radio broadcast, January 30. Accessed November 26, 2006. http://archives.cbc.ca/IDC-758835325/science_technology/tuberculosis/clip5.

–. 2013. "Premiers Back National Inquiry on Missing Aboriginal Women." *CBC News,* July 24. http://www.cbc.ca/news/canada/story/2013/07/24/pol-premiers-meeting-aboriginal-leaders-wednesday.html.

–. 2018. "$1.1B Class-Action Lawsuit Filed on Behalf of Former 'Indian Hospital' Patients." *CBC News,* January 30. https://www.cbc.ca/news/canada/toronto/indian-hospital-class-action-1.4508659.

CCHC (Charles Camsell History Committee). 1985. *The Camsell Mosaic: The Charles Camsell Hospital, 1945–1985.* Edmonton: Charles Camsell History Committee.

Centre to End All Sexual Exploitation (CEASE). 2019. http://www.ceasenow.org.

Chase, Steven. 2014. "Harper Continues to Resist Calls for Missing Aboriginal Women Inquiry." *Globe and Mail,* December 17. https://www.theglobeandmail.com/news/politics/harper-continues-to-resist-calls-for-missing-aboriginal-women-inquiry/article22133991/.

City of Edmonton. 2007. "Edmonton's Cultural Capital Program." http://www.edmontonculturalcapital.com/edmontonsccp.asp.

–. 2008. *The Quarters August Newsletter.* Accessed December 20, 2009. http://www.edmonton.ca/city_government/documents/CityGov/August_2008_Newsletter.pdf.

–. 2014. *The Quarters Downtown Area Redevelopment Plan.* https://www.edmonton.ca/city_government/documents/plans_in_effect/The_Quarters_Downtown_ARP_Consolidation.pdf.

–. 2019. "Population History." https://www.edmonton.ca/city_government/facts_figures/population-history.aspx.

Comack, Elizabeth, and Gillian Balfour. 2004. *The Power to Criminalize: Violence, Inequality, and the Law.* Halifax: Fernwood.

Conrad, Norman Charles. 1999. *Reading the Entrails: An Alberta Ecohistory.* Calgary: University of Calgary Press.

Cormier, Ryan, and Jim Farrell. 2005. "Victim Tried to Turn Life Around." *Edmonton Journal,* April 19. http://www.mapinc.org/drugnews/v05/n640/a02.html?3427.

Coulthard, Glen S. 2014. *Red Skin, White Masks: Rejecting the Colonial Politics of Recognition.* Minneapolis: University of Minnesota Press.

Culhane, Dara. 1998. *The Pleasure of the Crown: Anthropology, Law and First Nations.* Burnaby, BC: Talonbooks.

–. 2003. "Their Spirits Live within Us: Aboriginal Women in Downtown Eastside Vancouver Emerging into Visibility." *American Indian Quarterly* 27 (3–4): 593–606.

Cultural Memory Group. 2006. *Remembering Women Murdered by Men: Memorials across Canada.* Toronto: Sumach.

–. 2016. "Memorials for Women across Canada: The Politics of Remembering Women Murdered by Men." http://www.missingpeople.net/memorials_for_women.htm.

Cunningham, Pamela M. 2005. "Edmonton's 'Forgotten' Cemetery." In *Edmonton on Location: River City Chronicles,* ed. Heather Zwicker, 147–55. Edmonton: NeWest.

Daniel, Thomas M. 1997. *Captain of Death: The Story of Tuberculosis.* Rochester, NY: University of Rochester Press.

de Certeau, Michel. 1984. *The Practice of Everyday Life.* Trans. Steven Rendall. Berkeley: University of California Press.

Dean, Amber. 2009. "Hauntings: Representations of Vancouver's Disappeared Women." PhD diss., University of Alberta.

–. 2015. *Remembering Vancouver's Disappeared Women: Settler Colonialism and the Difficulty of Inheritance.* Toronto: University of Toronto Press.

Deer, Sarah. 2015. *The Beginning and End of Rape: Confronting Sexual Violence in Native America.* Minneapolis: Minnesota Press.

–. 2018. "Native People and Violent Crime: Gendered Violence and Tribal Jurisdiction." *Du Bois Review* 15 (1): 89–106. doi:10.1017/S1742058X18000012.

Dehaene, Michiel, and Lieven De Cauter, eds. 2008. *Heterotopia and the City: Public Space in a Postcivil Society.* New York: Routledge.

Deleuze, Gilles, and Felix Guattari. 1987. *A Thousand Plateaus: Capitalism and Schizophrenia.* Trans. Brian Massumi. Minneapolis: University of Minnesota Press.

–. 1994. *What Is Philosophy?* Trans. Hugh Tomlinson and Graham Burchell. New York: Columbia University Press.

Deloria, Vine. 1995. *Red Earth, White Lies: Native Americans and the Myth of Scientific Fact.* Golden, CO: Fulcrum.

Dempsey, Hugh A. 2006. "1870: A Year of Violence and Change." In *Alberta Formed, Alberta Transformed,* vol. 1, ed. Michael Payne, Donald Wetherall, and Catherine Cavanaugh, 208–34. Edmonton/Calgary: University of Alberta Press/University of Calgary Press.

Dickason, Olive. 1984. *The Myth of the Savage and the Beginnings of French Colonialism in the Americas.* Edmonton: University of Alberta Press.

Dransfeld, Rosie, dir. 2012. *Who Cares.* National Film Board of Canada.

Dubisch, Jill. 1989. "Death and Social Change in Greece." *Anthropological Quarterly* 62 (40): 189–200.

Edmonton Journal. 2009. "Murdered Aboriginal Women 'Not Garbage.'" May 1. https://www.pressreader.com/canada/edmonton-journal/20090501/281689725758437.

Ellis, Erin. 1990. "Cairn Tribute to Native TB Victims: Families at Peace with Knowing Fate of Forgotten Northerners." *Edmonton Journal,* June 24, B1.

Fanon, Frantz. 1963. *The Wretched of the Earth.* Trans. Richard Philcox. New York: Grove.

–. 1967. *Black Skin, White Masks.* Trans. Charles Lam Markmann. New York: Grove.

Farmer, Paul. 2004. "An Anthropology of Structural Violence." *Current Anthropology* 45 (3): 305–25.

Ferguson, Robert George. 1955. *Studies in Tuberculosis.* Toronto: University of Toronto Press.

Ferris, Shawna. 2007. "Dangerous Order: Globalization, Canadian Cities, and Street-Involved Sex Work." PhD diss., McMaster University.

–. 2015. *Street Sex Work and Canadian Cities: Resisting a Dangerous Order.* Edmonton: University of Alberta Press.

Fong, Petti. 2008. "Edmonton Killer Preying on Prostitutes." *Toronto Star,* January 6. https://www.thestar.com/news/canada/2008/01/06/edmonton_killer_preying_on_prostitutes.html.

Foucault, Michel. 1970. *The Order of Things: An Archaeology of the Human Sciences.* London: Tavistock.

–. 1977. *Discipline and Punish: The Birth of the Prison.* Trans. Alan Sheridan. Reprint, New York: Vintage Books, 1995.

–. 1980. *Power/Knowledge: Selected Interviews and Other Writings, 1972–1977.* Ed. Colin Gordon. Trans. Colin Gordon, Leo Marshall, John Mepham, and Kate Soper. New York: Pantheon Books.

–. 1990. *The History of Sexuality: An Introduction*. Vol. 1. Trans. Robert Hurley. New York: Vintage Books.

–. 2003. *"Society Must Be Defended": Lectures at the Collège de France, 1975–1976*. Trans. David Macey. New York: Picador.

Fowlie, Jonathan. 2003. "Edmontonians Fear Serial Killer Preying on Sex-Trade Workers." *Globe and Mail*, January 17. https://www.theglobeandmail.com/news/national/edmontonians-fear-serial-killer-preying-on-sex-trade-workers/article22393019/.

Francis, Daniel. 1997. *National Dreams: Myth, Memory, and Canadian History*. Vancouver: Arsenal Pulp.

Freud, Sigmund. 1914. *The Psychopathology of Everyday Life*. Trans. A.A. Brill. New York: W.W. Norton.

Fried, L. 1984. "Early Settlement: Sales of Land and Factors Leading to Settlement." In *South Edmonton Saga*, ed. Papaschase Historical Society, 29–32. Edmonton: Papaschase Historical Society.

Friesen, Gerald. 1987. *The Canadian Prairies: A History*. Toronto: University of Toronto Press.

Galloway, Gloria. 2017. "Inquiry into Missing and Murdered Women a Failure: Indigenous Group." *Globe and Mail*, May 16. https://www.theglobeandmail.com/news/politics/inquiry-into-missing-and-murdered-women-a-failure-indigenous-group-says/article35003027/.

Galtung, Johan. 1969. "Violence, Peace, and Peace Research." *Journal of Peace Studies* 6 (3): 167–91.

Geddes, Gary. 2017. *Medicine Unbundled: A Journey through the Minefields of Indigenous Health Care*. Toronto: Heritage House.

Gell, Alfred. 1992. *The Anthropology of Time: Cultural Constructions of Temporal Maps and Images*. Oxford: Berg.

Gibbs Van Brunschot, Erin. 2003. "Community Policing and 'John Schools.'" *Canadian Review of Sociology/Revue canadienne de sociologie* 40 (2): 215–32.

Goffman Erving. 1961. *Asylums: Essays on the Social Situation of Mental Patients and Other Inmates*. Harmondsworth, UK: Penguin.

Gordon, Avery. 1997. *Ghostly Matters: Haunting and the Sociological Imagination*. Minneapolis: University of Minneapolis Press.

Government of Canada. 2016. "A Better Future for Indigenous Peoples." In Government of Canada, *Growing the Middle Class*, 133–48. Ottawa: Department of Finance Canada. https://www.budget.gc.ca/2016/docs/plan/budget2016-en.pdf.

–. 2019. "Tuberculosis: Monitoring." https://www.canada.ca/en/public-health/services/diseases/tuberculosis/surveillance.html.

Granzow, Kara, and Amber Dean. 2007. "Revanchism in the Canadian West: Gentrification and Resettlement in a Prairie City." *TOPIA: Canadian Journal of Cultural Studies* 18: 89–106.

Graybill, Andrew R. 2007. *Policing the Great Plains: Rangers, Mounties, and the North American Frontier, 1875–1910.* Lincoln: University of Nebraska Press.

Gregory, Derek. 2004. *The Colonial Present: Afghanistan, Palestine, Iraq.* Malden, MA: Blackwell.

Grygier, Pat Sandiford. 1994. *A Long Way from Home: The Tuberculosis Epidemic among the Inuit.* Montreal and Kingston: McGill-Queen's University Press.

Hall, Stuart. 1992. "The Question of Cultural Identity." In *Modernity and Its Futures,* ed. Stuart Hall, David Held, and Anthony McGrew, 273–325. Cambridge: Polity.

–. 2006. "Black Diaspora Artists in Britain: Three 'Moments' in Post-War History." *History Workshop Journal* (61): 1–24.

Hanon, Andrew. 2007. "New Plaque for Slain Women Now Outdated." *Edmonton Sun,* July 12. http://www.flickr.com/photos/joshuatree/891384210/.

–. 2008. "Tortured by Memories: A Former Resident Dug Graves as a Youngster – A One-Handed Boy Haunts Him Still." *Edmonton Sun,* February 24. http://media.knet.ca/node/3495.

Haraway, Donna J. 1991. *Simians, Cyborgs, and Women: The Reinvention of Nature.* New York: Routledge.

Harding, Katherine. 2005a. "The 'Killing Fields' of Edmonton." *Globe and Mail,* August 2. https://www.theglobeandmail.com/news/national/the-killing-fields-of-edmonton/article984387/.

–. 2005b. "Mounties Finally Admit Serial Killer Is Prowling Edmonton." *Globe and Mail,* June 18. https://www.theglobeandmail.com/news/national/mounties-finally-admit-serial-killer-is-prowling-edmonton/article18230493/.

Harootunian, Harry D. 1996. "The Benjamin Effect: Modernism, Repetition, and the Path to Different Cultural Imaginaries." In *Walter Benjamin and the Demands of History,* ed. Michael P. Steinberg, 62–87. Ithaca, NY: Cornell University Press.

Haudenosaunee Confederacy. 2019. "Who We Are." https://www.haudenosauneeconfederacy.com/who-we-are/.

Healy, Veronica. 2008. Personal communication with author, February 4.

Heisz, Andrew, and Logan McLeod. 2004. *Low-Income in Census Metropolitan Areas, 1980–2000.* Ottawa: Statistics Canada. http://www.urbancenter.utoronto.ca/pdfs/elibrary/StatsCan_Low-Income-in-Citi.pdf.

Highet, Megan J. 2005. "Body Snatching and Grave Robbing: Bodies for Science." *History and Anthropology* 16 (4): 415–40.

Hodgson, Corrine. 1982. "The Social and Political Implications of Tuberculosis among Native Canadians." *Canadian Review of Sociology and Anthropology* 19 (4): 502–12.

Hubbard, Phil. 1999. *Sex and the City: Geographies of Prostitution in the Urban West.* Aldershot, UK: Ashgate.

Hubbard, Phil, Roger Matthews, and Jane Scoular. 2008. "Regulating Sex Work in the EU: Prostitute Women and the New Spaces of Exclusion." *Gender, Place and Culture: A Journal of Feminist Geography* 15 (2): 137–52.

Hubbard, Phil, and Teela Sanders. 2003. "Making Space for Sex Work: Female Street Prostitution and the Production of Urban Space." *International Journal of Urban and Regional Research* 27 (1): 75–89.

Human Rights Watch. 2013. *Those Who Take Us Away: Abusive Policing and Failures in Protection of Indigenous Women and Girls in Northern British Columbia, Canada.* http://www.hrw.org/reports/2013/02/13/those-who-take-us-away.

Humphreys, Peter. 1989. "*The Magic Mountain* – A Time Capsule of Tuberculosis Treatment in the Early Twentieth Century." *Canadian Bulletin of Medical History* 6 (2): 147–63.

Hunt, Sarah. 2014. "Ontologies of Indigeneity: The Politics of Embodying a Concept." *Cultural Geographies* 21 (1): 27–32.

–. 2017. "Foreword." In Julie Kaye, *Responding to Human Trafficking: Dispossession, Colonial Violence, and Resistance among Indigenous and Racialized Women,* ix–xv. Toronto: University of Toronto Press.

Huyssen, Andreas. 2003. *Present Pasts: Urban Palimpsests and the Politics of Memory.* Stanford, CA: Stanford University Press.

Institute for the Advancement of Aboriginal Women. 2019. "About Us." http://iaaw.ca/about-us/.

Jacobs, Beverly, and Andrea Williams. 2008. "Legacy of Residential Schools: Missing and Murdered Aboriginal Women." In *From Truth to Reconciliation: Transforming the Legacy of Residential Schools,* ed. Marlene Brant Castellano, Linda Archibald, and Mike DeGagné, 119–40. Ottawa: Aboriginal Healing Foundation.

Jeffs, Allyson. 2004. "Final Ceremony Honours Aboriginals Buried behind School." *Edmonton Journal,* September 5, A11.

Jiwani, Yasmin, and Mary Lynn Young. 2006. "Missing and Murdered Women: Reproducing Marginality in News Discourse." *Canadian Journal of Communication Studies* 31 (4): 895–917.

Jones, Reece. 2009. "Categories, Borders and Boundaries." *Progress in Human Geography* 32 (2): 174–89.

Kane, Paul. 1859. *Wanderings of an Artist among the Indians of North America from Canada to Vancouver's Island and Oregon through the Hudson's Bay Company's Territory and Back Again.* London: Longman, Brown, Green, Longmans, and Roberts.

Kaye, Julie. 2017. *Responding to Human Trafficking: Dispossession, Colonial Violence, and Resistance among Indigenous and Racialized Women.* Toronto: University of Toronto Press.

Kelm, Mary Ellen. 1998. *Colonizing Bodies: Aboriginal Health and Healing in British Columbia, 1900–1950.* Vancouver: UBC Press.

–. 2005. "Diagnosing the Discursive Indian: Medicine, Gender and the 'Dying Race.'" *Ethnohistory* 52 (2): 371– 406.

Kimmel, Michael, and Jacqueline Holler. 2011. *The Gendered Society: Canadian Edition.* New York: Oxford University Press.

Kirkup, Kristy. 2016. "Number of Missing and Murdered Indigenous Women Higher than Thought: Minister." *Toronto Star,* February 15. https://www.thestar.com/news/canada/2016/02/15/number-of-missing-and-murdered-indigenous-women-higher-than-thought-minister.html.

Kleiss, Karen, and Jim Farrell. 2004. "Grisly 'Dumping Ground' Discovery." *Edmonton Journal,* June 13, A1.

Kristeva, Julia. 1982. *Powers of Horror: An Essay on Abjection.* Trans. Leon S. Roudiez. New York: Columbia University Press.

Law, John. 2004. *After Method: Mess in Social Science Research.* London: Routledge.

Lawrence, Bonita. 2003. "Gender, Race and the Regulation of Native Identity in Canada and the United States: An Overview." *Hypatia* 18 (2): 3–31.

Lawrence, Bonita, and Enakshi Dua. 2005. "Decolonizing Antiracism." *Social Justice* 32 (40): 120–43.

Lefebvre, Henri. 1991. *The Production of Space.* Oxford: Blackwell.

Legacy of Hope Foundation. 2001a. "About the Partners and Funders." http://wherearethechildren.ca/en/about/.

–. 2001b. "Where Are the Children? Healing the Legacy of the Residential Schools." http://wherearethechildren.ca/en/.

Legislative Assembly of Alberta. 2005. *Alberta Hansard,* May 16. http://www.assembly.ab.ca/ISYS/LADDAR_files%5Cdocs%5Chansards%5Chan%5Clegislature_26%5Csession_1%5C20050516_1330_01_han.pdf.

Lett, Dan. 2013. "Emergency Department Problems Raised at Sinclair Inquest." *Canadian Medical Association Journal* 185 (17): 1483.

Little Bear, Leroy. 1998. "Aboriginal Relationships to the Land and Resources." In *Sacred Lands: Aboriginal World Views, Claims and Conflicts,* ed. Jill Oakes, Rick Riewe, Kathi Kinew, and Elaine Maloney, 15–20. Edmonton: Canadian Circumpolar Institute.

Ljunggren, David. 2009. "Every G20 Nation Wants to Be Canada, Stephen Harper Insists." *Global News,* September 26. Accessed October 22, 2009. http://news.

globaltv.com/money/Every+nation+wants+Canada+Stephen+Harper+insists/2037877/story.html.

Lowman, John. 2000. "Violence and the Outlaw Status of (Street) Prostitution in Canada." *Violence against Women* 6 (9): 987–1011.

Loyie, Florence, and Ryan Cormier. 2005. "Latest Body in Farm Field Another Prostitute." *Edmonton Journal,* May 10, A1.

Lutz, John Sutton, ed. 2007. *Myth and Memory: Stories of Indigenous-European Contact.* Vancouver: UBC Press.

Lux, Maureen. 1996. "Beyond Biology: Disease and Its Impact on the Canadian Plains Native People, 1880–1930." PhD diss., Simon Fraser University.

–. 1998. "Perfect Subjects: Race, Tuberculosis, and the Qu'Appelle BCG Vaccine Trial." *Canadian Bulletin of Medical History* 15 (2): 277–95.

–. 2001. *Medicine That Walks: Disease, Medicine, and Canadian Plains Native People, 1880–1940.* Toronto: University of Toronto Press.

–. 2006. "White Blood: Race, Tuberculosis, and Aboriginal People, 1920–1950." Paper presented at "A Day of History of Medicine," University of Alberta, Edmonton, April.

–. 2016. *Separate Beds: A History of Indian Hospitals in Canada, 1920–1980s.* Toronto: University of Toronto Press.

–. 2017. "Indian Hospitals in Canada." *Canadian Encyclopedia.* https://www.thecanadianencyclopedia.ca/en/article/indian-hospitals-in-canada.

MacGregor, James G. 1949. *Blankets and Beads: A History of the Saskatchewan River.* Edmonton: Institute of Applied Art.

MacIsaac, Daniel. 2008. "Tales of Buried Bodies." *Edmonton Sun,* January 4. http://archives.algomau.ca/main/sites/default/files/2010-061_013_027.pdf.

Mackey, Eva. 1999. *The House of Difference: Cultural Politics and National Identity in Canada.* London: Routledge.

MacLaren, Ian S. 1989. "'I Came to Rite Thare Portraits': Paul Kane's Journal of His Western Travels, 1846–1848." *American Art Journal* 21 (2): 7–22.

Mah, Bill. 2006. "New Day for Downtown East: City Hall Committed to Redeveloping Area; Tax Incentives Possible." *Edmonton Journal,* January 30, A9.

Mahaffy, Cheryl. 2007. "The Hidden Face of Prosperity." *Alberta Views,* November 1. https://albertaviews.ca/hidden-face-prosperity/.

Mahoney, Jill. 2004. "Serial Killer May Be at Work, Alberta Police Say." *Globe and Mail,* June 16. https://www.theglobeandmail.com/news/national/serial-killer-may-be-at-work-alberta-police-say/article1134038/.

Mair, Kimberly. 2016. *Guerrilla Aesthetics: Art, Memory, and the West German Urban Guerrilla.* Montreal and Kingston: McGill-Queen's University Press.

Manasc Isaac Architects. 2007. "Traditional Burial Grounds and Fort Edmonton Cemetery: Symbolism." https://apps.manascisaac.com/projects/rossdale_memorial.

Marlow, D. 2005. "6th Annual Memorial: Innocence Lost." *Envoy* Fall: 3. Accessed December 17, 2009. http://www.e4calberta.org/pdfs/envoy2005-fall.pdf.

Mason, Gail. 2002. "Recognition and Reformulation." *Current Issues in Criminal Justice* 13 (3): 251–68.

Mbembe, Achille. 2001. *On the Postcolony.* Berkeley: University of California Press.

–. 2003. "Necropolitics." Trans. Libby Meintjes. *Public Culture* 15 (1): 11–40.

McClintock, Anne. 1995. *Imperial Leather: Race, Gender and Sexuality in the Colonial Contest.* New York: Routledge.

McGillivray, Anne, and Brenda Comaskey. 1999. *Black Eyes All of the Time: Intimate Violence, Aboriginal Women, and the Justice System.* Toronto: University of Toronto Press.

McIvor, Sharon Donna. 2004. "Aboriginal Women Unmasked: Using Equality Litigation to Advance Women's Rights." *Canadian Journal of Women and the Law* 16 (1): 106–36.

McManus, Sheila. 2005. *The Line Which Separates: Race, Gender, and the Making of the Alberta-Montana Borderlands.* Edmonton: University of Alberta Press.

McNeill, Laurie. 2008. "Death and the Maidens: Vancouver's Missing Women, the Montreal Massacre, and Commemoration's Blind Spots." *Canadian Review of American Studies* 38 (3): 375–98.

Mitchell, Katharyne. 2006. "Geographies of Identity: The New Exceptionalism." *Progress in Human Geography* 30 (1): 95–106.

Moore, P.E. 1961. "No Longer Captain: A History of Tuberculosis and Its Control amongst Canadian Indians." *Canadian Medical Association Journal* 84 (18): 1012–16.

Morrison, Toni. (1987) 2004. *Beloved.* Reprint, New York: Vintage Books.

Moses, Dirk A. 2005. "Hayden White, Traumatic Nationalism, and the Public Role of History." *History and Theory* 44 (3): 311–32.

Moten, Fred, and Stefano Harney. 2004. "The University and the Undercommons: Seven Theses." *Social Text* 22 (2): 101–15.

Native Land Digital. 2019. "Native Land." Map. https://native-land.ca.

Native Women's Association of Canada (NWAC). 2009. *Voices of Our Sisters in Spirit: A Report to Families and Communities.* 2nd ed. https://nwac.ca/wp-content/uploads/2015/05/NWAC_Voices-of-Our-Sisters-In-Spirit_2nd-Edition_March-2009.pdf.

–. 2010. *What Their Stories Tell Us: Research Findings from the Sisters in Spirit Initiative.* https://nwac.ca/wp-content/uploads/2015/07/2010-What-Their-Stories-Tell-Us-Research-Findings-SIS-Initiative.pdf.

–. 2015. "Fact Sheet: Violence against Aboriginal Women." https://www.nwac.ca/wp-content/uploads/2015/05/Fact_Sheet_Violence_Against_Aboriginal_Women.pdf.

–. 2019. "Fact Sheet – MMIWG." July 25. https://www.nwac.ca/resource/fact-sheet-mmiwg/.

Nechi Insitute. 2017. "Welcome to Nechi." https://nechi.com/.

Northcott, Herbert, and Donna Wilson. 2001. *Dying and Death in Canada.* Peterborough, ON: Broadview.

O'Neill, Maggie, Rosie Campbell, Phil Hubbard, Jane Pitcher, and Jane Scoular. 2008. "Living with the Other: Street Sex Work, Contingent Communities and Degrees of Tolerance." *Crime, Media, Culture* 4 (1): 73–93.

Online Cree Dictionary. 2019. "Amiskwaciwâskahikan." http://www.creedictionary.com/search/index.php?q=amiskwaciw%C3%A2skahikan&scope=1.

Owram, Doug. 1980. *The Promise of Eden: The Canadian Expansionist Movement and the Idea of the West, 1856–1900.* Toronto: University of Toronto Press.

Palmater, Pamela D. 2011. "Stretched beyond Human Limits: Death by Poverty in First Nations." *Canadian Review of Social Policy* (65–66): 112–27.

–. 2016. "Shining Light on the Dark Places: Addressing Police Racism and Sexualized Violence against Indigenous Women and Girls in the National Inquiry." *Canadian Journal of Women and the Law* 28 (2): 253–84.

Palmater, Pamela D., and Sylvia McAdam. 2018. "Idle No More." In *Race and Racialization: Essential Readings,* 2nd ed., ed. Tania Das Gupta, Carl E. James, Chris Anderson, Grace-Edward Galabuz, and Roger C.A. Maaka, 690–94. Toronto: Canadian Scholars Press.

Pannekoek, Frits. 2006. "On the Edge of Great Transformation, 1857–58." In *Alberta Formed Alberta Transformed,* vol. 1, ed. Michael Payne, Donald Wetherell, and Catherine Cavanaugh, 181–207. Edmonton/Calgary: University of Alberta Press/University of Calgary Press.

Patton, Paul. 2003. "Concept and Politics in Derrida and Deleuze." *Critical Horizons* 4 (2): 157–75.

Peake, Linda, and Brian Ray. 2001. "Racializing the Canadian Landscape: Whiteness, Uneven Geographies, and Social Justice." *Canadian Geographer* 45 (1): 180–86.

Perreault, Samuel. 2011. "Violent Victimization of Aboriginal People in the Canadian Provinces, 2009." Statistics Canada. Retrieved from http://www.statcan.gc.ca/pub/85-002-x/2011001/article/11415-eng.htm.

Peters, Evelyn J. 1998. "Subversive Spaces: First Nations Women and the City." *Environment and Planning D: Society and Space* 16 (6): 665–85.

Phillips, S. 2006. "Gentrifying Downtown East Will Leave Poor Out in the Cold, Community Fears." *Vue Weekly*, April 6. Accessed December 20, 2009. http://www.vueweekly.com/article.php?id=3546.

Pickles, Katie, and Myra Rutherdale, eds. 2006. *Contact Zones: Aboriginal and Settler Women in Canada's Colonial Past.* Vancouver: UBC Press.

Pillow, Wanda. 2003. "Confession, Catharsis, or Cure? Rethinking the Uses of Reflexivity as Methodological Power in Qualitative Research." *International Journal of Qualitative Studies in Education* 16 (2): 175–96.

Poundmaker's Lodge. 2019. "Tansi and Welcome!" http://poundmakerslodge.ca/.

Povinelli, Elizabeth A. 2011. *Economies of Abandonment: Social Belonging and Exclusion in Late Liberalism.* Durham, NC: Duke University Press.

Pratt, Geraldine. 2005. "Abandoned Women and Spaces of the Exception." *Antipode* 37 (5): 1052–78.

Pratt, Mary Louise. 1992. *Imperial Eyes: Travel Writing and Transculturation.* London: Routledge.

Pruden, Jana G. 2011. "Eight Years in, Project Kare Counts Victories on Its Own Terms." *Edmonton Journal*, October 10. https://www.pressreader.com/canada/edmonton-journal/20111010/281595237286545.

Razack, Sherene. 1998a. *Looking White People in the Eye: Gender, Race, and Culture in Courtrooms and Classrooms.* Toronto: University of Toronto Press.

–. 1998b. "Race, Space, and Prostitution." *Canadian Journal of Women and the Law* 10 (2): 338–76.

–. 2000. "Gendered Racial Violence and Spatialized Justice: The Murder of Pamela George." *Canadian Journal of Law and Society* 15 (2): 91–130.

–, ed. 2002. *Race, Space and the Law: Unmapping a White Settler Society.* Toronto: Between the Lines.

–. 2007. *Casting Out: The Eviction of Muslims from Western Law and Politics.* Toronto: University of Toronto Press.

–. 2013. "Timely Deaths: Medicalizing the Deaths of Aboriginal People in Police Custody." *Law, Culture and the Humanities* 9 (2): 352–74.

–. 2014. "'It Happened More Than Once': Freezing Deaths in Saskatchewan." *Canadian Journal of Women and the Law* 26 (1): 51–80.

–. 2016. "Gendering Disposability." *Canadian Journal of Women and the Law* 28 (2): 285–307.

RCMP (Royal Canadian Mounted Police). 2014. *Missing and Murdered Aboriginal*

Women: A National Operational Overview. http://publications.gc.ca/collections/collection_2014/grc-rcmp/PS64-115-2014-eng.pdf.

–. 2015. "KARE/Pro-Active Team." http://www.rcmp-grc.gc.ca/ab/community-communaute/mis-dis/kare/index-eng.htm.

Regan, Paulette. 2010. *Unsettling the Settler Within: Indian Residential Schools, Truth Telling, and Reconciliation in Canada.* Vancouver: UBC Press.

Reitmanova, Sylvia, and Diane L. Gustafson. 2012. "Coloring the White Plague: A Syndemic Approach to Immigrant Tuberculosis in Canada." *Ethnicity and Health* 17 (4): 403–18.

Remember Our Sisters Everywhere (ROSE). 2009. "Women's Memorials." http://www.communitywalk.com/womensmemorials.

Rosenberg, Sharon. 2000. "Standing in a Circle of Stone: Rupturing the Binds of Emblematic Memory." In *Between Hope and Despair: Pedagogy and the Remembrance of Historical Trauma,* ed. Roger Simon, Sharon Rosenberg, and Claudia Eppert, 75–89. Lanham, MD: Rowman and Littlefield.

–. 2013. "Mediations on Turning toward Violently Dead." In *Democracy in Crisis: Violence, Alterity, Community*, ed. Stella Gaon, 220–40.Manchester: University of Manchester Press.

Rosenberg, Sharon, Amber Dean, and Kara Granzow. 2010. "Centennial Hauntings: Reckoning with the 2005 Celebration of Alberta's History." *Journal of Memory Studies* 3 (4): 395–412.

Roth, Pamela. 2012. "Edmonton Murder Capital of Canada." *Edmonton Sun,* January 1. https://edmontonsun.com/2012/01/01/edmonton-murder-capital-of-canada/wcm/dce5e39d-acdb-47da-aede-322c432caac4.

Royal Commission on Aboriginal Peoples. 1996. *Report of the Royal Commission on Aboriginal Peoples.* Vol. 1, *Looking Forward, Looking Back.* Ottawa: Minister of Supply and Services Canada. http://publications.gc.ca/site/eng/9.819007/publication.html.

Said, Edward W. 1979. *Orientialism.* New York: Vintage Books.

–. 1994. *Culture and Imperialism.* New York: Vintage Books.

Sampson, Robert J. 2002. "Organized for What? Recasting Theories of Social (Dis) organization." In *Crime and Social Organization,* ed. Elin Waring and David Weisburd, 95–110. New Brunswick, NJ: Transaction.

Sampson, Robert J., and Lydia Bean. 2006. "Cultural Mechanisms and Killing Fields: A Revised Theory of Community-Level Racial Inequality." In *The Many Colors of Crime: Inequalities of Race, Ethnicity and Crime in America,* ed. Ruth D. Peterson, Lauren J. Krivo, and John Hagan, 8–37. New York: New York University Press.

Sanchez, Lisa E. 1997. "Boundaries of Legitimacy: Sex, Violence, Citizenship, and Community in a Local Sexual Economy." *Law and Social Inquiry* 22 (3): 543–80.

Sanday, Peggy Reeves. 1996. "Rape-Prone versus Rape-Free Campus Cultures." *Violence against Women* 2 (2): 191–208.

Schaefer, Otto. 1959. "Medical Observations and Problems in the Canadian Arctic: Part I." *Canadian Medical Association Journal* 81 (4): 248–53. https://www.ncbi.nlm.nih.gov/pmc/articles/PMC1831059/.

Schatzki, Theodore R. 1996. *Social Practices: A Wittgensteinian Approach to Human Activity and the Social.* Cambridge: Cambridge University Press.

Sibley, David. 1995. *Geographies of Exclusion.* London: Routledge.

Silman, Janet. 1987. *Enough Is Enough: Aboriginal Women Speak Out.* Toronto: Canadian Scholars Press.

Silver, Jim, Joan Hay, Parvin Ghorayshi, and Darlene Klyne. 2006. *In Their Own Voice: Building Urban Aboriginal Communities.* Halifax: Fernwood.

Simon, Roger I. 2005. *A Touch of the Past: Remembrance, Learning, and Ethics.* New York: Palgrave.

Simon, Roger I., Sharon Rosenberg, and Claudia Eppert, eds. 2000. *Between Hope and Despair: Pedagogy and the Remembrance of Historical Trauma.* Lanham, MD: Rowman and Littlefield.

Simpson, Audra. 2014. *Mohawk Interruptus: Political Life across the Borders of Settler States.* Durham, NC: Duke University Press.

–. 2016. "The State Is a Man: Theresa Spence, Loretta Saunders and the Gender of Settler Sovereignty." *Theory and Event* 19 (4). https://www.muse.jhu.edu/article/633280.

Simpson, Audra, and Andrea Smith, eds. 2014. *Theorizing Native Studies.* Durham, NC: Duke University Press.

Simpson, Leanne Betasamosake. 2014. "Not Murdered, Not Missing: Rebelling against Colonial Gender Violence." https://www.leannesimpson.ca/writings/not-murdered-not-missing-rebelling-against-colonial-gender-violence.

–. 2016. "Indigenous Resurgence and Co-Resistance." *Critical Ethnic Studies* 2 (2): 19–34. doi:10.5749/jcritethnstud.2.2.0019.

–. 2017. *As We Have Always Done: Indigenous Freedom through Radical Resistance.* Minneapolis: University of Minnesota Press.

Simpson, Leanne [Betasamosake], Wanda Nanibush, and Carol Williams. 2012. "The Resurgence of Indigenous Women's Knowledge and Resistance in Relation to Land and Territoriality: Transnational and Interdisciplinary Perspectives." *InTensions* (6): 1–7.

Sinnema, Jodie. 2002. "Every 'Date' Can Be Her Last: Death Stalks Women Who Stroll City's Underworld." *Edmonton Journal,* March 18, B1.

Sinnema, Jodie, and C. Purdy. 2003. "Murder Puts Prostitutes on Edge: Dead Woman Could Have Been Any One of Them, They Fear." *Edmonton Journal,* January 15, B1.

Smith, Andrea. 2003. "Not an Indian Tradition: The Sexual Colonization of Native Peoples." *Hypatia* 18 (2): 70–85.

–. 2005. *Conquest: Sexual Violence and American Indian Genocide.* Cambridge: South End.

–. 2014. "Native Studies at the Horizon of Death: Theorizing Ethnographic Entrapment and Settler Self-Reflexivity." In *Theorizing Native Studies,* ed. Audra Simpson and Andrea Smith, 207–34. Durham, NC: Duke University Press.

Smith, Linda Tuhiwai. 1999. *Decolonizing Methodologies: Research and Indigenous Peoples.* London: Zed Books.

Smith, Neil. 1996. *The New Urban Frontier: Gentrification and the Revanchist City.* New York: Routledge.

Sparke, Matthew. 2005. *In the Space of Theory: Postfoundational Geographies of the Nation-State.* Minneapolis: University of Minnesota Press.

Sproule-Jones, Megan. 1996. "Crusading for the Forgotten: Dr. Peter Bryce, Public Health, and Prairie Native Residential Schools." *Canadian Bulletin of Medical History* 13 (2): 199–224.

Staples, Annalisa R., Ruth L. McConnell, and Jill Elizabeth Oakes. 1993. *Soapstone and Seed Beads: Arts and Crafts at the Charles Camsell Hospital, a Tuberculosis Sanatorium.* Edmonton: Provincial Museum of Alberta.

Stevenson, Lisa. 2014. *Life beside Itself: Imagining Care in the Canadian Arctic.* Oakland: University of California Press.

Stoler, Ann Laura. 1995. *Race and the Education of Desire: Foucault's* History of Sexuality *and the Colonial Order of Things.* Durham, NC: Duke University Press.

Strega, Susan, Caitlin Janzen, Jeannie Morgan, Leslie Brown, Robina Thomas, and Jeannine Carriere. 2014. "Never Innocent Victims: Street Sex Workers in Canadian Print Media." *Violence against Women* 20 (1): 6–25.

Swanson, Kate. 2007. "Revanchist Urbanism Heads South: The Regulation of Indigenous Beggars and Street Vendors in Ecuador." *Antipode* 39 (4): 708–28.

Taussig, Michael. 1989. "Terror as Usual: Walter Benjamin's Theory of History as a State of Siege." *Social Text* (23): 3–20.

–. 1999. *Defacement: Public Secrecy and the Labor of the Negative.* Stanford, CA: Stanford University Press.

Thobani, Sunera. 2007. *Exalted Subjects: Studies in the Making of Race and Nation in Canada.* Toronto: University of Toronto Press.

Thrift, Nigel. 1999. "Steps to an Ecology of Place." In *Human Geography Today,* ed. Doreen Massey, John Allen, and Phil Sarre, 295–322. Cambridge: Polity.

Timm, Jordan. 2007. "Landscape with Sexy Transvestite: Kent Monkman's Playful Subversions of an Old Form Tell a Different Story of the Frontier." *Maclean's,* December 31. http://archive.macleans.ca/article/2007/12/31/landscape-with-sexy-transvestite.

Todd, Zoe. 2016. "An Indigenous Feminist's Take on the Ontological Turn: 'Ontology' Is Just Another Word for Colonialism." *Journal of Historical Sociology* 29 (1): 4–22.

Tourangeau, Jerry, dir. 1999. *Lost Songs.* Documentary. Produced by Clint Tourangeau and Elaine Moyah. Montreal: National Film Board of Canada.

Truth and Reconciliation Commission of Canada (TRC). 2015. *Honouring the Truth, Reconciling for the Future: Summary of the Final Report of the Truth and Reconciliation Commission of Canada.* Ottawa: Truth and Reconciliation Commission of Canada. http://publications.gc.ca/site/eng/9.800288/publication.html.

Tuck, Eve. 2009. "Suspending Damage: A Letter to Communities." *Harvard Educational Review* 79 (3): 409–28.

Tuck, Eve, and K. Wayne Yang. 2012. "Decolonization Is Not a Metaphor." *Decolonization: Indigeneity, Education and Society* 1 (1): 1–40.

Van Wagenen, Aimee. 2004. *An Epistemology of Haunting: A Review Essay.* London: Sage Publications.

Veracini, Lorenzo. 2010. *Settler Colonialism: A Theoretical Overview.* Basingstoke, UK: Palgrave Macmillan.

Vowel, Chelsea. 2016. *Indigenous Writes: A Guide to First Nations, Métis and Inuit Issues in Canada.* Winnipeg: Highwater.

Waldram, James Burgess, D. Ann Herring, and T. Kue Young. 1995. *Aboriginal Health in Canada: Historical, Cultural, and Epidemiological Perspectives.* Toronto: University of Toronto Press.

Walker, Kathy. 2003. "Residential Students Dug Grave for Sick Classmates." *Edmonton Journal,* August 28, A1.

Walkowitz, Judith R. 1992. *City of Dreadful Delight: Narratives of Sexual Danger in Late-Victorian London.* Chicago: University of Chicago Press.

Warren, Peter. 2006. "The Evolution of the Sanatorium: The First Half-Century, 1854–1904." *Canadian Society for the History of Medicine* 23 (2): 457–75.

Watts, Vanessa. 2013. "Indigenous Place-Thought and Agency amongst Humans and Non-Humans (First Woman and Sky Woman Go on a European World Tour!)." *Decolonization: Indigeneity, Education and Society* 2 (1): 20–34.

Wherrett, George Jasper. 1977. *The Miracle of Empty Beds: A History of Tuberculosis in Canada.* Toronto: University of Toronto Press.

Withey, Elizabeth. 2005. "Killer 'Somebody's Neighbour.'" *Edmonton Journal,* June 18, A4.

Wolfe, Patrick. 2006. "Settler Colonialism and the Elimination of the Native." *Journal of Genocide Research* 8 (4): 387–409.

World Health Organization. 2019. "Tuberculosis." https://www.who.int/en/news-room/fact-sheets/detail/tuberculosis.

Wyatt, Kyle Carsten. 2013. "Losing the Land Again: The Risks of Privatizing Property on First Nations Reserves." *The Walrus,* January 28. https://thewalrus.ca/losing-the-land-again/.

Yaeger, Patricia. 2002. "Consuming Trauma; Or, the Pleasure of Merely Circulating." In *Extremities: Trauma, Testimony, and Community,* ed. Nancy K. Miller and Jason Daniel Tougaw, 25–51. Urbana: University of Illinois Press.

Young, James Edward. 1993. *The Texture of Memory: Holocaust Memorials and Meaning.* New Haven, CT: Yale University Press.

Zournazi, Mary. 2002. "The Art of Living – with Michel Serres." In *Hope: New Philosophies for Change,* 192–209. New York: Routledge.

Zwicker, Heather. 2004. "Dead Indians, Power Conglomerates and the Upper Middle Class: Commemorating Colonial Conflict in Edmonton's Rossdale." Paper presented at the Canadian Association of Cultural Studies 2nd Annual Conference, Edmonton. Accessed March 8, 2007. http://www.culturalstudies.ca/proceedings04/proceedings.html.

Index

Note: MMWIG refers to missing and murdered Indigenous women and girls.